P9-CQA-950

The Life of the Parties

The Life of the Parties

Activists in Presidential Politics

Edited by

Ronald B. Rapoport
Alan I. Abramowitz
John McGlennon

THE UNIVERSITY PRESS OF KENTUCKY

Scholarly publisher for the Commonwealth,
serving Bellarmine College, Berea College, Centre
College of Kentucky, Eastern Kentucky University,
The Filson Club, Georgetown College, Kentucky
Historical Society, Kentucky State University,
Morehead State University, Murray State University,
Northern Kentucky University, Transylvania University,
University of Kentucky, University of Louisville,
and Western Kentucky University.

Editorial and Sales Offices: Lexington, Kentucky 40506-0024

Library of Congress Cataloging-in-Publication Data

Main entry under title:

The Life of the parties.

Includes index.
1. Political conventions—United States—Addresses,
essays, lectures. 2. Political parties—United States
—Addresses, essays, lectures. 3. Presidents—United
States—Nomination—Addresses, essays, lectures.
I. Rapoport, Ronald. II. Abramowitz, Alan.
III. McGlennon, John.
JK2255.L54 1986 324.5′6′0973 85-22510
ISBN 0-8131-1559-0

Contents

Tables

Acknowledgments

In any large project like this one, there are many people who contribute to its success. The editors thank David Reed of the College of William and Mary whose assistance in merging the twenty-two separate data sets into a single master file was invaluable. Without his help this project would have been impossible. In each of the eleven states leaders of the Democratic and Republican parties provided us with access to their conventions and allowed us to collect the data on which this research is based. Only their cooperation made this project feasible. In addition, the College of William and Mary provided copious computer time, secretarial help, and summer grants for all three editors. Finally, five individuals not represented in this volume but who participated in the data collection—George Otte, Ronald Pynn, Thomas Sanders, Thomas Simmons, and Mary Thornberry—contributed enormously to the project.

The papers in this volume came out of a conference held at William and Mary in October 1981 and funded by the National Science Foundation. We are grateful to the foundation, and particularly to its political science program director, Gerald Wright, for his help and encouragement. In addition those conference participants who were not part of the project itself—Samuel Eldersveld, Barbara Farah, M. Kent Jennings, Clifton McClesky, and Warren Miller—are responsible not only for contributing to the success of the conference, but also for the many improvements that resulted from their comments on the papers. Finally, but certainly not least, we thank Malcolm Jewell for his encouragement, comments, and criticisms through the process which led to the publication of this volume.

Thanks also to the *Journal of Politics* for permission to quote at length, in chapter 4, from our article, "The Party Isn't Over: Incentives for Activism in the 1980 Presidential Nominating Campaign," which appeared in the November 1983 issue; to the *International Political Science Review*, and to Sage Publications for permission to quote at length, in chapter 3, from an article of the same title which appeared in the 1983, number 1 issue; and to the *American Political Science Review* for permission to reprint as chapter 5 the Stone and Abramowitz article, "Winning May Not be the Only Thing, But It's More Than We Thought: Presidential Party Activists in 1980," which appeared in the March 1984 issue.

Introduction and Methodology

Political scientists have traditionally focused their attention on the behavior of political elites—those in a society who occupy positions of authority in governmental institutions. Since the development of public opinion polling as a research tool during the 1940s, political scientists have also devoted considerable attention to the political beliefs and behavior of members of the general public in the United States and other industrial democracies. Much less attention has been paid to a group which occupies a crucial intermediate position between the political elite and the mass public, the informal political activists. These are people whose involvement in politics extends beyond the act of voting to more intensive forms of participation such as campaigning for candidates or contacting public officials.

The informal political activists play a vital role in a democracy because their interest, attention, and activity allow them to wield disproportionate influence on political decision-makers. In addition, political decision-makers are frequently recruited from the ranks of the informal activists. These informal activists therefore provide an important link between political elites and the mass public in a democracy.

One of the most important avenues of informal participation in democratic politics is the party organization. In all modern industrial democracies, party organizations play a crucial role in the recruitment of political elites. Participation in party affairs provides an opportunity for interested citizens to influence the selection of political leaders beyond the limited choice offered in elections. In the United States especially, the decentralized, permeable party structures provide multiple opportunities for citizen participation. Only in the United States do members of the general public have the opportunity to select party nominees in primary elections. The vast majority of local, state, and national officeholders in the United States are nominated in primary elections.

In addition to the state and local primaries, the Democratic and Republican parties provide many opportunities for citizens to participate in party activities. One of the most important of these activities, and the principal one for which the national parties exist in the United States, is the nomination of presidential candidates. Reforms adopted by both parties since 1968 have drastically altered the process by which delegates to the presidential nominating conventions are chosen and increased the opportunities for citizen participation in this process. In addition to the proliferation of presidential primaries in 1980—over 70 percent of the delegates to both the Democratic and Republican national nominating conventions were chosen in primaries—the rules governing party caucuses and conventions have been changed to increase opportunities for citizen participation.

The results of the post-1968 reforms of the presidential nominating process have been controversial. Some scholars and party leaders believe that these participatory reforms have allowed dogmatic ideological activists to exercise too much influence over the presidential nomination. According to the neoconservative critics of party reform such as Jeane Kirkpatrick and Aaron Wildavsky, the new activists are less representative of the political views of the electorate and less concerned about the viability of the party itself than the elected officials and party regulars they have displaced.

Research on the motivations, characteristics, and political beliefs of party activists in the United States has concentrated heavily on national party convention delegates, especially those who attended the 1972 Democratic National Convention, one of the most unusual party gatherings of modern times.

The research on which the papers in this volume are based was stimulated by a desire to broaden the data base on which our knowledge about American party activists rests. The caucus-convention states seemed to provide an ideal opportunity to examine the characteristics, motivations, and beliefs of a broad group of party activists in the postreform presidential nominating process.

Before the recent era of party reform, American political parties at the national level were generally characterized as loose-knit coalitions of state and local organizations controlled by pragmatic politicians for whom issues and ideology were subservient to the goal of winning elections. Events since 1968 have led to a thorough revision of this characterization. The national parties have greatly increased their control over the rules and procedures used by state and local organizations to select national convention delegates. Presidential primaries have proliferated, forcing candidates to appeal directly to the electorate rather than to state and local party leaders. Reforms of the caucus-convention system have opened up the process of selecting national convention delegates to a new breed of issue-oriented activists. Some students of American party politics have expressed fears that these changes threaten the viability of the parties as organizations. If the parties are dominated by activists who are more concerned with promoting issue positions than with winning elections, who identify more strongly with outside interest groups than with the party organization, and who owe their primary loyalty to a particular candidate rather than to party leaders, then these fears may be well founded.

The chapters in this book deal with a wide range of topics concerning the role of party activists in the presidential nominating system. All of these chapters, though, shed light on the condition of the parties as organizations in the postreform era. While the evidence examined here lends support to some of the findings of earlier studies concerning the characteristics and attitudes of contemporary party activists, the contributors to this book generally reach more optimistic conclusions regarding the viability of the parties as organizations.

Several of the chapters in this volume present evidence of a continuing nationalization of the party system. This process can be seen as both a cause and an effect of the increased centralization of the presidential nominating system. Abramowitz, McGlennon, and Rapoport ("A State Analysis") find that party activists in the eleven states included in this study have similar social characteristics and political beliefs. In all eleven states, Democratic activists were less affluent and included larger proportions of racial and ethnic minority groups than Republican activists. Similarly, Democratic activists were much more likely to be active in labor unions, teachers' organizations, women's rights, environmental, and civil rights organizations than Republican activists, while the latter were more likely to be active in business, religious, and anti-abortion groups. In all eleven states, Democratic activists were substantially more liberal than Republican activists—the most liberal group of Republican activists (from Iowa) were considerably more conservative than the most conservative group of Democratic activists (from Oklahoma).

Two chapters suggest possible explanations for the nationalization of the party system. Moreland, Steed, and Baker find that substantial proportions of the activists in several of the states included in the study were relatively recent migrants. The fact that so many newcomers to these states were delegates to the party conventions provides evidence of the permeability long regarded as a key characteristic of the American party system. In such traditionally one-party Democratic states as Texas, Virginia, and South Carolina, migrants have contributed to the emergence of strong Republican organizations. In addition, Moreland, Steed, and Baker show that Democratic migrants tended to be younger, better educated, and more liberal than Democratic activists who were long-term residents of their states. Thus, migration has contributed to the ideological polarization of the two parties.

In "The Permeability of Parties" Kweit and Kweit investigate another source of change in the composition of hte parties: conversion. In the traditionally one-party southern states, many of today's GOP activists are conservative former Democrats. By using the "exit" option to express their dissatisfaction with the direction of their traditional party, these ex-Democrats have contributed to the ideological realignment of party politics in the South and the emergence of genuine two-party competition. Furthermore, Kweit and Kweit show that converts to the Democratic party, especially during the 1960s, tended to be more liberal than activists who were lifelong Democrats. The net result of conversion has been increased ideological polarization of the parties.

Despite the increase in ideological polarization brought about by migration and conversion, the two parties are far from monolithic. Activists within each party display a wide variety of social background characteristics and represent a wide variety of interest groups. No single interest group comes close to achieving majority status in either party. In fact, Francis and Benedict find that multiple group memberships are common among party activists. This pattern of overlapping memberships may reduce the likelihood that activists will act as agents of outside interest groups.

Although diversity is found in both parties, several papers included in this book find evidence of important differences between the ideological and coalitional makeup of the two parties. A greater variety of interest groups are represented among the ranks of Democratic activists. Similarly, Brudney and McDonald show that issue and ideological divisions are much sharper in the Democratic party than in the Republican party. In 1980 many of the issues dividing the Democrats remained submerged because liberal activists were reluctant to abandon an incumbent president who appeared to offer a greater chance of victory than his more liberal challenger. However, the findings presented by Brudney and McDonald suggest a greater potential among Democratic activists for intraparty conflict along ideological lines than among the more ideologically homogeneous Republicans.

Many recent studies have emphasized the increased importance of ideology as a motivation for activism in the presidential nominating process since 1968. This volume provides considerable evidence of the importance of issues and ideology to activists in te 1980 presidential nominating campaign. In one chapter, Rapoport explores the extent of issue constraint among activists. His findings suggest a source of increased ideological thinking among contemporary activists: the rising level of education. Among activists, in contrast to the general public, issue constraint increases substantially with higher levels of education.

The salience of ideological concerns among contemporary activists has led to questions about their commitment to the party as an organization. Abramowitz, McGlennon, and Rapoport, however, show in "Incentives for Activism" that activists do not view concern with issues and party loyalty as conflicting values. They find a positive correlation between purposive (issue and candidate) and partisan motivations among state convention delegates in 1980. This finding suggests that activists' pursuit of ideological goals may be tempered by party loyalty. Similarly, Francis and Benedict find that interest group involvement is not associated with weaker commitment to the party organization. Even among delegates who were active in newer ideological groups such as environmental or anti-abortion organizations, party loyalties were generally quite strong.

Findings reported by Hauss and Maisel call into question the belief that party reforms, by encouraging participation of new types of activists, have led to domination of parties by extremist ideologues. They find that members of these new groups—women, youth, and racial minorities—were not significantly more likely to embrace extremist ideological positions or to reject the values of compromise and coalition-building than other types of activists.

Stone and Abramowitz examine the attitudes of activists toward the tradeoff between ideology and electoral success. As in previous studies, when activists were presented with an abstract choice between ideological purity and winning elections, most chose ideological purity. Yet these general orientations, which have been the focus of so much research, had very little impact on the behavior of activists in choosing among candidates seeking the presidential nomination. Faced with a concrete choice between candidates with differing ideological positions and electoral prospects, activists weighed electability more heavily than ideology.

It would be a mistake to conclude from the evidence presented in this volume that the new breed of party activists behaves no differently than the party regulars who controlled presidential nominations before the era of reform. Unlike the party regulars, most of today's presidential activists are not beholden to party leaders or elected officials for their positions. Few state convention delegates in 1980 were concerned about advancing their own political careers. Instead, most were motivated by a desire to promote their conception of good public policy. In this sense they were, in James Q. Wilson's terms, amateurs. But they were also realistic enough to recognize the necessity of compromise and coalition- building in order to achieve their ideological or policy objectives.

Collectively, the articles included in this volume show contemporary party activists to have more complex motivations, beliefs, and values than previous research had suggested, holding strong views on issues along with strong party loyalties and capable of pursuing ideological goals and electoral success simultaneously. In reforming the rules of the presidential nominating system, the parties have attempted to adapt to new demands arising from their political environment. These studies indicate that the new participants in the nominating process have also adapted to one of the most important demands arising from their political environment: the need for compromise and coalition-building.

METHODOLOGY

The data analyzed in this book come from a survey of delegates attending party conventions in eleven states between April and June of 1980. These eleven states all used a caucus-convention system (rather than a primary election) to select their delegates to the 1980 Democratic and Republican presidential nominating conventions. Delegates attending the state conventions were responsible for electing the delegates to the national nominating conventions. In each state, a team of political scientists distributed and collected self-administered questionnaires at the Demo-

Completed Questionnaires Returned at Each State Convention

State	Democrats	Republicans
Arizona	337	387
Colorado	1003	638
Iowa	1673	1107
Maine	1046	441
Missouri	317	380
North Dakota	623	404
Oklahoma	609	1244
South Carolina	621	739
Texas	440	564
Utah	452	1218
Virginia	1669	1716

cratic and Republican conventions. The questionnaires used in every state were identical except for their covers and a few optional questions dealing with state issues and political leaders.

The number of completed questionnaires returned at each party convention varied considerably depending upon the size of the convention itself as well as the response rate among delegates. The acompanying table shows the number of completed questionnaires returned at each convention.

A total of 17,628 delegates (8,790 Democratic delegates and 8,838 Republican delegates) returned completed questionnaires. It was not possible to compute a precise response rate to the survey in each state since the procedures for distributing the questionnaires (generally attaching them to or placing them on delegates' seats in the convention hall) did not allow us to determine how many delegates actually received questionnaires. However, the proportion of distributed questionnaires which were returned varied from approximately 25 percent to approximately 70 percent, with an average of approximately 50 percent.

We were able to compare the delegates who returned questionnaires with the entire population of delegates at each convention in terms of geographical distribution and candidate support. In only one case did we discover a major discrepancy between the survey respondents and the convention delegates. Among Maine Republicans, delegates from one of the state's two congressional districts were overrepresented among the survey respondents. Although there was very little difference in candidate support between delegates from the two districts, we weighted the Maine Republicans to equalize the representation of the two congressional districts in our sample.

Because of the large variation in the number of respondents at each convention, unless otherwise indicated, each of the papers included in this volume uses a weighted sample of delegates in which the representation of each state party convention is equalized. Therefore, the results presented in these papers reflect an average of the eleven states in each party. Many of the analyses presented in these papers were repeated with the unweighted data and almost no differences were found in the results.

PART ONE

The 1980 Delegate Study: Context and Overview

1

The Underexplored Nomination Process

STEVEN E. SCHIER

As the first comprehensive multistate survey of delegates to state party conventions, the highest echelon of state caucus-convention systems in the presidential nomination process, this book augments knowledge of the presidential nomination system in general and the 1980 nominations in particular, and provides sorely needed assistance to political scientists' attempts to fathom this complex, multidimensional process. Such a description of nomination operations is emphatically not hyperbole, for the process is as complex in its systemic import as in its baroque operations. By "systemic import" I mean the various functions the process actually performs in the American political system, which will be enumerated shortly.

This complexity can be illustrated by considering three ways that the nomination process can be conceived. It is first and most obviously a method of candidate nomination, essential to the conduct of quadrennial presidential elections. This most common understanding of the process focuses upon strategies of the candidates, interpretations of the national media and the "verdicts" (Marshall 1981, 81) from particular state caucuses, and primaries labeled of strategic moment by the media and candidates. These variables interact to produce "front runners" and (since 1952) national convention confirmation of them through first-ballot nominations. This is the nomination process as most politicos, reporters, and many political scientists conceive it.

Study of presidential nominations that settles upon the above sort of conceptualization does not, however, adequately consider other systemically important dimensions of political behavior evident within the process. Presidential nominations are also important exercises in state politics; each caucus and primary involves a campaign and "election" in a particular state. This ranks among the more consequential operations involving state parties, for it serves to represent the candidate preference opinions of party activists and to allow the articulation (in caucus-convention systems) of activist issue positions concerning the national agenda. Nomination operations within states might be more accurately described as unique interactions of national and state electoral processes. States are subject to national media and candidate organization invasions of varying magnitude, depending on the purported "strategic importance" of the contest.

It is the politically active segment of a state's electorate, those willing to vote in a primary or attend a caucus meeting, who are the focus of all this "outsider" attention. Analysis of their behavior in such instances informs our knowledge of the attributes of party activists within and across states. The studies in this volume in particular divulge much information about that stratum of activists who attend statewide conventions as delegates. This state-level perspective suggests a number of useful research questions: Do these elites vary in their attributes across states? Why or why not? What does such variation or the absence of it reveal to us about differences in electoral politics among these particular states? Very few nomination process studies have focused on single states (Marshall 1978; Lengle 1981) or multistate comparisons (Schier 1980). The data collected here, however, provide ample opportunity for this.

Presidential nominations also can be viewed as a nationwide elite process involving a hierarchy of political activism. By "elite process" I mean one involving "that political class that has more influence than others in shaping specified values through the political process." (Kirkpatrick 1976, 22) Several strata of participation occur in it, and the denizens of each in aggregate may vary on average from each other in certain social, economic, and political characteristics. Some studies have investigated the attributes of Presidential primary electorates (for example, Ranney 1972; Hedlund 1977; Kritzer 1977). National convention delegates at the top of this participatory structure have been thoroughly studied as well (Sullivan, Pressman, Page, and Lyons 1974; Soule and Clarke 1970; Soule and McGrath 1975; Sullivan, Pressman, and Arterton 1976; Jackson, Brown, and Brown 1978; Jackson, Brown, and Bositis 1982; Roback 1975; Costain 1980; Kirkpatrick 1975, 1976). Intervening echelons with few exceptions (Nyitray 1975; Hutter and Schier 1982) have been overlooked until the advent of this volume. Additional intra-elite and elite-mass comparisons are now possible with this 1980 state convention data, and all of the authors here pursue a variety of them. It is this conceptualization of state party conventions that most of the authors in this book implicitly adopt as the basis for their analysis.

In order for studies of presidential nomination activities to aid the understanding of broader national political processes, it is necessary to conceive of the elite behaviors investigated here in reference to their actual systemic functions. That is, what these elites actually do that is of consequence to national electoral and policymaking systems should be specified. The general functional importance of these elites of the "second order"—those activists below the formal policymakers—was identified by Gaetano Mosca: "the stability of any political organism depends on the level of morality, intelligence, and activity that this second stratum has obtained." (Mosca 1939, 404) Three specific functions that these elites perform are the act of candidate choice, descriptive and opinion representation, and opinion leadership. Each will be explained in turn.

CANDIDATE CHOICE

The most obvious conception of nominations involves the observed sequence of behaviors directly influencing the choice of nominee. These choices are made throughout the process hierarchy and constitute its most systemically consequential decisions. After all, these are the choices that determine the identity of the two major general election candidates. Prenomination candidate choice has been the object of recent formal theoretical works (Brams 1978; Aldrich 1980). John Aldrich hypothesizes choices to be dependent upon "a tradeoff of policy and electability that many citizens must face in preconvention campaigns," but that the actual decision depends "upon the specifics of the situation" (1980, 84). He then suggests that electability will be weighted more heavily later in the campaign when reliable information about candidate prospects is more available and costs for nonsupport of particular candidates can be more clearly perceived.

That these propositions were written in 1980 illustrates the paucity of our present understanding of exactly how candidate choices are made in the nomination process. A variety of studies have demonstrated the association of candidate preference with demographic and ideological characteristics of national delegates in several nomination years (Soule and Clarke 1970; Soule and McGrath 1975; Sullivan, Pressman, Page, and Lyons 1974; Kirkpatrick 1975, 1976; Jackson, Brown, and Brown 1978; Jackson, Brown, and Bositis 1982). Correlates of candidate preference, though, do not tell us how the choice itself is made. Several of these studies also measure the political "style" of delegates and draw inferences about candidate choice behavior from responses to abstract questions of "style."

The concept of activist behavioral "style" originates in the work of James Q. Wilson (1962, 1973). He identified "amateur" and "professional" activist styles entailing "mutually supportive sets of attitudes about principles, procedures and goals that relate to citizen and partisan political activity." (Roback 1975, 439) The behavior of the amateur is rooted in a clear expression of what constitutes the public interest and in a strong commitment to programmatic principles. Professionals in contrast tend to make political decisons on the basis of their electoral effects, and they define politics in terms of negotiable concrete events (Wilson 1962, chapters 1, 10, and 11).

Such styles supposedly manifest themselves in national delegate behavior in several ways. A common operationalization of style in delegate studies (Soule and Clarke 1970; Soule and McGrath 1975; Roback 1975) involves "no" (amateur) and "yes" (professional) responses to survey questions asking whether party unity is to be preferred to open participatory intraparty debate at conventions, whether a party worker should support a nominee even if he disagrees with him, and whether controversial items should be excluded from the party platform to insure party unity. Delegates were also asked whether one's self-conception is that of a loyal party worker (professional) or of an issues activist (amateur). The question concerning nominee support clearly taps abstract notions about candidate choice. The inference commonly made about an amateur response to this question is that the particular respondent actually chooses candidates on the basis of ideological proximity rather than electability.

As Walter Stone and Alan Abramowitz point out in their article in this volume, all recent studies of national convention delegates find them to respond overwhelmingly as amateurs to this candidate choice question. This has been the source of no little disquiet among "neoconservative" critics of post-1968 nomination arrangements, who decry the investment of authority over candidate choice in delegates who are "less oriented toward winning." (Kirkpatrick 1976, 153) These amateurs (or "purists" to use Polsby and Wildavsky's terminology) threaten through their choices to present to the electorate ideologically extreme candidates, resulting in extreme policy oscillation between administrations, increasing voter disaffection from nominees, and thus ultimately less legitimate and stable national electoral and policymaking systems. (For an overview and critique of this perspective, see Nakamura and Sullivan 1981.)

These dire predictions about the dysfunctional effects of the rise of amateurs depend in large part upon the assumption that responses to candidate choice-related survey questions strongly correlate with the actual rationale employed by delegates in their candidate choices. Abramowitz and Stone in this volume are the first to carefully investigate this relationship, and their findings refute the conventional wisdom. At 1980 state party conventions and the notoriously "purist ridden" 1972 Democratic National Convention, they find delegates "weighed electability more heavily than ideology" in their nomination choices, even though the respondents in their samples overwhelmingly in the abstract "prefer ideological purity to winning."

This is a major and controversial contribution to our understanding of candidate choice behavior. Their findings make logical sense; abstract stated ideals and actual behaviors often diverge in political life. The broader implication here is that actual delegate choice behavior in the nomination process may not have altered greatly since the reforms of 1968-1972. This is not to say that similar substantive choices have been made since the reforms, but rather that a similar choice process has been employed by new people. The authors do not claim that delegates judge electability as the old bosses and delegation leaders did, but that, however conceived, electability loomed as the foremost criterion of candidate choice among their 1972 and 1980 samples. Thus "new politics" Democratic liberals and "new right" Republican conservatives may choose candidates according to a criterion also employed by Mayor Daley and Boss Cox, but their substantive choice will vary from that of the old "pros" if they possess differing types of perceptions of what electability entails.

Neoconservative critics may need to redirect their arguments should further studies confirm these findings. The root of the neoconservative objection should perhaps no longer be the amateur choice process itself, but rather the intensity and substance of amateurs' ideological orientations as they influence perceptions involved in both this choice process and other substantive decisions (such as those regarding the platform). A common neoconservative criticism of these ideological orientations is that they are unrepresentative of those of party identifiers (Ranney 1974). This issue is pursued later in this essay.

Such insights into candidate choice behavior are the result of creative and careful survey instrument construction. Questions incorporated asked for relative ideological position and electability judgments concerning each major candidate. This permitted linkages between candidate preferences and these evaluative dimensions to be more carefully explored than in prior studies. Further survey research on candidate choice should incorporate comparable indicators.

REPRESENTATIVENESS

Representation is clearly a highly important function of electoral systems in constitutional democracies. Presidential nomination processes, as part of the American electoral system, have over the last fifteen years been the target of reformers seeking to alter their representational procedures. The controversial McGovern-Fraser reforms of the early 1970s ushered into nomination practice a variety of new procedures: proportional representation, demographic quotas, and more open participation in party caucuses and conventions. These procedures derived from divergent normative theories of representation and engendered much controversy.

What aspects of representation were at issue? The argument revolves around, in Hanna Pitkin's terms, "what are the politically salient features to be represented" (1967, 87). American electoral arrangements traditionally assume the opinions of electors to be the appropriate object of representation; it is opinion representation upon which modern electoral practice within American parties is based. Certain recent procedural reforms in nomination practices—proportional representation and more open participation—have altered the mechanism for opinion representation within this process. A rival concept of descriptive representation of social characteristics, the rationale for the controversial McGovern-Fraser "quotas" of 1972, remains the basis for the current Democratic national convention gender quota (half of the delegates must be female). Republicans at the national level currently employ no such descriptively based procedures. Overall, nomination procedures in both parties now have as their central purpose the representation of nomination participants' candidate preference opinions.

Candidate preference is but one of several aspects of representativeness observable of the elites constituting the nomination process hierarchy. Studies of other aspects of representativeness aid in defining and appraising the desirability of the particular characteristics of these elites. Political scientists have made two other aspects of representation the object of study in recent years: the representativeness of social characteristics and of issue opinions or ideology. The former involves the degree of similarity between elites and their mass base of party identifiers concerning social and demographic characteristics. The latter concerns the degree to which elites differ from the same mass base on specific issues and overall ideological orientation.

Major studies of national delegate representativeness (McCloskey et. al. 1960; Kirkpatrick 1976) show this elite to be socially unrepresentative of identifiers in all of the characteristics associated positively with political participation (education, age, income, and occupational status). Their findings concerning issue representativeness, however, varied considerably over time. McCloskey et. al. (1960) found 1956 Democratic national convention delegates to be ideologically closer to both Democratic and Republican identifiers than were Republican delegates. Kirkpatrick (1976) found in 1972 the opposite pattern—Republican national delegates were closer to both sets of identifiers than were Democratic delegates.

Relatively little has been known of the social and ideological characteristics of intervening elites in the nomination process, such as state convention delegates, until the advent of this volume. As previous research found for national delegates, the state delegates investigated here are unrepresentative of identifiers in social characteristics that correlate positively with participation. The studies here also consistently find large mean differences between Democratic and Republican state delegates on both ideological self-placement and most specific issue opinions. This suggests that party nomination elites now are conforming more closely to the role, long endorsed by responsible party proponents, of advocating distinct and contrasting programmatic alternatives from which the electorate can choose (Schattschneider 1942; Ranney 1954).

Despite these tendencies, it is in fact unlikely that such a role can be adequately performed by these elites, considering the at best fleeting attention given by the electorate to the programmatic statements articulated by national conventions. Presidential candidates themselves remain the primary providers of programmatic content of concern to the electorate. Certainly the delegates choose these candidates, but apparently not simply on the grounds of ideological proximity. The nomination process, aside from the candidates themselves, gives the electorate less than salient programmatic information for distinguishing the two parties from each other.

Notwithstanding this limited programmatic effect by nomination elites upon general election candidate choices by the electorate, the ideological unrepresentativeness of national convention delegates was the subject of repeated criticism by neoconservative analysts of the post-1968 nomination process. Nelson Polsby and Aaron Wildavsky identified as a primary goal of purist nomination activists the uncompromised articulation by the party nominee of their own (often extreme) views. Nomination processes for purists are exercises in "self expression": "in the purist conception of things, instead of a party convention being a place where a party meets to choose candidates who can win elections by pleasing voters, it becomes a site for finding a candidate who will embody the message delegates seek to express" (1980, 23). Purists or amateurs threaten the very electoral viability of parties by their expressive articulation of issue positions that are extreme in comparison with those of both party identifiers and the electorate as a whole—the McGovern and Goldwater nominations being cases in point. This formulation has been echoed by Austin Ranney (1975) and Jeane Kirkpatrick (1976).

Charles Hauss and Sandy Maisel in this volume identify those purist or amateur delegate characteristics that are the object of neoconservative opprobrium and describe their relative frequency among 1980 state convention delegates. Relatively few delegates are evident who are "extremist" in ideology and who disapprove strongly of candidates' compromising their principles in order to win. The authors then conclude that reports of extremist takeover of the nomination process, much like certain accounts of Mark Twain's death, were greatly exaggerated. These conclusions depend crucially upon the authors' operational definitions of extremism, which are certain to spark controversy. Have they in this erected a straw man?

The controversy over the presence of "extremists" among party activists is in large part a debate over definitions. How many extremists are required to constitute a threat, and how extreme must they be? Hauss and Maisel set high limits on each. An alternative formulation employed by

McCloskey (1960) and Kirkpatrick (1976) measures the *relative* degree of extremism of ideological self-placement by national convention delegates in comparison to that of party identifiers. Which definition is to be preferred? Relative location informs us more about the location of certain activists in the ideological space of the electoral system, but more absolute measures tell us more about activist "outliers" and their distinctive characteristics. Each, then, has its uses.

Though the specter of rampant purism is somewhat allayed by the findings of Hauss and Maisel and of Stone and Abramowitz, other recent tendencies suggest neoconservative arguments should not be entirely dismissed. Ideological distance between delegates and identifiers is widening (Farah, Jennings, and Miller 1981). Given such tendencies, the neoconservative fear of an ideologically unrepresentative nomination process may be now, in fact, being slowly realized. It is important to qualify this by noting that ideologically more extreme delegates may not behave as prototypical purists; Stone and Abramowitz give evidence of this. To further comprehend the actual political import of this growing divergence, more research is needed on how ideological attributes of delegates at all levels influence their nomination process behaviors. This first requires a more thorough understanding of the degree of ideological variation among elites located at various echelons of the process hierarchy.

A number of studies in this volume contribute to such an understanding by investigating state convention delegate ideology and its correlates, most notably those evident in the social characteristics of the delegates. Jeffrey Brudney and Jean McDonald discover that 1980 Democratic and Republican state convention delegates "conceive of the issues in comparable dimensions" but from decidedly different perspectives. Candidate preference strongly relates to ideological grouping among Democratic delegates, Kennedy supporters being more thoroughly ideological than any other preference group in either party. Public officeholding among Democratic delegates also associates positively with ideological moderation. No such difference occurs among the ideologically more homogeneous Republicans. Thus the purist specter looms as influencing delegate behavior more among Democrats. In this party alone did issue constellations, public officeholding, and candidate preference vary together, and this covariance suggests that Democratic Kennedy delegates who were not officeholders might most closely fit this purist description.

Further study of the behavior of this group could more thoroughly test this proposition.

Robert and Mary Kweit study the "permeability" of state party organizations as evident in the characteristics of state convention delegates. Their findings imply that the parties have been somewhat permeable—for example, a substantial number of party "switchers" were 1980 delegates—and that this permeability is enhancing somewhat the ideological distinctiveness of the two parties, at least at this elite level. Those who switched parties during the sixties in particular have more extreme ideological positions. Overall, though, the ideological differences between long-time and less experienced party activists were small. It does not seem that the presence of new or switcher activists in these states is a major source of more extreme ideological positions among delegates.

An additional aspect of state party permeability with implications for the ideological variation of state convention delegates is the influx of new migrants into state nomination politics. Laurence Moreland, Robert Steed, and Tod Baker find the new migrants among Democratic delegates to be more liberal in their responses to a series of issue questions. This ideological tendency is a function of the youth and high education of these migrants. Democratic migrants were also less supportive of Jimmy Carter. No substantial ideological or candidate preference differences obtained between Republican migrants and other Republican delegates. "Upscale" young migrant Democratic delegates thus are more ideologically extreme and prefer a candidate closest to them ideologically. This is another subgroup worth investigating further for evidence of purist behavior.

John Francis and Robert Benedict find comparable patterns of Democratic heterogeneity and Republican homogeneity in their investigations of the interest group activism of state delegates as it relates to party support, ideological self-identification, and specific issue positions. Many Democratic members of newer interest groups—women's rights, environmental, and civil rights organizations—are both more liberal and less committed to the party than other Democratic delegates. Anti-abortion group members are the most divergent Republicans in their ideological and candidate support perspectives (a small divergence, by Democratic standards). These Democratic and Republican group members also possess supposedly purist attributes, but do they evidence purist behavior?

What composite portrait of the ideological and related social characteristics of 1980 state convention delegates is evident from these studies? The delegates are on average socially and economically elite, a finding consistent with other studies of nomination activists. Greater ideological and social homogeneity is evident among Republican delegates in comparison to Democrats. Certain types of Democratic delegates may be more likely to exhibit purist or amateur behavior: party switchers during the sixties, highly educated younger delegates, and members of newer interest groups. This hardly indicates, however, that the Democratic party is now dominated by operational purists. Purist attitudes in the abstract, as we have noted, do not necessarily entail purist candidate choice behavior. The types of delegates who potentially might display such behavior constitute a minority of Democratic delegates in all of the above studies.

Though the degree of operational purism among state Republican delegates in 1980 remains difficult to assess, the studies here do indicate that Republican delegates are more uniformly ideologically extreme than their Democratic counterparts. Republican state delegates in 1980 may not behave as purists in their candidate choices, and relatively few may fall at the poles of indicator scales measuring extremism. It nonetheless is possible that such an overwhelmingly conservative group's perceptions of electability could differ from that of more moderate party identifiers, thus making their candidate choices somewhat less representative of identifiers. Such a divergence was evident in the substantive issue choices of national Republican delegates in 1980, resulting in a national platform to the right of the issue preferences of party identifiers. Perhaps the ideological homogeneity of Republican delegates threatens to make their collective behavior more unrepresentative of party identifiers than that of the Democrats, who are on average equally extreme but more heterogeneous.

The Republican and Democratic state delegates possessed on average two distinctly different programmatic perspectives in a fashion roughly similar to that desired by "responsible party" advocates. Programmatic distinctiveness of this sort is somewhat unrepresentative of the party-in-the-electorate. To what extent is this unrepresentativeness a problem? After all, nomination procedures provide for representation of candidate preference opinions of actual participants, not of the issue preferences of party identifiers. This sort of unrepresentativeness will be dysfunctional for the broader electoral system if conventions nominate candidates widely considered "extreme" on the issues by the electorate. Abramowitz and Stone demonstrate that candidate choice processes of 1980 state delegates do not necessarily guarantee this result. We thus must continue to be concerned with the consequences. If ideologically extreme process participants choose candidates largely on the grounds of ideological proximity, electoral dysfunctions—alienated voters, lower turnout—will probably result. The quality of opinion representation in nomination processes in this way fundamentally influences the legitimacy of the American electoral system. Studies of purist nomination behavior (as opposed to attitudes) therefore must rank high on the agenda of future research. Future surveys should incorporate, in addition to indicators of candidate preference behavior such as those used in this 1980 survey, comparable measures of activities such as platform decisions. These measures can identify behavior that indicates the degree of representativeness of nomination activists.

OPINION LEADERSHIP

Opinion leadership is the least commonly acknowledged systemic function of nomination process elites. By "opinion leadership" I mean direct or indirect influence upon the opinions of others through the articulation of one's own opinion. Such leadership commonly operates in two modes: a personal mode involving personal contact with others that is both direct and indirect (for example, through friends as intermediaries); and an impersonal mode entailing direct and indirect contact with others through media mechanisms. Personal opinion leadership is largely a function of personal political activism. Through interest group and party activities, one acquires skills and knowledge that permit personal influence upon the opinions of others both within and without the nomination process. The quality of this leadership in specific instances depends also upon a variety of psychological and social variables as well. The paucity of studies of opinion leadership of this sort is testimony to the difficulty of systematically observing such complex and (in the scientific sense) uncontrollable interactions. Much of our understanding of how this operates in the nomination process comes from journalistic accounts of such incidents as activists' interaction with voters. (For example, see White 1961, 1965, 1969, 1973; Witcover 1978; Schram 1977).

Impersonal opinion leadership in the nomination process is more commonly the object of academic and journalistic attention. This involves impersonal dissemination of various symbolic and substantive messages from nomination process participants through the media, where activists do not control the content of the disseminated messages to the extent that they can in personal opinion leadership. Are the delegates united? How do they stand on important platform issues? Why do they support their nominee? Answers to these sorts of questions are supplied by the media to mass audiences throughout the nomination process. This conduit permits delegates to at least indirectly communicate advocacy of their opinions to a far larger group than personal opinion leadership can reach. The impact of impersonal leadership is greatly diluted by its very mechanism of transmission, however. Not many people seek out media interpretations of delegate opinions, much less weigh them heavily. As noted earlier, it is the candidates themselves who inject into the electoral process the programmatic content to which the electorate actually pays attention. Delegates in the aggregate nonetheless do create images of national conventions in the minds of voters which probably influence their electoral choices, the exotic image of the 1972 Democratic national convention being a case in point (Wattenberg 1973).

Both sorts of opinion leadership perform certain systemic functions through the nomination process. Personal opinion leadership can serve to reinforce or alter the opinions of party and group identifiers and to clarify the programmatic commitments of activists. This contributes to the patterning of opinion among both nomination process elites and those party identifiers who regularly interact with them. Impersonal opinion leadership through the media can influence both the issue opinions and candidate evaluations of the electorate.

These opinion leadership functions are more thoroughly understandable from the perspective of agenda-building theory. Cobb and Elder (1972) identify two sorts of opinion agendas in the American political system: a systemic agenda, defined as "all issues that are commonly perceived by members of the political community as meriting public attention and as involving matters within the legitimate jurisdiction of existing governmental authority" (1972, 85), and an institutional agenda, "that set of items explicitly up for active and serious consideration of authoritative decision makers" (1972, 86). The authors contend that both party platforms and media coverage are conduits for the emergence of issues on the systemic agenda (1972, 91).

The processes of opinion leadership sketched here involve a set of behaviors by nomination process activists entailing interactions with others personally and impersonally that, independent of the actual nomination candidate contest itself, influence the content of national systemic and institutional agendas. Issues promoted by these nomination elites are deemed legitimate by a broader public and accorded systemic and even institutional attention. How substantial is this activist influence? I have already suggested that such agenda-influencing attempts are dwarfed by the influence that party nominees themselves have upon the agenda status of particular issues. Precious little attention, though, has been paid to such functions by students of the nominating process. The agenda effects of personal and impersonal opinion leadership both within and without the nomination process deserve more systematic scholarly pursuit.

Certain studies in this volume do relate to this research question. Francis and Benedict's study of interest group affiliations of state delegates identifies several arenas of delegate opinion leadership. Moreland, Steed, and Baker demonstrate the changing composition of opinion leaders in state nomination processes resulting from migration of activists. Ronald Rapoport devotes perhaps the most thorough attention to this dimension of activist behavior in his analysis of the attributes of attitudinal constraint among 1980 state convention delegates. He finds that attitudinal constraint or consistency in this sample correlates positively with education, even when controlling for self-professed ideology, motivation for activism, and previous political involvement. This contrasts with earlier studies of mass samples in which constraint was more strongly related to involvement than to education. The findings suggest that education among nomination process elites affects their agenda-influencing activities, since attitude structuring among delegates should be reflected in their opinion leadership behaviors.

Rapoport also identifies a group of attitudinal purists among the delegates who possess high levels of constraint. He constructs a purism index that identifies purists as those delegates who score particularly low on personalism and pragmatism scales, high on an ideology scale and are motivated by single issues. Rapoport finds these delegates rank higher in constraint than those at the opposite ends of the scales of this index. However, purists consist of only 19 percent of the delegates—hardly a flood tide. Further research should identify social and demographic characteristics of these attitudinal purists: do they include the types evidencing purist characteristics in other studies in this volume? The effects of high constraint among this purist group upon actual behavior also bears investigation, since distinctive purist behavior is the source of concern for neoconservatives.

The neoconservative critique, then, can be understood as also a criticism of the opinion leadership activities of certain types of delegates. Ideological extremism and tactical amateurism, if ascendant in both parties, should serve to broaden the systemic agenda and encourage polarization around its central issues. This polarization may then in turn produce massive voter alienation. These speculations are based upon hypothetical assertions about delegate behavior that as yet have not been systematically proved or disproved. The studies here by Stone and Abramowitz and by Hauss and Maisel do suggest that such behavior was not greatly in evidence at 1980 state conventions. We can further understand opinion leadership by nomination activists only by investigating relevant behaviors as they relate to the neoconservatives' hypothetical correlates of constraint, ideology, party support, and motivation. Such analysis should also encompass an appreciation of the systemic functions performed by delegate opinion leadership.

In this essay's title I termed the presidential nomination process "underexplored" because political scientists have not yet thoroughly pursued the rich and varied theoretical implications of process behavior. This essay attempted to illustrate several perspectives usefully employable in the study of nomination participants' activities, and to indicate those sorts of activist behaviors that particularly bear further scrutiny. If this essay is of heuristic value, it has fulfilled its purpose.

The studies in this volume in various ways address the theoretical concerns I have raised here. Certainly much about nomination process behavior remains to be discovered, but the studies here sizably contribute to our understanding of who the people in the middle of this process are and how they behave.

REFERENCES

Aldrich, John. 1980. *Before the Convention*. Chicago: University of Chicago Press.

Brams, Steven J. 1978. *The Presidential Election Game*. New Haven: Yale University Press.

Cobb, Roger W. and Charles D. Elder. 1972. *Participation in American Politics: The Dynamics of Agenda-Building*. Boston: Allyn and Bacon.

Costain, Ann N. 1980. "Changes in the Role of Ideology in American National Nominating Conventions and Among Party Identifiers." *Western Political Quarterly* 33: 73-86.

Farah, Barbara G., M. Kent Jennings, and Warren E. Miller. 1981. "Convention Delegates: Reform and Representation of Party Elites, 1972-1980." Paper presented at the Conference on Presidential Nomination Activism, College of William and Mary, Williamsburg, Virginia.

Hedlund, Ronald D. 1977. "Cross-over Voting in a 1976 Open Presidential Primary." *Public Opinion Quarterly* 41: 498-514.

Hutter, James L. and Steven E. Schier. 1982. "Iowa Political Party Activists: Social and Opinion Representation." Paper presented at the 1982 annual meeting of the Western Social Science Association, Denver, Colorado.

Jackson, John S., Barbara Leavitt Brown, and David Bositis. 1982. "Herbert McCloskey and Friends Revisited: 1980 Democratic and Republican Party Elites Compared to the Mass Public." *American Politics Quarterly* 10: 158-80.

Jackson, John S. III, Jesse C. Brown, and Barbara L. Brown. 1978. "Recruitment, Representation and Political Values: The 1976 Democratic National Convention Delegates." *American Politics Quarterly* 6: 187-212.

Kirkpatrick, Jeane J. 1976. *The New Presidential Elite*. New York: Russell Sage.

______. 1975. "Representation in the American National Conventions: The Case of 1972." *British Journal of Political Science* 5: 265- 322.

Kritzer, Herbert M. 1977. "The Representativeness of the 1972 Primaries." *Polity* 10:121-29.

Lengle, James I. 1981. *Representation and Presidential Primaries*. Westport, Conn.: Greenwood Press.

Marshall, Thomas R. 1981. *Presidential Nominations in a Reform Age*. New York: Praeger.

______. 1978. "Turnout and Representation: Caucuses Versus Primaries." *American Journal of Political Science* 22:169-82.

McCloskey, Herbert F., Paul J. Hoffman, and Rosemary O'Hara. 1960. "Issue Conflict and Consensus among Party Leaders and Followers." *American Political Science Review* 54: 406-27.

Mosca, Gaetano. 1939. *The Ruling Class*. New York: McGraw-Hill.

Nakamura, Robert, and Denis G. Sullivan. 1981. "A Critical Analysis of the Neoconservative Critique of Presidential Nomination Reform." Paper presented at the 1981 annual meeting of the American Political Science Association, New York.

Nyitray, Joseph P. 1975. "Amateur and Professional Democrats at the 1972 Texas

Pitkin, Hanna F. 1967. *The Concept of Representation*. Berkeley: University of California Press.

Polsy, Nelson and Aaron Wildavsky. 1980. *Presidential Elections*. 5th edition. New York: Scribners.

Ranney, Austin. 1975. *Curing the Mischief of Faction*. Berkeley: University of California Press.

———. 1974. "Comment on 'Changing the Rules Changes the Game'." *American Political Science Review* 68: 43-44.

———. 1972. "Turnout and Representation in Presidential Primary Elections." *American Political Science Review* 66: 21-37.

———. 1954. *The Doctrine of Responsible Party Government*. Urbana: University of Illinois Press, 1962.

Roback, Thomas H. 1975. "Amateurs and Professionals: Delegates to the 1972 Republican National Convention." *Journal of Politics* 37: 436-467.

Schattschneider, Elmer E. 1942. *Party Government*. New York: Farrar and Rinehart.

Schier, Steven E. 1980. *The Rules and the Game: Democratic National Convention Delegate Selection in Iowa and Wisconsin 1968-1976*. Washington, D.C.: University Press of America.

Schram, Martin. 1977. *Running for President: A Journal of the Carter Campaign*. New York: Pocket Books.

Soule, John W. and James Clarke. 1970. "Amateurs and Professionals: A Study of Delegates to the 1968 Democratic National Convention." *American Political Science Review* 64: 888-99.

Soule, John W. and Wilma E. McGrath. 1975. "A Comparative Study of Presidential Nomination Conventions: The Democrats of 1968 and 1972." *American Journal of Political Science* 19: 501-17.

Sullivan, Denis G., Jeffrey L. Pressman, and F. Christopher Arterton. 1976. *Explorations in Convention Decisionmaking: The Democratic Party in the 1970's*. San Francisco: W.H. Freeman.

Sullivan, Denis G., Jeffrey L. Pressman, Benjamin I. Page, and John J. Lyons. 1974. *The Politics of Representation: The Democratic Convention 1972*. New York: St. Martin's.

Wattenberg, Ben. 1973. Testimony before the Mikulski Commission on Delegate selection. (Mimeographed.)

White, Theodore H. 1973. *The Making of the President 1972*. New York: Atheneum.

______. 1969. *The Making of the President 1968*. New York: Atheneum.
______. 1965. *The Making of the President 1964*. New York: Atheneum.
______. 1961. *The Making of the President 1960*. New York: Atheneum.
Wilson, James Q. 1962. *The Amateur Democrat*. Chicago: University of Chicago Press.
______. 1973. *Political Organizations*. New York: Basic Books.
Witcover, Jules. 1978. *Marathon: The Pursuit of the Presidency 1976*. New York: Signet Books.

2

Between Light and Shadow: The Political Context

L. SANDY MAISEL

The blood on the streets of Chicago, Mayor Daley gesturing ominously at Abraham Ribicoff, the frustration of those who worked within the political system to unseat Lyndon Johnson only to have his handpicked successor capture the presidential nomination—these are the indelible memories of the 1968 Democratic convention. But just as these events left an imprint on the political minds of all of those who participated in that troubled convention, so too did they leave a permanent mark on the way in which we nominate our presidential candidates. Nothing has been the same since 1968.

When Nelson Polsby and Aaron Wildavsky wrote the first edition of *Presidential Elections* (1964), they were undoubtedly convinced that revision for all subsequent additions would be routine. All that would be necessary would be to include examples from each successive presidential election. After all, the process was not constantly under revision. The rules had remained substantially the same since the Democrats eliminated the two-thirds rule in 1936. The candidates' strategies did not differ significantly from year to year. The number of states holding primaries had remained roughly the same since 1920, and roughly the same percentage of delegates (about 40 percent) were chosen in primary elections. The importance of party bosses who controlled large delegations could not be underestimated.

Polsby and Wildavsky themselves have noted how much has changed in the two decades since their first edition appeared.

> Anyone who claims that there is no such thing as real and fundamental change in American politics need only glance at our account of what has happened [since the publication of their first edition]—procedures for making nominating decisions, the kinds of people who are influential in making them, the characteristics of the delegates, and their basic dispositions towards politics have all

> undergone drastic alterations over the years (Polsby and Wildavsky 1980, vii).

Not only has the process changed, but how political scientists study the process has changed as well. What we know about the "old process" comes largely from anecdotal material. For example, according to Schlesinger (as cited in Polsby and Wildavsky 1964, 119) James Farley opposed the attempt to defeat the two-thirds rule in 1932, "knowing well that not all delegates who were for Roosevelt were against the rule, and fearing that a defeat on this issue might set back the whole Roosevelt drive." How did Schlesinger know that Farley felt this way? How did Farley get his information? More important, was Farley right? We simply do not know. We have relied heavily on conventional wisdom, the wisdom of our elders. Key wrote that state and local party leaders' "influence may be decisive in the action of state primaries and conventions" (1964, 402) and that "though the conventions may not be bossed, selection of delegates becomes a matter handled exclusively by party professionals" (1964, 408). Generations of political scientists have explained the process to their students in these terms or terms similar to them. Key cites no sources; on what data did he base his findings?

In more recent years delegates to national conventions have been closely studied. Polsby and Wildavsky know who delegates are and what they think about politics because these delegates have been studied over and over (see, as examples, Sullivan et al. 1974; Kirkpatrick 1976; Sullivan et al. 1976). From the National Election Studies series we know a great deal about what the voting public thinks as they are deciding whom to support during the presidential selection process. But we know virtually nothing about the process through which delegates to national conventions are chosen if they are not chosen through presidential preference primaries.

The state convention is part of today's political world, and it is a fallback to the political world described by V.O. Key and his contemporaries. It is a world of party loyalists and political activists; it is a world of one-time amateur participants. Most important, it gives us a good overall view of the kinds of people active in politics in the 1980s. Perhaps the best analogy is to that famous television show of the era when caucus-convention politics was more prevalent, Rod Serling's *The Twilight Zone*. These delegates might not be "between light and shadow, between science and superstition," but they are in a twilight zone of politics, between the formal procedures of the past and those of the present and future, between boss-dominated parties and participatory democracy, between party loyalty and issue, or candidate, activism.

The goal of this chapter is to demonstrate how the process has evolved to the present state and to describe the part of the process which leads to state conventions choosing national convention delegates in some of the states.

THE DELEGATE SELECTION PROCESS

Hubert Humphrey won the Democratic presidential nomination in 1968 without winning a single presidential preference primary. The foundations of the Democratic party and of the presidential nominating process were shaken during the spring and summer of 1968. First Senator Eugene McCarthy and then Senator Robert Kennedy asked hundreds of thousands of Americans to seek to alter the country's foreign policy by working within the system. Many did work within the system and they succeeded at the task they were given. They unseated Lyndon Johnson, but the prize they sought, their party's nomination of a peace candidate, was denied to them by a complex, archaic, and ultimately undemocratic process.

The convention delegates, even as they were nominating Hubert Humphrey, saw that the process was badly flawed. They approved a majority report from the convention's credentials committee which called for giving Democrats a "meaningful and timely opportunity" to participate in the selection of their party's nominee, and they also accepted a minority report of the rules committee which called for changes to guarantee a "full and timely" opportunity for participation. Shortly after the convention, National Chairman Fred Harris appointed a Commission on Party Structure and Delegate Selection (commonly referred to as the McGovern-Fraser commission after its original chair and his successor) to carry out the mandate of the convention to alter the rules for delegate selection.

The McGovern-Fraser commission took its mandate seriously. The sense of urgency which pervaded its deliberations is expressed clearly in the concluding section of *Mandate for Change*, the commission's final report: "If we are not an open party; if we do not represent the demands for change, then the danger is not that the people will go to the Republican Party; it is that there will no longer be a way for people committed to orderly change to fulfill their needs and desires within our traditional political system. It is that they will turn to third or fourth party politics or to the anti-party politics of the street" (McGovern-Fraser commission 1971).

The reforms instituted as a result of the McGovern-Fraser commission's report took note of the fact that many state parties had no written rules, that the delegate selection process was often concluded before it was clear who the candidates were or what the significant issues would be, and that many rank-and-file Democrats had no opportunity at all to participate, much less to participate in a full and meaningful way. To correct these situations, state party rules had to be written down and widely disseminated, the process could not begin before the calendar year in which a presidential election was to be held, all meetings had to be widely publicized and opened to all Democrats, parties had to make significant efforts to see that those groups traditionally underrepresented in Democratic party decision-making circles—women, minorities, and younger voters—were involved in numbers roughly equivalent to their proportion of the voters in an area, and party meetings had to be run under rules which guaranteed the fairness of those proceedings.

The McGovern-Fraser commission's recommendations specifically recognized that states should have a good deal of leeway in determining how they would choose delegates to national conventions. Primary systems and caucus-convention systems, each with a number of variations, could conform with the new rules. However, by adopting these new rules, the national party sought to assure that certain basic standards were met.

To put the matter most bluntly, the changes had not only the desired impact, but also far-reaching consequences not envisioned by those who wrote the rules. This is not the appropriate place to reopen the debate over whether these rules were dysfunctional for the Democratic party. However, it is appropriate to note the effects of the McGovern-Fraser reforms and subsequent reforms on the presidential nominating process. For our purposes, the most significant consequence is that many state parties found that the easiest way to conform with the new Democratic party rules was to hold presidential preference primaries. In 1972, state delegations were successfully challenged on the basis that the caucus-convention procedure had not been carried out in a manner which complied with the new rules. Thereafter, state parties felt that they were on less dangerous ground if they selected delegates through primaries. Here the rules were

Table 2.1. Presidential primaries and percentage of delegates chosen, 1964–1980

Year	Democrats		Republicans	
	Number of primaries	Percentage of delegates	Number of primaries	Percentage of delegates
1964	17	45.7	17	45.6
1968	15	40.2	15	38.1
1972	22	65.3	21	56.8
1976	30	76.0	30	71.0
1980	32	71.8	34	76.0

Source: 1964 through 1976 comes from Wayne 1981, 84; 1980 derived by the author from Congressional Quarterly Service sources.

quite simple and could be administered through one central election mechanism, as opposed to caucuses spread throughout the state and administered by local officials less concerned about or even aware of the procedural rules.

The McGovern-Fraser reforms affected only the Democratic party. However, because delegate selection rules are most frequently written into state law, changes in how the Democrats operated had effects on Republican party procedures as well. Table 2.1 lists the number of presidential preference primaries and the percentage of delegates chosen in those primaries for each party since 1964. The trend toward more primaries in which an increasing percentage of the delegates are chosen is clear. There appears to have been a slight aberration for the Democrats in 1980, because a smaller percentage of Democrats were chosen in these primaries than had been the case in 1976. However, this too can be explained by rule changes. In 1980 the Democrats were more insistent on closed primaries than they had been in the past. Michigan, which has traditionally held a primary, found that it was unable or unwilling to change state law to conform to Democratic party rules. Consequently, the Michigan Democrats held a nonbinding primary on the same day that the Republicans held their primary. However, the delegates to the national convention were elected in separate caucuses, which had been held nearly a month earlier. If Michigan's 141 delegates were added to the total selected in primary elections, the upward trend would have continued.

It should be further noted that there are a number of different kinds of presidential preference primaries. Those listed in Table 2.1 are only those primaries through which delegates are actually chosen to the national convention. New York Republicans are included in this list, even though the delegates' presidential preferences are not listed on the ballot. So too are those states such as Illinois in which the presidential preference poll and the delegate selection poll are conducted separately, though at the same time. I have also included the Vermont Republican primary, which determines the delegates chosen only if one candidate receives 40 percent of the votes cast, which did not happen in 1980. Nonbinding presidential preference primaries held by Idaho, Michigan, Texas, and Vermont Democrats and by Montana and District of Columbia Republicans are not included in the table.

Most, but not all, of the largest states are included in the group which holds presidential preference primaries. However, twenty states for the Democrats (plus Guam, the Virgin Islands, Democrats Abroad, and Latin American Democrats) and eighteen for the Republicans (including Vermont, which really had a dual system) selected their national convention delegates through some sort of caucus-convention system.

These systems too can be usefully broken down, with different categorization schemes appropriate depending on the problem confronting the analyst. In some cases a tiered-caucus system exists, one in which delegates are elected at one caucus level to go on to the next caucus level and so forth up to the state convention which chooses delegates to the national convention. For instance, Oklahoma Democrats met first at the precinct level, then at the county level, then at the congressional district level, and only finally at the state convention. Some of the delegates were chosen at the district conventions, which in fact convened at the site of the state convention. Others were chosen as the state convention met as a body. In other cases, for example both Republicans and Democrats in Maine, local caucuses elected delegates directly to the state convention at which national convention delegates were selected. In the case of the "nonstate" Democrats, such as those on Guam, delegates to the national convention were elected directly at the caucus, with no intermediate step.

Another useful way to categorize caucuses deals with the amount of competition. Senator Howard Baker referred to the January caucuses in Iowa as "the functional equivalent of a primary" (Germond and Witcover 1981, 93ff.). The same could be said of the caucuses in Maine and perhaps in other states. A second distinct group includes those states in which there was competition for delegate slates, but not intense competition. These states can be separated from those above by factors such as personal effort by the presidential candidates and/or turnout (though only estimates are available for turnout in many states). Colorado and North Dakota Democrats seem to fit into this category. Finally, there were several caucus states in which there was essentially no competition. This seems to have been the case in many Republican states, e.g., Oklahoma or Vermont, whose caucuses were held after it was clear that Ronald Reagan had the nomination in hand.

However, the clearest distinction seems to be between the Democratic party caucuses and the Republican party caucuses. They differed in terms of formal rules and informal norms as well as level of competition. In an effort to place the data on which the rest of this book is based into as clear a context as is possible, a discussion of some of the important differences between Democratic and Republican activities in caucus-convention states follows.

THE 1980 CAUCUSES

The rules governing the *Call to the 1980 Democratic National Convention* specified the ways in which delegates chosen through the caucus-convention system were to be selected. Specifically, the rules mandated that the Democrats in a particular state convene all caucuses on the same day, that the presidential preference of the delegates at each successive stage in the selection of delegates to the national convention accurately reflect the presidential preferences of those participating at the next lower stage (except that those preferencees receiving less than 20 percent of the expressed support need not receive delegates to the next higher level) and that at least three-quarters of the delegates be chosen in a district not larger than a congressional district. Within these guidelines states had a good deal of leeway; however, these rules themselves were quite determinative of the composition of delegations to state conventions, all of which were chosen through a process the rules of which were restricted by the national rules.

Because delegates at each stage in the process had to reflect the presidential preferences of those at earlier stages, the first stage in the total process was the most important. Thus it was the Iowa caucuses on January 21, not the county or district caucuses held later in the process,

Table 2.2. Democratic caucuses and presidential preferences of delegates

State	Date of first stage	Presidential preference of national delegates		
		Carter	Kennedy	Other
Iowa	January 21	31	17	22
Maine	February 10	11	11	—
Minnesota	February 26	38	—	37
Delaware	March 9	10	4	—
Hawaii	March 9	15	4	—
Washington	March 9	36	21	1
Alaska	March 11	0.6	1.8	8.6
Oklahoma	March 11	34	3	5
Mississippi	March 15	32	—	—
South Carolina	March 15	34	1	2
Wyoming	March 15	8	3	—
Virginia	March 22	59	5	—
Idaho	April 17	8	5	4
North Dakota	April 19	2	4	8
Michigan	April 26	70	71	—
Missouri	April 22/May 6	57	5	15
Texas	May 3	104	38	10
Colorado	May 5	19	13	8
Utah	May 19	10	4	6
Vermont	May 24	5	7	—

Source: Congressional Quarterly articles at time of caucuses and on the eve of the Democratic National Convention (August 9, 1980: 2268).

which received the most press attention and which in fact determined the composition of the Iowa State Democratic Convention and the Iowa delegation to the Democratic National Convention. Because of the importance of the local-level caucuses, it is important to note when these were held. These dates are listed in Table 2.2.

It is important to note that the first stage in twelve of the twenty caucus-convention states was held early in the presidential nominating process. The Iowa caucus, of course, received the most publicity. However, caucuses in other states were also hotly contested between supporters of the various presidential hopefuls. Records were set in state after state for caucus attendance. Those at the caucuses were often encouraged to come to support their presidential favorite in much the same way that party faithful are prodded into voting on primary day in other states. The delegates elected at these caucuses were elected because of their support for one presidential hopeful or another, or because they were well-known party workers who preferred to stay uncommitted and convinced a significant proportion of those at the caucus to do the same. However, they did not go on to the next stage, nor eventually to the state conventions, just because they were long-time party faithfuls. They had to play an active role in the 1980 presidential selection process to be selected to go on.

In other states, however, the caucuses were less hotly contested. In the southern caucus states, for instance, Senator Kennedy's campaign did not make a major effort because they did not feel such an effort would bear fruit. These states typically do not have a history of contested, open caucuses such as that which exists in Iowa, Maine, or Minnesota. Therefore, caucuses were less well attended, contests less frequent, and delegates more like those conforming to the conventional wisdom of years ago, loyal party followers and workers, receiving rewards for past efforts.

In still other caucus states the first round was not held until after it was clear that President Carter had built an insurmountable lead over Senator Kennedy and would be renominated. The experiences in those states differed according to local factors. In Missouri, as an example, the candidates did little active campaigning, but supporters of Senator Kennedy—union liberals (especially the International Association of Machinists), pro-abortion and pro-ERA supporters, blacks, and others—persisted in their campaigns, particularly in the local enclaves where they had most support, even though by late April and early May when the Missouri caucuses were held it was evident that their candidate would not be the nominee. In Michigan, on the other hand, the Kennedy campaign worked hard and had strong support from labor. The Michigan caucuses were strongly contested by the Kennedy campaign because they were viewed as a last-ditch effort. Kennedy strategists saw that they could gain a symbolic victory quite cheaply, largely because the caucuses were poorly advertised, poorly understood by the voters, and consequently poorly attended. The organizational efforts of the pro-Kennedy unions paid significant dividends. In other states with late caucuses, however, the fight was over before it began. The campaigns did not wage major battles, and the caucuses were poorly attended. The delegates selected tended to be those who had been active in party organization in the past.

A number of factors stand out in looking at the experiences in the states in which the Democratic party elected delegates to the national convention through the caucus/convention method. First, of course, the rules played a major role. There was no chance for delegates to switch their presidential preference after the first stage in the process was completed. Thus those delegates from early states could not respond to the campaign as it unfolded. More important for our point of view, the delegates selected to state convention were supporters of particular presidential candidates and often viewed their role primarily in that light. Thus, it is unclear whether they would have wanted to change their presidential preference even if they had had the opportunity.

However, the rules were not the only factor influencing the choice of delegates. Level of competition was also important. Determined by different factors in different states, level of competition was to some extent determined by outside forces—i.e., did the major presidential contenders put significant campaign resources into these caucuses? In some cases they felt this was necessary because of the timing of the caucuses and the media attention; Iowa and Maine stand out as examples here. In other cases the effort was either put in or not put in because of perceived payoffs. However, factors peculiar to individual states also determined the level of competition. This was particularly apparent in those states which have a rich history of caucuses and meaningful state convention. In North Dakota, despite the fact that the first-level caucuses were not held until mid-April and no presidential hopeful made a major effort in the state, delegates at the state convention fell into five separate camps—Carter supporters, Kennedy supporters, uncommitted delegates, and delegates not committed to either presidential hopeful but united under the banner in one case of the state's education lobby and the other of the Prairie Campaign for Economic Democracy. The last two groups received two and six presidential delegates from the state convention respectively.

The delegates to Democratic state conventions, then, represent a diverse group. They are Carter loyalists and Kennedy loyalists. They are party regulars and one-time activists. They are those who fought hard for the positions they received and those who attended conventions almost as a matter of routine. They are those active in their state party and those whose activity was stimulated by others outside of their states. They are certainly not a unified bloc, but they do represent the wealth of experiences which define activists in a political system as decentralized as ours.

Table 2.3. Dates of Republican caucuses and presidential preferences of delegates

State	Date of first stage	Presidential preferences of national delegates		
		Reagan	Bush	Other
Iowa	January 21	37	—	—
Arkansas	February 2	9	8	2
Alaska	February 21	19	—	—
Minnesota	February 26	26	17	—
Maine	all of February	—	6	4
Delaware	March 9	4	—	2
Missouri	March 22-29	34	—	3
Oklahoma	April 7	34	—	—
Washington	April 13	34	2	1
Vermont	April 22	16	—	3
Virginia	May 10-13	51	—	—
Arizona	May 3	28	—	—
Colorado	May 5	31	—	—
Wyoming	May 10	16	—	3
North Dakota	May 15	12	1	4
Hawaii	May 17	3	—	11
Montana	June 6	20	—	—
Utah	June 28	21	—	—

Source: Congressional Quarterly articles on eve of Republican National Convention. (July 12, 1980: 1928). Many delegates switched to Reagan at the convention as other candidacies collapsed.

Politicians and political scientists spend a good deal of time and effort attempting to differentiate Republicans from Democrats. One very clear difference has emerged strikingly in recent years: the Republicans have specifically rejected the Democratic National Committee's efforts to dictate how states should select delegates to national nominating conventions. The Republicans have had a reform commission; they do encourage more participation by women and minorities. However, they have assiduously avoided requiring their state party organizations to follow any particular rules or guidelines. "And that," as the Mad Hatter said, "has made all the difference."

Table 2.3 lists the Republican states which held caucuses in 1980, along with the dates of the first stage of the caucus-convention process and with the allocation of delegates among presidential candidates after the state convention. Only seven of the eighteen states held the first round of their caucuses relatively early in the nominating season. The other eleven states held their first caucuses well after the Reagan nomination was assured. Even more important is recognition of the fact that the first stage of the nominating process is not as significant for the Republicans as it is for the Democrats. While the Democrats insist that the presidential preference of those at the first stage in the nominating process is reflected at the next and subsequent stages, the Republicans mandate no such representation. To the contrary, in many states those attending the first round caucuses are not even asked their presidential preference. In Iowa, where the Republican caucuses probably were given more media attention than those of the Democrats, presidential preference was determined. George Bush went from the position of an asterisk in public opinion polls to that of a legitimate challenger to Ronald Reagan because of his showing in those caucuses. However, the Iowa Republicans do not freeze delegates selected at the local caucuses into their presidential choice for the rest of the process. There was a good deal of shifting away from Bush and toward Reagan at subsequent county and district conventions, before the final delegation to the national convention was chosen.

Even with that shifting permitted, Iowa is somewhat atypical of the Republican pattern. Colorado is perhaps most typical. In the case of Colorado, Republicans, as identified by registration procedures outlined in state law, caucused at the precinct level in order to elect delegates to county conventions. Approximately 3 to 5 percent of the eligible Republicans attended the caucuses, though no accurate turnout statistics were reported. Those attending the precinct caucuses were not polled as to their presidential preference. At the county conventions, delegates were elected to the state and congressional district conventions. Again the norm was for straw polls not to be taken; even when they were taken, these votes on presidential preference were not used to allocate delegates to the next stage convention.

But even the Colorado example shows more "regularity" than was seen in other Republican states. In Arizona, for example, rank and file Republicans had virtually no say in the process at all. In the spring of 1978, rank and file Republicans elected precinct committeemen. These individuals were the only ones eligible to attend the first round of the Arizona caucus, held in May of 1980. Thus the total potential electorate for the county caucuses for Arizona Republicans was only about 200. Oklahoma provides another interesting case for the Republicans. All registered Republicans are permitted to attend the precinct meetings, which were held on April 7 in 1980. Delegates were elected at these meetings to attend county conventions; at those conventions delegates were elected to the district and state convention, regardless of whether they were elected by the county conventions or not. Thus the process stays open to a larger number of party activists for a much longer period of time.

It is not necessary or appropriate to make value judgments on the differences between Republican procedures and those of the Democrats. It is not far from accurate to say that the Republican caucus state procedures in 1980 look very much like those which the Democrats employed prior to 1972. The main changes within the Republican party have involved states moving from caucus-convention systems to primary systems, often following changes in state laws which were implemented because of the needs of the Democrats to comply with their party's national rules. Thus the Republican party caucus states have not had to comply with the rules of the McGovern-Fraser commission and have not done so. In not doing so, they have not had the benefits of those reforms in terms of openness and timeliness and the like; nor have they had to deal with the problems caused by those reforms and commented on so frequently by critics of the new Democratic procedures.

What one can say with some certainty is that, compared with Democratic delegate selection, the process by which the Republican delegates to the 1980 state conventions were chosen looked a lot like the process in operation throughout the nation before the reforms. But were the results the same as before the reforms? If so, we might expect the delegates to be party regulars and party workers attending the convention as a reward for past work, joining in a statewide meeting with others who share their views, to reinforce those views, to rebuild the spirit of the party which will carry them on to the fall campaign. As we shall see, findings on these points are not so clear cut.

The purpose of this chapter has been to provide some background for those reading the chapters drawn from analysis of the survey of delegates to state conventions in 1980. Certainly these delegates do not stand as a random sample of political activists. They were chosen as part of a process which itself is undergoing change. They represent only one group out of a number who together constitute the decision-makers that process has designated. Moreover, because these delegates come from different states which chose delegates with different political situations, they are not homogeneous.

However, they are an important group of political activists to examine for the exact reason that they represent a wide range of political activists. The Republicans, particularly, represent something of a throwback to the politics of another era. As such, they are undoubtedly different from Republicans who are active in states which do not maintain the caucus-convention system. The Democrats themselves represent a diverse group, some not unlike their Republican counterparts, some not unlike their copartisans in primary states.

The presidential nominating process is often criticized because it lacks coherence. The diversity of rules—and consequently the diversity of types of people chosen as delegates—is symptomatic of this lack of coherence. The delegates analyzed in this study do represent activists who have played key roles in state and local political organizations, but perhaps without decision-making power. So long as we understand what these delegates represent and what they do not, they do stand as an important group to study in order to learn more about those active on the American political scene.

REFERENCES

Germond, Jack W. and Jules Witcover. 1981. *Blue Smoke and Mirrors*. New York: Viking.

Key, V. O. 1964. *Politics, Parties, and Pressure Groups*. 5th ed. New York: Thomas Y. Crowell.

Kirkpatrick, Jeane. 1976. *The Presidential Elite*. New York: Russell Sage Foundation and the Twentieth Century Fund.

McGovern-Fraser Commission. 1971. *Mandate for Change,* the Final Report of the Commission on Party Structure and Delegate Selection. Washington, D.C.: Democratic National Committee.

Polsby, Nelson W. and Aaron Wildavsky. 1980. *Presidential Elections,* 5th ed. New York: Scribner's.

———. 1964. *Presidential Elections*. 2nd ed. New York: Scribner's.

Sullivan, Denis G., Jeffrey L. Pressman, and F. Christopher Arterton. 1976. *Explorations in Convention Decision Making*. San Francisco: W. H. Freeman.

Sullivan, Denis G., Jeffrey L. Pressman, Benjamin I. Page, and John J. Lyons. 1974. *The Politics of Representation*. New York: St. Martin's.
Wayne, Stephen J. 1981. *The Road to the White House*. post- election ed. New York: St. Martin's.

3

An Analysis of State Party Activists

ALAN I. ABRAMOWITZ, JOHN McGLENNON,
RONALD B. RAPOPORT

The question of how best to study American state and local parties has long been in dispute. Some scholars (e.g., Burnham 1970) have relied heavily on aggregate election results; others (e.g., Gibson, Cotter, Bibby, and Huckshorn 1981) have sought information about the staffing, budgets, and other operating details of party organizations. In between are studies of county chairmen (Jackson and Hitlin 1981), and of state chairmen (Huckshorn 1976). Gibson et al. (1981) are clearly correct in their contention that organizations can be fruitfully studied in terms of "institutional party strength," but it is also true that this party strength is, over a period of time, dependent on the financial and manpower support of large numbers of volunteer activists. It is this group of activists at the state level that we propose to examine.

State party activists are not homogeneous across the United States. As Frank Sorauf recently noted, "what we blithely call the national parties are merely coalitions of jealous, wary, and diverse state and local party organizations" (Sorauf 1980, 109). In spite of this diversity, however, we will argue that there are some very important commonalities among the activists in each state party—commonalities in the demographic makeup of the activist group and in the ideological and issue positions of activists. Furthermore, we will show that much of the regionalism of the party system, discussed by Key and those who followed (Key 1949; Lockhard 1959; Fenton 1966) is no longer so prevalent. Findings at the mass level (Beck and Lopatto 1982) indicating that even the South has become much less distinct, also apply at the level of party activists. In the second part of the article, we will focus on how state party differences in past and present electoral success have produced parties with distinctive activist bases.

DEMOGRAPHIC CHARACTERISTICS

More than in other countries, political activity in the United States is highly correlated with social class (Nie and Verba 1975, 42). Whether we look at voting or more demanding activities, education and income are strongly related to participation (Milbrath and Goel 1977). It should not be surprising then to find that the incomes and education levels of our activists are substantially above the average for their states. Overall, 18 percent of our activists earn $45,000 or more a year, while only 16 percent earn under $15,000. In every state, at least 10 percent of the activists earn over $45,000. In terms of education, the unrepresentativeness of the activists is, if anything, more apparent. Over half are college graduates, and more than 80 percent have at least some college.

More interesting than the aggregate findings, however, are party and state differences in demographics. Traditionally, among mass samples, Republican voting has borne at least a mild relationship to income, race, and education (Miller, Miller, and Schneider 1980). However, among eligible voters, the relationship with income and education has diminished substantially in the last two decades, particularly among the young (Abramson 1974; Ladd 1982). What we should expect to find for elites, across states, is not self-evident. Particularly in states dominated by one party or the other, we might expect to find class differences more commonly expressed in factional disputes within the majority party rather than between the parties. Samuel Patterson (1963) found that in Oklahoma, a Democratic dominated state, Democratic activists were substantially higher in income, education, and age than were their Republican counterparts. Patterson then argued that a dominant state party might be expected to draw on the dominant social group. If so, states in our study like South Carolina and Texas might be expected to show the same reversal that Patterson found, rather than reflecting the traditional partisan coalitions.

As Table 3.1 shows, however, party activist differences in income do reflect traditional differences in the coalitional bases of the parties. In all eleven states, Republican activists are wealthier. They are both more likely to make $45,000 or more (23 percent compared to 13 percent for Democrats) and less likely to make under $15,000 per year (13 percent compared to 19 percent for the Democratic activists). It is important to note that this difference is not determined by the degree of minority representation among Democratic activists, as it is found in all states,

Table 3.1. Income and education of activists

State	Percentage over $45,000		Percentage under $15,000		Percentage college grad		*Ns**	
	Repub-lican	Demo-crat	Repub-lican	Demo-crat	Repub-lican	Demo-crat	Repub-lican	Demo-crat
Arizona	17.9	10.5	14.1	21.1	45.5	58.1	387	337
Colorado	26.2	11.2	9.7	19.1	58.9	57.6	638	1003
Iowa	22.1	8.8	10.5	22.1	56.6	45.9	1107	1673
Maine	15.7	6.4	20.9	28.2	59.4	53.6	441	1046
Missouri	21.0	14.7	14.0	16.4	45.4	40.7	380	317
North Dakota	34.3	16.1	11.7	22.0	44.8	50.2	404	623
Oklahoma	21.7	13.7	16.0	14.3	40.4	37.0	1244	609
South Carolina	20.2	12.9	13.4	19.8	60.9	60.0	739	621
Texas	37.8	16.7	8.7	15.0	59.0	60.0	564	440
Utah	11.7	9.0	17.6	18.5	59.0	56.1	1218	452
Virginia	27.7	21.3	9.3	15.3	56.9	59.1	1716	1669

*This is the total *N* for each state party. In cases of missing data percentages are calculated on the basis of a reduced *N* throughout the paper. In no case are *N*s reduced by more than 20 percent.

regardless of whether blacks number less than 5 percent of the Democratic delegates as in North Dakota, or over 30 percent of the Democratic delegates as in South Carolina.

Our support for Patterson's hypothesis is rather weak. Although the four most Republican states according to Ranney's Index of Party Competition (Ranney 1976) do show four of the five highest Republican income advantages, Democratic dominant and majority states do not show particularly small Republican advantages. More striking is the relationship between Republican and Democratic incomes across states ($r = .74$ between percentage of Democrats under $25,000 in a state, and the percentage of Republicans earning under $25,000). Consistently then, Republicans earn more than do Democratic activists, and those states with wealthier Republican activists also have wealthier Democratic activists.

Studies of party elites have consistently found small differences between educational attainment of Democratic and Republican elites (Jackson and Brown 1982, 12). Ours is no different. This is not surprising given the overall high level of education among our activists, and the increasingly large role played by public school teachers in the Democratic

Table 3.2. Sex, minority representation, and age of activists

State	Percentage female		Percentage minority		Percentage under 30		Percentage over 60	
	Repub-lican	Demo-crat	Repub-lican	Demo-crat	Repub-lican	Demo-crat	Repub-lican	Demo-crat
Arizona	46.7	47.1	1.8	20.4	4.3	22.0	30.7	18.0
Colorado	39.7	50.3	2.9	9.4	8.3	18.1	14.2	12.0
Iowa	37.4	50.4	1.2	2.0	14.2	22.9	15.2	11.9
Maine	43.5	52.1	0.0	1.6	*	*	*	*
Missouri	42.8	48.7	*	*	15.6	15.8	22.0	15.5
North Dakota	33.9	46.6	1.3	2.0	9.0	23.5	18.2	18.6
Oklahoma	47.7	53.4	3.6	12.5	19.7	18.3	18.4	15.9
South Carolina	35.7	58.7	1.5	38.3	18.0	14.2	15.3	13.1
Texas	44.8	40.0	3.1	16.5	12.6	21.1	13.2	10.8
Utah	22.3	37.6	0.8	4.8	22.0	22.5	9.5	13.9
Virginia	46.6	50.8	1.9	18.0	14.7	18.6	17.9	17.3

*Data unavailable for state party.

party (an average of one in four Democratic delegates were active in educational organizations, compared with less than one in seven at the Republican conventions). Once again state differences are rather small, as Table 3.1 shows.

Although openness of the parties without regard to age, race, and sex categories is specifically mentioned in the charters of both parties (Harmel and Janda 1982), the Democratic commitment to affirmative action is unmatched in Republican party rules. Recently, the Democratic party has debated, and, at various times, instituted quotas for women and minorities (Ranney 1978).

This might lead to an expectation of a substantially higher percentage of young, women, and minority delegates at Democratic state conventions. However, while race has consistently and strongly been related to vote, this has not been the case for either age or sex (Miller, Miller, and Schneider 1980). We should expect then that party differences in race will be reinforced by both electoral coalition composition and by affirmative action guidelines, while only the latter will affect sex and age distributions (Mitofsky and Plissner 1980, 43). This should lead to large party differences in minority representation, but much smaller age and sex differences.

Table 3.2 strongly supports this expectation. In every state with a sizable nonwhite population, Democratic activists mirror or exceed the percentage of minority group members in the population, while for Republicans, the percentage of nonwhite activists is almost entirely unrelated to the percentage of nonwhites in the state population. For example, Iowa Republicans, with 2.6 percent nonwhites in the state, had 1.2 percent minority representation at their convention, while South Carolina, with 31.2 percent minorities, had only 1.5 percent minority representation at their Republican convention.

Youth and female representation are less related to party. In ten of eleven states, Democrats had more female activists than did Republicans. However, because of affirmative action mandates, it is difficult to infer from this that a higher percentage of Democratic activists are female. Overall, Democrats had an average of 49 percent female delegates and Republicans 40 percent. Within each party female representation was quite consistent across states, with the exception of Utah, which is heavily influenced by a strongly patriarchal Mormon Church. Once again we see consistent (although in this case small) differences between parties, and broad homogeneity across states.

Age differences, as Table 3.2 shows, are even less consistent. Although a majority of states show more Democratic delegates under thirty, the differences exceed 10 percent for only Arizona and North Dakota. The Republican advantage in delegates over sixty, although present in a majority of states, reaches 5 percent in only Arizona and Missouri. Unlike income and education, in which delegates come from the higher echelons, age and sex breakdowns of delegates are much less skewed, although, not surprisingly in view of participation research (Verba and Nie 1972), the young are underrepresented in both parties. Women are slightly underrepresented in the Republican party, but not in the Democratic party.

PARTISANSHIP AND IDEOLOGY

But demographic attributes, important as they may be symbolically, are clearly important to issue representation. The study of social background characteristics is often based on the assumption that they will affect the issue positions supportive of the groups represented (Putnam 1976). American political parties are often viewed as ideologically decentralized, even comprising different political cultures (Elazar 1972). We do know, for instance, that Southern Democrats vote consistently more

Table 3.3. Ideology and partisanship of activists

State	Ideological placement[a]		Issue scale[b]		Percentage strong national partisans		Percentage strong state partisans	
	Republican	Democrat	Republican	Democrat	Republican	Democrat	Republican	Democrat
Arizona	4.40	2.25	4.4	16.4	93.3	83.6	93.6	85.7
Colorado	4.30	2.34	5.4	15.5	87.3	62.8	85.7	71.7
Iowa	3.80	2.32	8.3	17.1	80.1	75.9	78.4	74.0
Maine	3.78	2.43	9.7	15.8	71.7	63.2	70.8	61.5
Missouri	4.32	2.67	5.2	13.0	83.6	85.7	79.2	82.7
North Dakota	4.07	2.36	6.3	16.2	93.5	61.5	92.7	74.2
Oklahoma	4.41	2.80	4.7	12.3	83.9	78.6	80.6	81.4
South Carolina	4.38	2.47	4.3	13.5	84.9	70.9	78.1	81.3
Texas	4.53	2.35	3.9	15.0	88.4	77.7	81.2	79.4
Utah	4.38	2.47	4.6	13.7	79.3	55.6	74.5	69.6
Virginia	4.27	2.51	5.5	14.4	85.0	77.8	82.5	81.7

[a]On this scale 1 is very liberal and 5 is very conservative.

[b]On this scale 0 means that all 13 issues responses were in the conservative direction; 26 would mean that all issue positions were in the liberal direction.

conservatively than do northern Democrats in the Congress (Manley 1973). Kenneth Janda (1980), comparing U.S. parties with forty-two others in Western Europe, found the U.S. Democratic and Republican parties to be the two lowest in centralization of power. On the other hand, surveys of national convention delegates have found wide differences between mean positions of the delegates from the two parties. This finding applied to the pre-amateur days of the 1950s (McClosky et al. 1960) as well as for the radically altered environment of the 1970s (Kirkpatrick 1976; Farah et al. 1981). In our survey, we had respondents rate themselves on a one-to-five scale ranging from very liberal (one) to very conservative (five). In addition, we asked them for their positions on thirteen national issues, on the basis of which we computed a liberalism scale.[1] As Table 3.3 shows, the most striking differences are between parties in a given state. On the five- point scale the average difference in self-placement between Democratic and Republican delegates was 1.8 units. Although interparty differences are not the same in all states, the smallest difference is still substantial (1.34 units in Maine). Furthermore, the most conservative Democratic party (Oklahoma) is still to the liberal side of center on the ideological scale, and is closer to the most liberal Democratic party (Arizona) than it is to the nearest Republican party (Maine). Similarly the most liberal Republican Party (Maine) is still closer to the most conservative Republican party (Texas) than it is to the nearest Democratic party.

Of course self-placement is a subjective matter. Liberal in Texas may not mean the same as in Maine. Turning to our objective measure of ideology (based on the thirteen issue responses), we find almost identical results. In fact, the correlation (r) between mean state party score on self-placement and objective ideology is − .88 for the Democrats, and − .98 for the Republicans (because the scales are in opposite directions, the correlations have negative signs). Again, although there is a range on our liberalism scale among Democrats (from 12.3 to 17.1) and among Republicans (from 3.9 to 9.7), the most liberal Republican Party (still Maine) is substantially more conservative than the most conservative Democratic Party (still Oklahoma). Furthermore, each state Democratic party is substantially more distant from its Republican counterpart than it is from any other Democratic party, and the same holds for each state Republican party.

What stands out from this examination of ideology of activists is the consistent liberalism of the Democrats and the consistent conservatism of the Republicans. Even in the most conservative Democratic state, delegates are much more likely to call themselves liberals than conservatives, while even in the most liberal Republican state, delegates are more than seven times as likely to call themselves conservatives as to call themselves liberals. Activists in traditional strongholds of conservative Democrats, like South Carolina, Virginia, and Texas, are not even clearly more conservative than those in states like Maine, North Dakota, and Iowa. American party politics has clearly become less regional and more national, at least at the party activist level.

Nationalization of parties, however, implies not only ideological similarity, but loyalty to the national party as well. To what degree do these convention delegates identify with the national party whose state convention they are attending? While it is clearly the case that we would not expect many delegates at a party convention to identify with the other party, we might expect to find, given the tradition of regionalism and localism, that the degree of identification with the national party would vary across states. There has recently been a rebirth of regional caucuses in the Congress (Arieff 1980) and during Carter's term westerners, even Democrats, were known to be unhappy with many of his programs (Fenton, Cook, and Buchanan 1980). This could produce lower levels of national identification, even given the high level of ideological homogeneity within each party.

Our measure of the degree of party identification in a state is simply the percentage of delegates from that state party convention saying that they strongly identify with that party. (We asked respondents about their identification with national and state parties in different questions.) Even at a national convention we might expect to find some variance on partisan strength. Lee (1981) reports that 74 percent of 1976 Democratic National Convention delegates and 72 percent of 1976 Republican delegates were strong partisans. Overall, the level of national partisanship among our activists is even higher than Lee found; an average of 78 percent of our respondents were strong identifiers (72 percent among Democrats and 85 percent among Republicans). There is, however, substantial variation across states, particularly among the Democrats.

The percentage of Democratic delegates calling themselves "strong Democrats" ranges from slightly over half (56 percent) in Utah to 86 percent in Missouri. What is particularly striking is the lack of aggregate relationship among state parties between ideology and national partisanship. Oklahoma, which was the most conservative Democratic party, is the third most partisan at the national level. Equally surprising is that, of the five border and southern states, four are above average (72 percent) for Democrats in their national partisanship, and even South Carolina is only 1 percent below average. Southern parties look increasingly like other Democratic parties outside of the South. Although the South does not show low partisanship, however, two of the three western states do (Utah and Colorado).

Low levels of national partisanship can be a result of a differentiation between state and national parties or of simply a low identification with party in general. Of the four states lowest in national partisanship, three (Utah, Colorado, and North Dakota) show substantial increases in loyalty when we look at state partisanship.[2] Only Maine does not. What sets Maine apart from other Democratic parties is its large number of delegates who are new to the process. More than one-half of Maine Democratic delegates had been active less than five years, and almost 60 percent had been active in few or no recent political campaigns.[3]

Republicans show substantially less variation in partisanship across states. In every state except Maine, 79 percent or more of the delegates are strong partisans. Maine Republicans resemble Maine Democrats in that almost half (46 percent) have been active less than five years, and in that over 60 percent are usually active in few or no campaigns. Once again, it is the absence of previous party contact, either national or state, which is responsible for the low level of partisanship (which does not increase at the state level). One surprising fact about Republicans, compared with the Democrats, is that state partisanship is weaker than national partisanship in ten of the eleven states. Clearly regionalism plays less of a role in the Republican party. This lack of regionalism may be attributed to the ideological homogeneity of the national Republican party (Ladd 1982), as well as to the greater visibility of national Republican organizations such as the Republican National Committee, giving the party members a more national focus.

ORGANIZATIONAL CHANGE

In addition to regional and party differences among our activists, our data also allow us to look at organizational differences among state party organizations and to examine how party activists in different organizational situations might differ from one another. Parties may differ in a variety of ways. The differences we will examine relate to changes in party dominance (measured by the Ranney index) over the last thirty years. If a minority party has any hope of eventual success, it is under pressure to try to expand its appeal, both to the voting electorate and to the set of more involved or involvable activists. Over the last forty years, party competition has increased markedly across the country. This is reflected in our eleven states. Using 1946-1963 data, Ranney categorized twenty-five states as either one-party states or modified one-party states, and twenty-three as two-party competitive states (Ranney 1965). Eight of our eleven states were either one-party or modified one-party states. On the basis of 1962-1973 data, only sixteen states—including only five of our eleven—still had scores that would put them in these categories using the criteria Ranney used in 1965 (Ranney 1976).

In order to increase levels of competition, the minority party had to

Table 3.4. Migration, conversion, and pragmatism of activists

State	Percentage childhood out of state		Percentage switching parties		Percentage pragmatic	
	Republican	Democrat	Republican	Democrat	Republican	Democrat
Arizona	78.0	62.5	19.5	5.4	37.9	39.5
Colorado	64.1	55.1	24.0	17.5	31.4	33.6
Iowa	23.4	22.7	18.1	16.7	41.7	30.8
Maine	46.3	47.6	*	*	37.3	26.8
Missouri	31.0	18.6	22.2	7.0	31.1	38.9
North Dakota	17.8	17.9	9.5	19.0	52.9	36.5
Oklahoma	39.5	25.2	31.1	11.0	27.6	32.9
South Carolina	52.3	23.7	29.2	9.4	31.8	34.5
Texas	*	*	35.8	9.8	36.1	39.8
Utah	*	*	17.9	27.1	20.3	35.0
Virginia	55.8	39.6	31.0	12.6	38.7	45.6

*Data unavailable for state party group.

recruit partisans from the majority party, recruit voters and activists disproportionately among migrants to the state, or recruit heavily among the young. Our data allow us to examine the first two of these processes in detail. If we take as our base point for party strength the average of the 1946-1973 period (averaging the 1946-1963 and 1962-1973 Ranney indices), we find Democratic majorities (average index ratings over .55) in South Carolina, Texas, Oklahoma, Arizona, Virginia, and Missouri. Republican majorities (average index ratings of .45 or lower) existed in North Dakota, Colorado, Maine, and Iowa. Utah was closely divided throughout the period. In all states with a majority party, except for Missouri, which showed little change, and Colorado, in which the Republican position improved, the minority party has registered substantial gains over the baseline period (Jewell and Olson 1982, 25-27).[4]

As Table 3.4 shows, with the single exception of Iowa, there are strong effects of either migration, conversion, or both, benefiting the erstwhile minority party. In states of the South, conversion effects are particularly strong with an average of one-third of Republican delegates from Virginia, Texas, and South Carolina having switched from the Democratic party. By comparison, only about 10 percent of Democratic delegates from the same states had been Republicans. The South also shows strong migration effects with a majority of both Virginia and South Carolina Republicans having spent their childhoods out of state. Missouri and Oklahoma, border states, show similar trends, and both trends are stronger in Oklahoma where the Republican gains have been greater. In states with Democratic gains, similar processes have clearly been at work to the advantage of the Democrats. Because these are states with less immigration, migration effects are rather low for both parties and do little to differentiate between the parties. Unfortunately, data on conversion were unavailable for Maine, but in North Dakota, Democrats were twice as likely to be former Republicans as the reverse. Iowa provides the only negative findings.

Colorado shows that the majority party may, in increasing its majority, be dependent on conversion and migration, just as the minority party would be. Both migration and conversion differences favored the Colorado Republicans over their Democratic counterparts. We are able, then, by looking at the background of activists, to get some handle on processes of change in the party systems of the various states.

But changes in the status of parties should be expected to affect not only the formerly disadvantaged party. Activists who have seen their state party's dominance evaporate over a period of time could be expected to regroup and begin to look for ways to stop the decline. It is to be expected that among such parties we should find particularly high levels of pragmatism, since such parties should be particularly interested in expanding their base and in winning elections even at the price of ideological purity.[5]

Five states ranked as modified one-party states over the 1946-1963 period moved into two-party competition over the 1962-1982 period. Three are Republican (Iowa, North Dakota, and Maine), and two are Democratic (Virginia and Arizona). In our eleven-state sample, an average of 35.8 percent of Democrats and 35.2 percent of Republicans rated high on pragmatism. Each of our five declining state parties rated above the average for either party and above the pragmatism level of the opposing party in their state (by an average of 9.3 percent). In only one other state did differences between pragmatism levels of the parties exceed 8 percent, and that was Utah where the difference can again be ascribed to the extremely heavy influence of Mormon delegates in the Republican convention compared with the Democratic. Even though this use of cross-sectional data to infer a dynamic process (increasing pragmatism) is far from conclusive, it does suggest an interesting and plausible organizational adjustment to the partisan environment.

We see then that changes over time in the electoral success of parties result in parties with a different makeup from their forerunners. The improving minority party becomes more reliant on converts and outsiders; the declining majority party may become less purist and more pragmatic. Organizational factors are, then, reflected in the activists who make up the party elite.

At first glance, our findings seem inconsistent. In many ways activists are all similar to one another. Regardless of party, activists are highly educated and are well-off relative to others in their state. Although Democrats are, in general, likely to have more women and youths in their ranks, the differences are not particularly striking. Only on race do we find consistently strong party differences.

But demography can certainly not explain the strong ideological differences we consistently find between the parties. Even in the most conservative states, Democratic activists are consistently more likely to call themselves liberals rather than conservatives and to take issue positions far different from those of their Republican neighbors. American parties may, as Janda (1980) suggests, be decentralized, but even without central direction, Democratic and Republican activists are broadly similar in ideology to their fellow partisans in other areas of the country. Furthermore, these state party activists, with a few exceptions, show consistently high levels of identification with the national party—higher, in the aggregate, than delegates to the 1976 national conventions (Lee 1981).

Finally, in spite of ideological differences, state organizations from both parties are subject to the same organizational imperatives. The rising parties must find new recruits from converts and migrants, and the declining party must try to expand its base of support by broadening its appeal and becoming more pragmatic. Clearly, then, American state party activists are in some ways similar to others of their party, in some ways similar to other activists in their state, and in some ways similar to other party activists simply because their respective state parties confront the same organizational problems.

NOTES

1. The issues included were ERA, abortion, defense spending, National Health Insurance, nuclear power, domestic spending cuts, affirmative action for minorities, oil deregulation, wage-price controls, inflation, the draft, SALT II, and U.S. presence in the Middle East. Liberal responses were counted as 2, neutral responses as 1, giving the scale a range of 0 to 26, with 13 being the equivalent of all neutral responses. In Maine the National Health Insurance question was not asked and all respondents were coded at the neutral point.

2. These four states are also distinguished in that they are the four lowest in terms of the percentage of respondents saying that a very important motivation in becoming active was "to support my party."

3. Maine is unusual in that Brown, Crane, and Anderson did particularly well in these states. The strength of these insurgent, outsider candidates might mean that Maine delegates were less representative of the Maine party activists in general than is true for other states.

4. Ranney's index is based on vote for governor, seats in the state legislature held by each party, and control of the state legislature and governorship. Change is ascertained by comparing the 1946-73 period with the 1960-82 period. This latter classification is taken from Jewell and Olson (1982) who use the same criteria as Ranney, including as well the percentage of offices contested by each party. Because the periods of comparison overlap, our measure is intrinsically conservative.

5. The pragmatism index consists of a simple additive scale based on five Likert-type questions (question 14 in the appendix). The questions asked about the relative importance to the delegate of winning elections versus ideological purity. The resulting scale ranged from 5 (all ideology oriented responses) to 25 (all winning oriented responses). The scale was then trichotimized into high, medium, and low pragmatism categories.

REFERENCES

Abramson, Paul. 1974. "Generational Change in American Electoral Behavior." *American Political Science Review* 68 (March): 93-105.

Arieff, Irwin. 1980. "State Delegations Strive to Protect Their Interests Through Concerted Effort." *Congressional Quarterly* 38 (August): 2185-2189.

Beck, Paul Allen and Paul Lopatto. 1982. "The End of Southern Distinctiveness." In *Contemporary Southern Political Attitudes and Behavior,* edited by Laurence Moreland, Tod Baker, and Robert Steed. New York: Praeger.

Burnham, Walter Dean. 1970. *Critical Elections and the Mainsprings of American Politics*. New York: Norton.

Elazar, Daniel. 1972. *American Federalism: A View from the States*, 2nd ed. New York: Crowell.

Farah, Barbara, M. Kent Jennings, and Warren Miller. 1981. "Convention Delegates: Reform and the Representation of Party Elites, 1972-1980." Paper prepared for Conference on Party Activists, Williamsburg, Virginia.

Fenton, John H. 1966. *Midwest Politics*. New York: Holt, Rinehart & Winston.

Fenton, John, Rhodes Cook, and Christopher Buchanan. 1980. "Carter Plans Keyed to Going on the Offensive." *Congressional Quarterly* 38 (August): 2347-2349.

Gibson, James L., Cornelius P. Cotter, John F. Bibby, and Robert J. Huckshorn. 1981. "Assessing Institutional Party Strength." Paper prepared for annual meeting of Midwest Political Science Association.

Harmel, Robert and Kenneth Janda. 1982. *Parties and Their Environments*. New York: Longman.

Huckshorn, Robert. 1976. *Party Leadership in the States*. Amherst: University of Massachusetts Press.

Jackson, John and Barbara Brown. 1982. "A Comparison of Democratic and Republican Party Elites." Paper prepared for annual meeting of Midwest Political Science Association.

Jackson, John, and R. A. Hitlin. 1981. "The Nationalization of the Democratic Party." *Polity* 13 (Summer): 617-633.

Janda, Kenneth. 1980. "A Comparative Analysis of Party Organizations: The United States, Europe, and the World." In *The Party Symbol*, edited by William Crotty. San Francisco: W. H. Freeman.

Jewell, Malcolm and David Olson. 1982. *American State Political Parties and Elections*, 2nd ed. Homewood, Ill.: Dorsey.

Key, V. O. 1949. *Southern Politics*. New York: Knopf.

Kirkpatrick, Jeane J. 1976. *The New Presidential Elite*. New York: Russell Sage.

Ladd, Everett. 1982. *Where Have All the Voters Gone?* 2nd ed. New York: Norton.

Lee, Frederick P. 1981. "Trends in the Strength of Party Identification Among Party Leaders, 1976-1980." Paper prepared for annual meeting of Midwest Political Science Association.

Lockard, Duane. 1959. *New England State Politics*. Princeton: Princeton University Press.

Manley, John. 1973. "The Conservative Coalition in Congress," *American Behavioral Scientist* 17 (November/December): 223-247.

McClosky, Herbert, Paul Hoffman, and Rosemary O'Hara. "Issue Conflict and Consensus Among Party Leaders and Followers." *American Political Science Review* 54 (June): 406-427.

Milbrath, Lester and M. L. Goel. 1977. *Political Participation*. Chicago: Rand McNally.

Miller, Warren, Arthur Miller, and Edward Schneider. 1980. *American National Election Studies Data Sourcebook, 1952-1978*. Cambridge: Harvard University Press.

Mitofsky, Warren J. and Martin Plissner. 1980. "The Making of the Delegates 1968-1980." *Public Opinion Quarterly* 3 (October/November): 37-43.

Nie, Norman and Sidney Verba. 1975. "Political Participation." *Handbook of Political Science,* vol. 4, edited by Fred Greenstein and Nelson W. Polsby. Reading, Mass.: Addison-Wesley.

Patterson, Samuel. 1963. "Characteristics of Party Leaders." *Western Political Quarterly* 16 (June): 332-352.

Putnam, Robert. 1976. *Comparative Study of Political Elites*. Englewood Cliffs: Prentice-Hall.

Ranney, Austin. 1965. "Parties in State Politics." In *Politics in the American States,* edited by Herbert Jacob and Kenneth Vines. Boston: Little, Brown. See also 3rd ed.

Ranney, Austin. 1978. "The Political Parties: Reform and Decline." In *The New American Political System,* edited by Anthony King. Washington, D.C.: American Enterprise Institute.

Sorauf, Frank J. 1980. *Party Politics in America,* 4th ed. Boston: Little, Brown.

Verba, Sidney and Norman Nie. 1972. *Participation in America*. New York: Harper and Row.

PART TWO

INCENTIVES AND MOTIVATIONS

4

Incentives for Activism

ALAN I. ABRAMOWITZ, JOHN McGLENNON,
and RONALD B. RAPOPORT

One of the central tenets of organization theory is that the incentives that motivate individuals to participate in an organization have important consequences for the character of that organization (Clark and Wilson 1961). Many studies in recent years have pointed to a shift in the types of incentives that motivate individuals to participate in party politics in the United States. There is broad consensus among students of American political parties that material rewards and party loyalty have been declining in importance as incentives for activism while candidates and issues have become increasingly important as motivations for participation in party affairs (Wilson 1962; Hirschfield et al. 1962; Bowman et al. 1969; Ippolito 1969; Wiggins and Turk 1970; Roback 1974; Polsby and Wildavsky 1980; Sorauf 1980). Moreover, this shift in the nature of the incentives for activism is generally seen as having negative consequences for the vitality of the parties as organizations. The "new breed" of issue-oriented activists have been characterized as dogmatic purists more concerned with advancing their issue concerns within the party than with maintaining the effectiveness of the organization in order to win elections (Wildavsky 1965; Sullivan et al. 1974; Soule and McGrath 1975; Polsby and Wildavsky 1980; Kirkpatrick 1976, 1978). In addition, it has been argued that purposive motivations (defined as concern with candidates and issues) are unlikely to sustain long-term involvement in party affairs: individuals whose involvement is stimulated by a particular issue or candidate are unlikely to remain involved once that issue or candidate is gone. Activists motivated by idealistic goals may also easily become disillusioned by the bargaining and compromise necessary in politics. Hence, party organizations which rely on purposive motivations to attract activists are likely to suffer high rates of attrition (Wilson 1962; Conway and Feigert 1968; Sorauf 1980).

The involvement of issue-oriented activists in party affairs has been particularly evident in the presidential nominating process as a result of reforms which have reduced the ability of elected and party officials to control the selection of delegates to the national conventions (Ranney 1974; Polsby and Wildavsky 1980; Marshall 1981). The proliferation of presidential primaries and the democratization of party caucuses and conventions have made it possible for individuals with little or no commitment to the party as an organization to influence the selection of a candidate and even to become delegates to the national conventions. In 1972, for example, many of the McGovern and Wallace delegates at the Democratic national convention expressed very little loyalty to the Democratic party as an organization. Their commitment was to their own candidate and the issue concerns represented by that candidate (Kirkpatrick 1976). On the basis of her massive study of Democratic and Republican national convention delegates in 1972, Jeane Kirkpatrick concluded that "by 1972 the attenuation of attachment to party had affected the elites of both parties and all elite factions but was especially strong among newcomers to politics and the elite supporters of Wallace and McGovern. Because attachment to party is related to many aspects of political behavior, a continued trend away from solidary incentives will probably mean a major and fundamental change in the American political system" (1976, 114).

Examining evidence from a survey of 17,628 delegates attending twenty-two state party conventions in connection with the 1980 presidential nominating campaign, this chapter will argue that the fears expressed by Kirkpatrick and other scholars concerning the dangers to the parties from the growing involvement of issue-oriented activists have been generally exaggerated. While our evidence does support the conclusions of earlier studies regarding the importance of purposive motivations among contemporary party activists, we also find strong party attachments among these activists. Moreover, there was a positive correlation between purposive and partisan motivations among state party convention delegates in 1980 and both purposive and partisan motivations were related to length and regularity of party involvement. Finally, we show that party loyalty played an important role in determining the outcome of the Democratic nominating campaign among these activists by dampening the influence of ideology on candidate preference.

MOTIVATIONS OF PARTY ACTIVISTS

In order to assess the motivations for participation of delegates to state party conventions in 1980, our survey included a question, similar to

Table 4.1. Motivations of state convention delegates

	Democrats	Republicans
Party loyalty	62	67
Issues	76	84
Candidate	71	80
Career	8	4
Excitement	21	13
Meet people	32	22
Visibility	14	8
Civic duty	52	53
(minimum *N*)	(7602)	(7772)

Note: Each entry is percentage of delegates rating motivation as "very important."

those used in other studies of party activists, asking delegates to rate the importance of various motivations for their decisions to participate in the 1980 nominating campaigns (see appendix, question 15). When the responses were factor analyzed, two distinct factors emerged.[1] The first factor included four items: career advancement, the excitement of participating in the campaign, the opportunity to meet other people with similar interests, and the visibility of serving as a delegate. While seemingly disparate in content, all of these items involve personal benefits received from participation in the campaign. The second factor included only two items: advancing issue concerns and working to nominate a particular candidate. These two items clearly correspond to the more impersonal or purposive motivations for participation. Finally, two items—party loyalty and civic duty—did not load clearly on either factor. The results of the factor analysis were generally consistent with previous studies of motivations among party activists, which have distinguished between personal and impersonal goals. Since party loyalty and civic duty were not clearly tied to either set of motivations, these items were analyzed separately.

Table 4.1 presents the delegates' ratings of the importance of each of the eight motivations included in the survey. As other recent studies had led us to expect, purposive motivations were rated as the most important by delegates in both parties; overwhelming majorities of Democratic and Republican delegates rated issues and candidates as "very important" factors in their decisions to participate in the 1980 nominating campaigns. What is somewhat more surprising is that party loyalty was rated right behind purposive motivations in importance. In contrast, the personal benefits received from participation in the nominating process were rated much lower in importance by delegates in both parties. Although Democratic delegates rated the personal motivations as somewhat more important than did Republican delegates, while Republican delegates rated purposive motivations somewhat higher in importance than did Democratic delegates, activists in both parties clearly saw party loyalty along with concern with issues and candidates as the primary reasons for their involvement in the nominating campaign.

We have seen that Democratic and Republican state convention delegates rated the importance of party loyalty almost as high as the importance of issue and candidate concerns as a motivation for their involvement in the nominating campaigns. Moreover, there was a positive correlation between partisan and purposive motivations in both parties ($r = .23$ for Democratic delegates, $r = .13$ for Republican delegates). Of the delegates in each party who rated both issue and candidate concerns as "very important" motivations for participating, 70 percent also rated party loyalty as a "very important" motivation. Thus our findings do not support the contention of scholars like Kirkpatrick that the growing importance of purposive motivations has led to a decline in party loyalty among activists. Among the delegates in our survey, these two orientations were quite compatible with one another. Like the local committee members studies by Burrell (1982), most of these state convention delegates were concerned about issues and candidates *and* loyal to their party.

Table 4.2 shows the relationships between partisan and purposive motivations (appendix, question 15) and a variety of political background characteristics and attitudes.[2] Not surprisingly, there was a strong relationship between strength of party identification (question 11) and partisan motivation. The prevalence of partisan motivation among Democratic and Republican activists was a reflection of the fact that the large majority of these activists (72 percent of Democratic delegates and 85 percent of Republican delegates) were strong party identifiers. There was also a fairly strong positive relationship between strength of party identification and purposive motivation. Among these delegates, issue and candidate concerns were not only compatible with party loyalty, they were actually stronger among delegates with strong party loyalties. Moreover, purposive motivations were just as prevalent among party and elected officials as among other delegates. "Professionals" were no less

Table 4.2. Motivations correlated with political experience

	Democrats (minimum N = 7072)		Republicans (minimum N = 7548)	
	Partisan motivation	Purposive motivation	Partisan motivation	Purposive motivation
Party identification	.77	.31	.76	.27
Conservatism	.09	−.10	.11	.37
Years active in party	.46	.16	.32	.12
Regularity of campaign involvement	.43	.18	.33	.18
Organizational experience	.30	.04	.24	.02
Electoral experience	.29	.07	.24	.03

Note: Entries shown are gamma coefficients.

concerned about candidates and issues (although they were more concerned about their party) than were "amateurs."

The findings presented in Table 4.2 do not support the contention that purposive motivations become less important the longer one remains active in the party. In fact, issue and candidate concerns were positively related to both length of involvement in the party (question 2) and regularity of campaign participation (question 8). Far from being the "morning glories" derided by Tammany Hall leader George Washington Plunkitt, purposive activists tended to be the most experienced and dedicated party workers. Nor is there any evidence in our data that personal motivations tend to replace purposive motivations with longer involvement in the party, as Conway and Feigert (1968) argued in their study of members of local party committees in Maryland and Kentucky. In fact, there was no relationship between strength of personal motivations and either length of party involvement or regularity of participation among Democratic or Republican delegates.[3] The only group of delegates who demonstrated significantly stronger personal motivations in both parties were the very youngest age group—those under the age of twenty-five. It was among these political novices, almost all of whom were participating in their first convention, that the excitement, social contacts, prestige, and career opportunities associated with the campaign loomed largest in importance.[4] Among the older and more experienced delegates, these personal benefits were much less significant attractions. Thus, while personal benefits may play an important role in stimulating initial involvement in party affairs, they appear to have little to do with sustained and regular participation. Frequent and sustained involvement in party affairs appears to be motivated by concern with issues and candidates and, especially, by party loyalty.

The findings presented in Table 4.2 provide further evidence for the crucial role of party loyalty as a motivation for political activism. Partisan motivation was strongly related to both length and regularity of participation in party affairs among Democratic and Republican delegates. Of course, partisanship may be both a cause and an effect of party activity. Partisanship can stimulate activity on behalf of the party and its candidates. In addition, involvement in party affairs probably reinforces and strengthens partisan orientations. Whatever the direction of causality, it is clear that despite the decline of party loyalties in the electorate, partisanship remained an important motivation for political participation among these activists.

MOTIVATIONS AND CANDIDATE PREFERENCE

Thus far we have demonstrated that partisan motivations were an important stimulus to participation among state party convention delegates in 1980 and that strong party loyalties were quite compatible with strong purposive orientations among these delegates. We are also interested in whether these motivations had any impact on the most important activity of these delegates—the selection of a presidential candidate. Kirkpatrick and other scholars have argued that activists with strong purposive orientations will seek to nominate candidates who represent their own issue concerns, regardless of the electoral consequences for the party. However, if party loyalty is an important consideration in the minds of activists, it may temper their enthusiasm for candidates who appeal to their issue concerns but who threaten to undermine the party as an organization.

The 1980 campaign for the Democratic nomination provides a particularly good opportunity to test the relationship between issue concerns and party loyalty, because it involved a challenge to the renomination of the incumbent president.[5] Although he had originally campaigned for the presidency in 1976 as an outsider without close ties to the Washington establishment or to the leadership of his own party, in 1980 Jimmy Carter clearly sought to identify himself with the traditions and past leaders of the Democratic party. Carter appealed to loyal Democrats for support as an incumbent whose relatively moderate record and positions offered the party the best hope of retaining the White House. In general, we would expect party loyalty to lead activists to rally behind an incumbent president of their own party when the incumbent is challenged for the nomination; the incumbent president is the national leader of his party and a successful challenge to the incumbent would be seen by party loyalists as a repudiation of the party's leadership and record.

Edward Kennedy's challenge to Jimmy Carter for the Democratic presidential nomination in 1980 was based largely on his outspoken support for liberal positions on general issues. As a result, we would expect Kennedy to have appealed primarily to liberal activists with strong purposive orientations. We are interested in whether party loyalty reduced support for Kennedy among these purposive liberal activists.

In contrast to the Democratic contest, neither of the two major candiates seeking the Republican nomination could stake out a clear claim to the support of activists based on party loyalty. Despite the backing of some party leaders associated with former President Ford and the tacit support of the ex-president himself, George Bush had never held an elective office which would have established him as the recognized leader of the Republican party. However, because of his long association with the conservative cause, Ronald Reagan should have appealed strongly to purposive conservative activists in the Republican party.

Table 4.3 shows the joint effect of purposive and partisan motivations on support for the two major candidates in each party among state convention delegates. As expected, among Republican delegates, purposive motivation was related to support for Reagan, while partisan motivation had no effect on candidate support. Moreover, the relationship between purposive motivation and support for Reagan remained fairly strong after controlling for ideology. As a candidate long noted for his issue-oriented appeal, Ronald Reagan appealed to Republican activists with strong purposive orientations. Even among moderate-to-liberal Republicans, purposive motivation was related to support for Reagan. Only 32 percent of moderate-to-liberal Republicans with low purposive motivation supported Reagan compared with 53 percent of moderate-to-liberal Republicans with high purposive motivation. Apparently, despite their ideological differences with Reagan, purposive Republican moder-

Table 4.3. Candidate preference and motivation

Partisan motivation	Purposive motivation Low	Medium	High
	Democrats (percentage for Kennedy)		
Low	21 (*N* = 441)	35 (*N* = 667)	50 (*N* = 1123)
High	14 (*N* = 384)	21 (*N* = 817)	28 (*N* = 2928)
	Republicans (percentage for Reagan)		
Low	63 (*N* = 246)	75 (*N* = 503)	86 *N* = 1439)
High	58 (*N* = 263)	71 (*N* = 685)	87 (*N* = 3342)

Note: Only delegates supporting Kennedy or Carter for Democratic nomination and Reagan or Bush for Republican nomination are included.

ates were attracted by Reagan's personal style and issue-oriented approach.

Among Democratic delegates, purposive motivation was related to support for Kennedy, as expected. However, party loyalty clearly worked against Kennedy's challenge to the incumbent among these activists. Table 4.4 shows that the effect of partisanship was greatest among the most liberal activists in the Democratic Party—those who belonged to Kennedy's natural ideological constituency. Support for Kennedy was thirty percentage points lower among "very liberal" Democrats with strong partisan motivations than among "very liberal" Democrats with weak partisan motivations.

It appears that party loyalty caused many liberal Democrats to ignore their ideological inclinations and back the incumbent. Among liberal Democratic delegates (including those who described themselves as either "very liberal" or "somewhat liberal"), 63 percent viewed Edward Kennedy as closer to their own ideological position than Jimmy Carter while only 18 percent viewed Carter as closer to themselves (questions 16 and 20).

Yet these liberal Democratic activists supported Carter over Kennedy for the nomination by a decisive 58 to 42 percent margin. Why did Kennedy receive so little support from his own ideological constituency

Table 4.4. Preference for Kennedy among delegates

Partisan motivation	Very liberal	Somewhat liberal	Moderate to conservative
Low	78 (*N* = 453)	42 (*N* = 947)	21 (*N* = 843)
High	48 (*N* = 720)	29 (*N* = 1737)	16 (*N* = 1905)

Note: Based on delegates supporting either Kennedy or Carter for Democratic nomination.

within the Democratic party? The main reason was that 58 percent of these liberal activists viewed Jimmy Carter as having a better chance to win the November election while only 24 percent believed that Kennedy would have a better chance of winning (question 23). Contrary to the image of contemporary party activists as dogmatic ideologues, our evidence indicates that in choosing a nominee, many of these delegates were quite willing to sacrifice ideological purity for the sake of a greater chance of victory in November. (The following chapter, which provides a full analysis of the impact of ideology and electability on candidate choice, shows the much greater effect of electability.)

In conclusion, then, party loyalty, along with issue and candidate concerns, were the most important motivations for participation in the presidential nominating campaign among state party convention delegates in 1980. Personal benefits such as career advancement, social contacts, prestige, and the excitement of the campaign were rated as much less important reasons for participation by these delegates. The importance of candidate and issue concerns to these activists did not undermine their attachment to their party, as some studies of party activists would have led us to expect. In fact, there was a positive correlation between partisan and purposive motivations. The large majority of Democratic and Republican delegates in our survey were interested in issues and candidates and in achieving success for their party.

Our evidence did not support the contention that personal motivations tend to replace purposive motivations over time. Both partisan and purposive motivation were positively related to the length and regularity of participation in party affairs among these delegates. Personal motivations for participation were actually most prevalent among the very youngest delegates in both parties, suggesting that these motivations may stimulate a person's initial involvement in party politics but do not play an important role in sustaining a long-term commitment to the party. Partisanship itself seems to be the most important factor in maintaining a high level of involvement in party affairs over a long period of time.

Our evidence indicates that party loyalty was also an important factor in the outcome of the contest between Jimmy Carter and Edward Kennedy for the Democratic presidential nomination in 1980. Kennedy's challenge to the incumbent, based largely on his outspoken support for liberal positions on a wide range of domestic and international issues, might have been expected to appeal strongly to issue-oriented liberal activists within the Democratic party. But most of these liberal activists were also motivated by party loyalty, which made many of them reluctant to repudiate their party leader, even though they preferred the challenger's ideological stance.

Neither of the major contenders for the Republican presidential nomination in 1980 was able to appeal for support on the basis of party loyalty, since neither George Bush nor Ronald Reagan had held national elective office. Reagan was supported by the large majority of Republican activists in our survey because of his conservative ideological appeal and, primarily, because he was viewed as more electable than George Bush (see the chapter by Stone and Abramowitz in this volume). Reagan had come very close to defeating the incumbent president, Gerald Ford, for the Republican nomination, but Ford's position as an incumbent who had never been chosen by his own party probably weakened the impact of party loyalty on Republican activists. In general, we would expect partisanship to influence activists most strongly when an incumbent president is seeking renomination. To a lesser extent, a vice-president or former vice-president may be able to appeal to activists for support on partisan grounds as the heir to the position of national party leader.

In general, our findings indicate that partisanship is alive and well among presidential party activists. Perhaps these findings reflected conditions peculiar to the 1980 Democratic and Republican campaigns or to the states included in our study. But this does not appear very plausible. The contests in both parties in 1980 involved candidates—Edward Kennedy for the Democrats and Ronald Reagan for the Republicans—with strong appeal to issue-oriented activists. While the eleven states we studied cannot be described as "typical" of the country, they did vary considerably in size, regional location, economic development, and partisan orientation.

The rather pessimistic view of party activists which is prevalent in the political science literature is based to a large extent on the 1972 Democratic National Convention. This convention has unquestionably been studied more thoroughtly than any other party gathering. As the first presidential campaign following the major reforms adopted by the Democratic party in the aftermath of the 1968 presidential election, it was believed that the 1972 Democratic nominating campaign and convention would establish a pattern for future postreform nominating campaigns. Yet in some ways the 1972 contest for the Democratic nomination was extremely unusual. George McGovern was an unusually strong "insurgent" candidate who skillfully exploited the new rules and appealed to issue-oriented liberal activists largely on the basis of his dovish stance on the war in Vietnam. The McGovern delegates at the 1972 Democratic convention tended to be liberal newcomers with relatively weak party ties. In 1976, however, the Democrats chose the relatively moderate Jimmy Carter as their standard-bearer and in 1980 they rejected a challenge to the incumbent's renomination from the most visible and glamorous spokesman of the party's liberal wing.

On the basis of our evidence, party activists do not appear to be dogmatic purists. They are motivated by concern with issues and candidates but they are also motivated by loyalty to their party. In choosing a candidate for the nomination, they appear to be concerned about electability as well as ideology. In a period of mass-media campaigns, single-issue interest groups, and declining party identification in the electorate, the party activists are one of the last remaining bastions of partisanship. Far from being a threat to the viability of the parties, our evidence indicates that these activists are the life of the parties. As far as these activists are concerned, columnist David Broder was wrong—the party isn't over.

NOTES

1. After a varimax rotation was performed the following factor loadings were obtained:

	Factor 1	Factor 2
Party loyalty	.226	.287
Career	.522	−.054
Excitement	.737	.026
Meeting people	.642	.233
Candidate	.005	.568
Issues	−.100	.566
Visibility	.686	.058
Civic duty	.209	.263

2. Delegates were classified as high in partisan motivation if they indicated on question 15 that party loyalty was a "very important" reason for their involvement in the campaign. All others were classified as low in partisan motivation. Purposive motivation was measured by combining the candidate and issue motivation items. Delegates were classified as high in purposive motivation if they indicated that concern with issues and support for a candidate were both "very important" reasons for their participation. Delegates who indicated that only one of these factors was very important were classified as moderate in purposive motivation and delegates who indicated that neither factor was very important were classified as low in purposive motivation.

3. The correlations (Pearson's r) between personal motivations (combining career advancement, excitement, visibility, and social contacts) and length of party activity were −.05 for Democratic delegates and −.04 for Republican delegates. The correlations between personal motivations and regularity of participation were −.05 for both Democratic and Republican delegates.

4. Among Democratic delegates under the age of 25, 54 percent indicated that three or four of the personal motivations were at least "somewhat important" compared with only 31 percent of all other delegates. Similarly, among Republican delegates under the age of 25, 51 percent indicated that three or four of the personal motivations were at least "somewhat important" compared with only 17 percent of all other delegates.

5. Our analysis will focus on the choice between the two leading contenders for the 1980 nomination in each party: Jimmy Carter and Edward Kennedy for the Democrats, and Ronald Reagan and George Bush for the Republicans. Almost 90 percent of the delegates in each party supported one of the two leading candidates and no other candidate in either party was supported by more than two percent of the delegates.

REFERENCES

Bowman, Lewis, Dennis Ippolito, and William Donaldson. 1969. "Incentives for the Maintenance of Grassroots Political Activism." *Midwest Journal of Political Science* 13: 126-139.

Burrell, Barbara C. 1982. "The Congruence of Purposive Incentives and Party Loyalty of Local Party Officials: Implications for Party Maintenance." Paper delivered at the annual meeting of the Midwest Political Science Association, Milwaukee, Wisconsin.

Clark, Peter, and James Q. Wilson. 1961. "Incentive Systems: A Theory of Organizations." *Administrative Science Quarterly* 6: 129-166.

Conway, M. Margaret, and Frank Feigert. 1968. "Motivations, Incentive Systems, and the Political Party Organization." *American Political Science Review* 62: 1159-73.

Hirshfield, Robert, Bert Swanson, and Blanche Blank. 1962. "A Profile of Political Activists in Manhattan." *Western Political Quarterly* 15: 489-506.

Ippolito, Dennis. 1969. "Motivational Reorientation and Change Among Party Activists." *Journal of Politics* 31: 1098-1101.

Kirkpatrick, Jeane J. 1976. *The New Presidential Elite*. New York: Russell Sage.

______. 1978. *Dismantling the Parties*. Washington, D.C.: American Enterprise Institute.

Marshall, Thomas R. 1981. *Presidential Nominations in a Reform Age*. New York: Praeger.

Polsby, Nelson W., and Aaron Wildavsky. 1980. *Presidential Elections: Strategies of American Electoral Politics*. New York: Scribner's.

Ranney, Austin, 1974. "Changing the Rules of the Nominating Game." In *Choosing the President*, edited by James David Barber Englewood Cliffs: Prentice-Hall.

Roback, Thomas. 1974. *Recruitment and Incentive Patterns Among Grassroots Republican Officials: Continuity and Change in Two States*. Beverly Hills: Sage Publications.

Sorauf, Frank. 1980. *Party Politics in America*. Boston: Little, Brown.

Soule, John W., and Wilma McGrath. 1975. "A Comparative Study of Presidential Nominating Conventions: The Democrats of 1968 and 1972." *American Journal of Political Science* 19: 501-17.

Stone, Walter J., and Alan I. Abramowitz. 1982. "Activist Support for Presidential Candidates: Ideology and Electability in 1980." Paper delivered at the annual meeting of the Midwest Political Science Association, Milwaukee, Wisconsin.

Sullivan, Dennis G., Jeffrey L. Pressman, Benjamin I. Page, and John J. Lyons. 1974. *The Politics of Representation: The Democratic Convention 1972*. New York: St. Martin's.

Wiggins, Charles W., and William L. Turk. 1970. "State Party Chairmen: A Profile." *Western Political Quarterly* 23: 321-32.

Wildavsky, Aaron. 1965. "The Goldwater Phenomenon: Purists, Politicians, and the Two-Party System." *The Review of Politics* 27: 386-413.

Wilson, James Q. 1962. *The Amateur Democrat*. Chicago: University of Chicago Press.

5

Ideology, Electability, and Candidate Choice

WALTER J. STONE,
ALAN I. ABRAMOWITZ

Since the 1960s, the American party system has undergone dramatic change in response to the emergence of new issues such as Vietnam, abortion, and women's rights, and the involvement of growing numbers of issue-oriented activists in party affairs. Both parties have reformed their rules governing presidential candidate selection and these reforms have helped to increase the influence of issue-oriented activists in the presidential nominating process (Marshall 1981). The new activists frequently have seemed unwilling to compromise their ideological principles for the sake of appealing to a larger constituency in the general election. The presidential candidacies of Barry Goldwater, Eugene McCarthy, and George McGovern relied heavily on the support of activists whose ideological concerns appeared to outweigh their interest in winning the November election.

The increased role of "amateurs" (Wilson 1962) and "purists" (Polsby and Wildavsky 1980) in the presidential nominating process may have dangerous consequences for the parties. Party activists are often unrepresentative of the general electorate in their policy preferences (McClosky, Hoffman, and O'Hara 1960; Nexon 1971; Verba and Nie 1972; Farah, Jennings, and Miller 1981; and Jackson, Brown, and Bositis 1982). The single-minded pursuit of ideological goals by such activists may contribute to the fragmentation of the political parties. If their loyalties are to a particular candidate because that candidate is perceived to agree with their ideological views, they may have little or no loyalty to the party organization. Thus supporters of candidates who lose the nomination may not actively support the party nominee in the general election campaign (Johnson and Gibson 1974; Abramowitz, McGlennon, and Rapoport 1980).

A large number of studies, focusing primarily on national convention delegates, have pointed to the changing character of American party activists since the 1960s (see, for example, Soule and McGrath 1975; Roback 1975; Kirkpatrick 1976; and Jackson, Brown, and Brown 1978). This literature is unanimous in supporting the hypothesis that since 1972, party activists have tended to be "purist" in their orientation, supporting the candidate who best represents their ideological views rather than the candidate with the best perceived chance of winning the general election. Soule and McGrath (1975) showed that the proportion of "amateurs" at the Democratic National Convention in 1972 was more than twice the percentage in 1968.[1] Their concluding sentence sounded a warning for the party organizations commonly found in the literature: "American centrist parties have survived ideological conflict in the past, but with the added ingredient of political amateurs, compromise and unity will become more problematic in the future" (p. 516). Kirkpatrick's massive study of the 1972 conventions reached similar conclusions with respect to the changing character of party activists: "in 1972 we were moving away from a traditional organizational style toward one featuring parties that are less permanent, less broadly based, and less oriented toward winning" (Kirkpatrick 1976, 153).

The evidence which we will present does not support the predominant view of contemporary party activists as dogmatic ideologues more concerned with nominating a candidate who represents their issue concerns than with winning the November election. We believe that the literature on party activists has substantially underestimated the importance of electability because it has relied on general measures of purism vs. pragmatism which involve asking activists to consider, in the abstract, the tradeoff between ideology and electability.[2] We will show that such questions do not predict the behavior of party activists in selecting a presidential candidate. Despite a strong tendency among our respondents to opt for ideological purity over electability in the abstract, our data from 1980 indicate that Democratic and Republican activists were actually more concerned with electability than with ideology in choosing a party nominee.

ELECTABILITY VS. IDEOLOGY IN 1980

Activists in both parties in 1980 had to confront a potential conflict between ideology and electability. The Democrats were "blessed" with an incumbent president running for renomination. The problem for them was deciding whether Jimmy Carter was more blessing than curse. Incumbents are normally a good bet in the general election, but Carter's ratings in the polls had been low, his competence was widely questioned, and his administration was saddled with the blame for nearly unprecedented rates of inflation. Carter was, however, viewed as more of a centrist than Senator Edward Kennedy in a year when liberalism was widely perceived to be a liability. Kennedy could claim to be more electable than President Carter because he was not the incumbent, because he had clearly separated himself from the administration, because of the Kennedy name, and because he had a loyal personal following within and beyond the party. Of course, apart from his relative "extremism," his liabilities included serious questions about his character and his abilities as a national leader.

On the Republican side, similar ambiguities faced activists attempting to weigh their ideological preferences and their desire to regain control of the White House. Ronald Reagan, the clear frontrunner for the nomination following his strong challenge to Gerald Ford in 1976, a familiar national figure, and a popular former governor of the most populous state in the nation, was perceived by many to be too "extreme" to be a viable presidential candidate. Former President Ford was claiming as late as the spring of 1980 that Ronald Reagan was not electable, raising in the minds of some Republicans the specter of "another Goldwater." George Bush, the principal alternative to Reagan, could plausibly claim to be more electable because he was more a centrist. His major problems were his limited national visibility and an electoral record much less impressive than Reagan's.

Thus activists participating in the state conventions were faced with choices between candidates offering plausible claims to being the most electable candidate in their party, and presenting clear ideological choices. Many political scientists, familiar with the work of Anthony Downs (1957) and the literature on the "purist" character of contemporary activists, would be likely to assume that supporters of relatively "extreme" candidates like Ronald Reagan in 1980 and George McGovern in 1972 sacrificed electability in order to protect their ideological interests. This assumption, however, errs by linking attitude on the electability-ideology tradeoff directly to the support of a particular candidate. We will show that many of the supporters of Reagan in 1980 and McGovern in 1972 were concerned with supporting an electable candidate even if that meant compromising their personal ideological interests.

We begin by replicating the work of others and presenting the results of

Table 5.1. Support for ideological purism

Item (purist response)	Democrats	Republicans
A political party should be more concerned with issues than with winning elections (agree)	76 (*N* = 8278)	70 (*N* = 8318)
A candidate should express his convictions even if it means losing the election (agree)	86 (*N* = 8350)	86 (*N* = 8456)
I'd rather lose an election than compromise my basic philosophy (agree)	76 (*N* = 8255)	77 (*N* = 8426)
The party platform should avoid issues that are too controversial or unpopular (disagree)	80 (*N* = 8283)	80 (*N* = 8442)
Broad electoral appeal is more important than a consistent ideology (disagree)	63 (*N* = 7958)	70 (*N* = 8223)

Note: Entries are percentage of delegates giving a purist response to each item plus one-half of the percentage of delegates with no opinion. The largest percentage of no opinion was 15 percent and the average for all items was 7 percent with no opinion.

Table 5.2. Candidate preference by ideology

	Democrats		
Candidate preference	Very liberal (*N* = 1217)	Fairly liberal (*N* = 2756)	Moderate to conservative (*N* = 2830)
Carter	40	66	85
Kennedy	60	34	15
Total	100	100	100
	Republicans		
	Moderate to liberal (*N* = 734)	Fairly conservative (*N* = 3168)	Very conservative (*N* = 2977)
Bush	51	22	5
Reagan	49	78	95
Total	100	100	100

Note: All entries are percentages.

a series of general questions measuring "purism vs. pragmatism" among party activists. These questions posed the tradeoff between ideological satisfaction and electoral success in the abstract. As in other recent studies, the results presented in Table 5.1 show that party activists appear overwhelmingly to prefer ideological purity to winning. Findings such as these have led observers of the presidential nominating process to conclude that party activists threaten the ability of the parties to nominate presidential candidates with broad electoral appeal.[3]

Abstract generalizations such as those incorporated in our measures of "purism vs. pragmatism" may seem attractive but fail to predict the specific behavior (candidate support) in which we are interested. We also have measures of ideological proximity and estimated chances of victory in November associated with each major contender for the nomination. The question is, do activists follow their general purist inclinations when faced with specific choices between candidates?

IDEOLOGY AND CANDIDATE CHOICE

Democratic and Republican delegates in our survey were sharply polarized in their ideological preferences. When asked to place themselves on a five-point liberal-conservative scale, the majority of Democratic delegates described themselves as either "very liberal" (19 percent) or "fairly liberal" (39 percent). Republican delegates overwhelmingly described themselves as either "very conservative" (41 percent) or "fairly conservative" (46 percent). Moreover, delegates' ideological preferences were strongly related to their positions on thirteen national issues ranging from the Equal Rights Amendment and national health insurance to draft registration and the SALT II Treaty with the Soviet Union.[4]

Table 5.2 demonstrates that delegates in both parties based their decisions to support a candidate for their party's nomination at least partially on ideological grounds.[5] Among Democratic activists, liberals were much more likely to prefer Senator Kennedy over President Carter than were moderates or conservatives. However, fully two-thirds of the Democratic delegates who labeled themselves "fairly liberal" backed Jimmy Carter's renomination, and even among those who described themselves as "very liberal," two-fifths supported the incumbent over his more liberal challenger. While there was a clear relationship between ideology and candidate preference, the failure of Senator Kennedy's challenge to President Carter in these caucus states was due to his inability to gain the support of more than a minority of the liberal activists who constituted his natural ideological constituency.

Ideology was also an imperfect predictor of candidate support among Republican activists. Although Ronald Reagan's strongest backing came from delegates who described themselves as "very conservative," he was also supported by a large majority of delegates who were "fairly conservative," and by almost half of the delegates who described themselves as moderate-to-liberal in ideology. Like Edward Kennedy, George Bush failed to gain the support of many of those activists in his party who belonged to his natural ideological constituency.

In addition to asking delegates to describe their own ideological leanings, we also asked them to place each of the major contenders for Democratic and Republican nominations on the same five-point liberal-conservative scale. By combining these questions, we can determine the relative ideological proximity of the delegates to the two major candidates for their party's nomination. Based on these proximity measures, Edward Kennedy and George Bush should have received much greater support than they actually did. Among Democrats, 40 percent placed themselves closer to Kennedy than to Carter, while 44 percent placed themselves closer to Carter and 16 percent placed themselves equally close to both candidates. Of the delegates who described themselves as "very liberal," 86 percent placed themselves closer to Kennedy while only 5 percent placed themselves closer to Carter. Even among those who were "fairly liberal," 51 percent placed themselves closer to Kennedy while only 24 percent placed themselves closer to Carter. If the Democratic delegates in our survey had chosen a candidate on the basis of ideological proximity, the result would have been close to an even split between Carter and Kennedy rather than an easy victory for the incumbent.

A similar result occurs when we examine Republican delegates. Fifty percent placed themselves closer to Ronald Reagan, while 26 percent were closer to Bush, and 24 percent were equally close to both candidates. Among moderate-to-liberal Republicans, 71 percent were closer to Bush while only 6 percent were closer to Reagan. Even among those delegates describing themselves as "fairly conservative," Bush was perceived as closer in ideology by 37 percent compared with 28 percent who perceived Reagan as closer. Only among "very conservative" Republicans was Reagan clearly seen as closer in ideology than Bush (by a margin of 86 to

1 percent). If Republican delegates had based their candidate choice solely on ideology, George Bush would have lost to Ronald Reagan by a much narrower margin than he actually did.

THE IMPACT OF ELECTABILITY

In addition to our measures relating to ideology, we included a series of questions asking delegates to rate each of the major candidates' chances of winning the November election, if the candidate were nominated by his party. By combining these questions, we can measure delegates' perceptions of the relative electability of the contenders for their party's nomination. Among Democrats, 67 percent rated Jimmy Carter as more electable than Edward Kennedy, while only 18 percent rated Kennedy as more electable and 15 percent gave Carter and Kennedy an equal chance of winning the general election. The incumbent, despite his political liabilities, was seen by the large majority of Democratic activists as more likely to win in November than his challenger. What is perhaps more surprising is that Republican delegates overwhelmingly viewed the conservative Ronald Reagan as more electable than the relatively moderate George Bush. Seventy percent of Republican delegates gave Reagan a better chance of winning, while only 8 percent gave Bush a better chance of winning, and 22 percent gave them an equal chance of winning the November election.

Delegates' perceptions of the relative electability of the candidates seeking their party's nominations were moderately related to their ideological leanings (a point we explore in more detail below). But even among Democratic delegates who were ideologically closer to Kennedy, Carter was seen as more electable than Kennedy by a margin of 44 to 34 percent. Likewise, among Republican delegates who placed themselves closer to George Bush on the liberal-conservative scale, Reagan was viewed as more electable than Bush by a margin of 46 to 19 percent. Moreover, the perceptions of Democratic and Republican delegates regarding the relative electability of the candidates seeking their own party's nomination were consistent with the perceptions of the opposing party's activists: Republican delegates saw Carter as a stronger opponent than Kennedy (by a margin of 66 to 5 percent) and Democratic delegates saw Reagan, despite his conservatism, as a stronger opponent than Bush (by a margin of 55 to 11 percent). Thus there was widespread agreement among

Table 5.3. Candidate preference by perceived electability and ideological proximity

	Democrats		
	Carter more electable	Both equally electable	Kennedy more electable
Closer to Carter	98 (N = 2180)	57 (N = 148)	7 (N = 128)
Equal distance	94 (N = 643)	57 (N = 106)	4 (N = 91)
Closer to Kennedy	78 (N = 921)	18 (N = 409)	2 (N = 760)
	Republicans		
	Reagan more electable	Both equally electable	Bush more electable
Closer to Reagan	99 (N = 2348)	75 (N = 257)	24 (N = 34)
Equal distance	91 (N = 776)	60 (N = 324)	8 (N = 76)
Closer to Bush	83 (N = 586)	29 (N = 422)	2 (N = 217)

Note: Entries are percentages of Democratic delegates supporting Carter and percentages of Republican delegates supporting Reagan.

activists in both parties that Jimmy Carter and Ronald Reagan would be the strongest candidates for their parties in the November election. As a result, many delegates (about two-fifths in each party) faced a conflict between their ideological inclination and their judgment about which candidate in their party was most electable.

Table 5.3 shows the joint effect of ideological proximity and perceived electability on candidate support among Democratic and Republican delegates. It is clear that delegates' perceptions of the candidates' chances of winning in November had a greater impact on their candidate preference than did their perceptions of the candidates' ideological proximity. Regardless of which candidate delegates found more ideologically compatible, they tended to support the candidate they felt was more electable. Among Democrats who were closer to Kennedy in ideology but who

Table 5.4. Base of candidate support by candidate preference

	Democrats		Republicans	
	Carter delegates (N = 3734)	Kennedy delegates (N = 1652)	Reagan delegates (N = 4060)	Bush delegates (N = 980)
Electability	35	13	31	11
Ideology	3	32	5	38
Both	58	44	56	22
Neither	4	11	8	29
Total	100	100	100	100

Note: All entries are percentages.

thought that Carter was more likely to win in November, fully 78 percent supported Carter for the nomination. Similarly, 83 percent of the Republicans who were closer in ideology to Bush but viewed Reagan as more electable, gave their support to Reagan. Ideological proximity had a marked impact on candidate preference only among the minority of delegates who saw no difference between the candidates' chances of victory. The overriding importance of electability in determining candidate preference is evident in these results and directly contradicts the impression, based on the findings presented in Table 5.1, that the 1980 delegates tended to be ideological purists with little interest in winning the November election.

We are able to analyze the bases of support for the major candidates by examining the consistency of delegates' candidate preferences with ideology, electability, both of these factors, or neither one (see Table 5.4). For example, 35 percent of the Carter delegates viewed their candidate as more electable than Edward Kennedy but were just as close or closer in ideology to the Massachusetts senator (Table 5.4, column 1). Only 3 percent of the Carter delegates were closer to their candidate in ideology but viewed Senator Kennedy as equally or more likely to win the November election.

Table 5.4 suggests that there were substantial differences in the criteria on which supporters of the two leading candidates in each party based their decisions. Among the Democrats, over a third of the Carter delegates apparently based their choice on electability alone (even though they viewed themselves as closer to Kennedy in ideology), while very few Carter supporters preferred their candidate for purely ideological reasons. In contrast, almost a third of the Kennedy delegates favored their candidate because of his ideological stance and despite viewing Carter as more electable, while very few Kennedy delegates based their choice solely on electability.

From the beginning of his campaign for the nomination, Senator Kennedy emphasized his liberal record and positions as the basis of his challenge to the incumbent, so it is not surprising that his support was based largely on ideological grounds. In contrast, President Carter appealed to Democratic activists as an incumbent whose moderate record and positions offered the best hope of retaining control of the White House. Our results for Republican delegates are somewhat surprising, however. The candidate taking the more extreme position (in this case Ronald Reagan) might be expected to appeal to party activists (who are relatively extreme themselves) on ideological grounds and the more moderate candidate (George Bush) to attract the support of those activists concerned with electability. Table 5.4 shows that just the opposite was true among Republican party activists in 1980. Very few Republican delegates supported Ronald Reagan for purely ideological reasons, but almost a third of the Reagan delegates apparently based their decision on electability (despite viewing themselves as closer to George Bush in ideology). In contrast, a plurality of the Bush delegates supported their candidate for ideological reasons (despite viewing Ronald Reagan as more electable). In the Republican party, it was the moderate candidate whose appeal was based primarily on ideology and the conservative candidate who attracted the support of party activists concerned primarily about electability. That both Edward Kennedy and George Bush were soundly defeated suggests that candidates whose appeal to party activists is limited to ideology have little chance of success.

We have contrasted the results of our analysis of the impact of ideological proximity and electability on candidate support with the conclusions suggested by our attitudinal measures of purism vs. pragmatism. In order directly to examine the relationship between attitudinal purism-pragmatism and candidate support, we have combined our five classified delegates according to their score on this index as "purist," "mixed," or "pragmatic" in orientation.[6] Table 5.5 presents the results of a discriminant analysis of the effects of ideological proximity and electability on

Table 5.5. A discriminant analysis of candidate preference

Predictor variable	Democrats			Republicans		
	Purist	Mixed	Pragmatic	Purist	Mixed	Pragmatic
Electablility	.886	.910	.916	.850	.869	.856
Ideological proximity	.399	.349	.371	.444	.385	.422
% Correctly classified	91	90	89	88	86	84
(*N*)	(1680)	(1873)	(1429)	(1684)	(1684)	(1276)

Note: Entries are standardized discriminant function coefficients.

candidate support, controlling for the purism-pragmatism score.[7] Regardless of where delegates were classified on the purism-pragmatism index, electability was far more important in determining candidate preference than ideological proximity. Even delegates who consistently subscribed to the purist ideal in the abstract were much more influenced by their perceptions of the candidates' electability than by ideological proximity when they faced the problem of deciding whom to support for their party's nomination. There was little variation in the effects of electability and ideological proximity with position on the purism-pragmatism index, which supports our contention that these general items do not measure the criteria used by activists to select a candidate for the nomination.

ELECTABILITY AS A RATIONALIZATION

We have noted that activists' judgments about candidate electability and their perception of ideological proximity to the candidate are correlated, although the correlation is hardly perfect. Almost two-fifths of the delegates in each party perceived a conflict between their ideological preference and electability, and among those who did experience this conflict, over two-thirds in each party resolved it in favor of the candidate they viewed as more electable. But since ideological proximity and electability are correlated, what are the implications for our analysis?

One plausible hypothesis for the correlation is that activists tend to perceive the candidate whom they are closest to ideologically as most

Table 5.6. A path analysis of the rationalization hypothesis

Democrats (*N* = 5386)	*Republicans* (*N* = 5040)
Ideological proximity → Electability: .444	Ideological proximity → Electability: .389
Electability → Candidate preference: .697	Electability → Candidate preference: .570
Ideological proximity → Candidate preference: .205	Ideological proximity → Candidate preference: .229
$R^2 = .66$	$R^2 = .48$

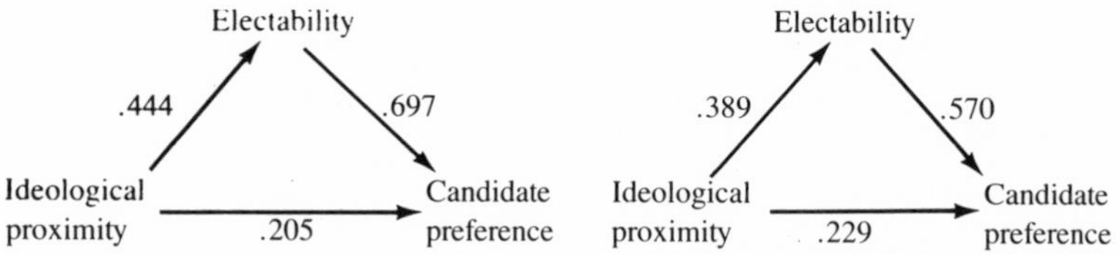

Compound path analysis

	Democrats		Republicans	
	Ideological proximity	Electability	Ideological proximity	Electability
Direct effect	.205	.697	.229	.570
Indirect effect	.309	—	.222	—
Total effect	.514	.697	.451	.570

Note: Coefficients are standardized regression or "path" coefficients.

likely to win. Judging the electability of presidential aspirants is a difficult business because so many imponderables are involved, including the candidates' credibility outside the parties, personality factors, the relevance of past electoral record, and, of course, the ideological positions of the candidates. Activists may maintain cognitive balance simply by rationalizing their ideological favorite as the most electable. If the evidence supports this hypothesis, the postreform interpretation of activists as predominantly purist could be salvaged, despite our criticism of the indicators prior studies have employed.

The analysis presented in Table 5.6 permits a test of the rationalization hypothesis.[8] For this analysis we assume that ideological proximity is causally prior to perceived electability, an assumption which is most antagonistic to our substantive argument. As the analysis in the figure shows, the direct effects of electability in both parties outweigh the direct effects of ideology. The figure also shows that ideology and electability are related. Both of these findings are consistent with the analysis we have presented so far. But even under the relatively unfriendly assumptions of this analysis, the compound path analysis shows that among both Democrats and Republicans the effect of electability on candidate preference was greater than the effect of ideological proximity. If we were to acknowledge that judgments about electability may also affect perceived ideological proximity, the relative effect of electability would increase. However, even the model most compatible with the "purist" hypothesis cannot prevent the conclusion that these presidential activists in 1980 were more influenced by their desire to nominate a winner than they were by their ideological interests.

ELECTABILITY VS. IDEOLOGY IN 1972

We are inevitably led to speculate about the generality of our findings. Is the concern with electability evident in our data a development among party activists after a period of idealism in which concern with victory was subordinated to ideological goals? Are these results somehow applicable only to the stratum of state party activists which we have studied? Or, because caucus-convention states do not constitute a fully representative subset of all states, can it be said that these results apply only to these states where party organizations may be relatively strong? These are legitimate questions which cannot be addressed fully without a complete replication and a new design. We do assert at the outset, however, that any attempt to explain away our findings would have to deal with the fact that the activists in our study subscribed overwhelmingly to "purist" values when offered the choice, in the abstract, between ideology and electability. That, coupled with the results of our analysis of the impact of electability and ideological proximity on candidate choice, gives us considerable confidence that our findings are not merely peculiar to 1980 or to the activists we happened to study.

Although a complete replication of our study is not possible with the data available from past surveys of party activists, the CPS survey of delegates attending the 1972 national nominating conventions did include questions which permit a partial replication. The 1972 Democratic National Convention offers a particularly interesting point of comparison because that convention followed on the heels of the reforms in the Democratic party which have often been linked to the increased influence of purists in the presidential nominating process. There was significant competition for the Democratic nomination in 1972 with the eventual winner, George McGovern, commonly seen as having depended almost exclusively on the support of liberal purists. Indeed, scholars like Kirkpatrick (1976) and Soule and McGrath (1975) relied on studies of the 1972 Democratic convention delegates in pointing to growing purist influence in the presidential nomination process. Analysis of the 1972 data permits us to compare our findings on party activists in eleven states with those from a truly national sample of higher level activists in the presidential nominating process.

As among the state convention delegates in our study, ideology was clearly related to candidate choice among the 1972 Democratic convention delegates. Among those who described themselves as either "radical" or "very liberal" in ideology, 83 percent indicated that George McGovern was their first choice for the nomination. Forty-six percent of those describing themselves as "somewhat liberal" supported a McGovern candidacy, and only 13 percent of moderate to conservative delegates favored the South Dakota senator. These results are consistent with our understanding of the 1972 Democratic contest as highly ideological in character.

Fortunately for our replication, delegates were also asked to indicate which candidate from a list of nine had the best chance of winning the November election. They were not asked to judge the electability of each candidate separately, so the question is not identical to ours, but the concept being measured is certainly the same. This measure of electability is strongly related to support for McGovern: 86 percent of the delegates who judged McGovern as most likely to win the election in November supported him, while only 21 percent of those who thought some other candidate most likely to win supported Senator McGovern for the nomination. However, the most important results are presented in Table 5.7, which compares the effects of ideology and electability on candidate choice.[9] The effect of ideology, while strong, is exceeded by the effect of electability. Comparing the left and right ends of the ideological spectrum, we find a difference in support for McGovern of 37 percent among those who gave him the best chance of winning and a difference of 47 percent among those who gave another candidate the best chance of winning. However, the difference in support for McGovern between those who rated him as the most electable candidate and those who did not is 43 percent, 58 percent, and 54 percent within each of the three categories of

Table 5.7. Candidate preference among Democratic National Convention delegates, 1972

	Ideology		
	Radical to very liberal	Somewhat liberal	Moderate to very conservative
McGovern more electable	93 (N = 625)	74 (N = 234)	57 (N = 63)
Other more electable	50 (N = 182)	16 (N = 228)	3 (N = 253)

Note: Entries are percentage of Democratic delegates supporting McGovern.

ideology. Thus, on average, the effect of electability was greater than the effect of ideology in this most ideological of postreform national conventions.[10]

We have now examined the effects of electability and ideology on party activists' support for candidates seeking their party's presidential nomination. These two factors are widely recognized in the literature but they have been analyzed on the basis of rather general and abstract measures. We have used more specific measures of ideological proximity and electability tied to the individual candidates. These allow us directly to assess the relative impact of ideology and electability on candidate support. While the general attitudinal measures appear to tap a widespread feeling among activists that philosophical principles should not be compromised in order to increase the chances of winning the election, these same activists are quite willing to do just that in practice.

We believe that this conclusion has important implications for the vitality of American political parties in the years ahead. If we assume from evidence like that presented in Table 5.1 that the parties are dominated by activists of a purist stripe, it is not difficult to imagine disastrous consequences for the party organizations. If activists are unwilling to compromise, if they choose candidates purely for ideological reasons, and if they hold views more extreme than the electorate at large, then the parties are likely to nominate candidates whose views are unrepresentative of the vast majority of ordinary citizens. Moreover, the task of reuniting warring ideological factions after the convention may be extremely difficult. But these consequences, commonly speculated upon in the literature, should not be as likely to occur if activists are primarily interested in winning the election. An important next step in researching this question will be to investigate the post convention behavior of presidential activists in order to determine precisely how divisive the prenomination campaign is, and whether activists supporting nomination losers because they judged them more electable do in fact switch their support to the nominee of the party.

Given our findings, how can we explain the support by party activists in previous nomination campaigns for such candidates as Barry Goldwater and George McGovern? We have no data from 1964, but our glance at the 1972 Democratic convention suggests that party activists simply miscalculated Goldwater's and McGovern's chances of winning. Our data indicate that activists are concerned about nominating a winner, not that their perceptions of who is likely to win are always accurate. Indeed, among the Democratic delegates in 1972, 58 percent thought that McGovern was the most likely of all candidates (Democratic and Republican) to win the November election. Judging a candidate's electability is never easy, for future events in the campaign or the world in general cannot be predicted. In one sense, Democratic delegates who supported McGovern thinking he was most electable were not very "pragmatic." Yet prior to the Eagleton fiasco, and without the benefit of hindsight, many Democrats might reasonably have believed that public discontent over Vietnam could carry George McGovern to the White House.

We think it quite possible that the relative effects of ideology and electability vary over time according to the kinds of issues on the agenda, and the kinds of candidates seeking the nomination. In many respects, 1980 is an ideal year to examine the relative weight of ideology and electability in the decision-making of party activists because the principal contenders in both parties were divided along ideological lines, and their claims to being most electable were plausible. In 1964, however, the contest for the Republican nomination probably involved a deeper ideological split between the moderate and conservative wings of the GOP than in 1980. Likewise, the Democrats in 1972 were sharply divided over Vietnam and other emotional issues, a fact which may account (differences in question wording aside) for the apparently greater effect of ideology in that year than in 1980. Similarly, Coleman (1973) has suggested that activists in the party out of power, facing a popular incumbent in the opposing party, may weigh electability less in their decision-making and opt for a candidate who best represents their ideological preferences.

These ideas are worth pursuing in future research on party activists. But while there may be variations in the effects of ideology and electability over time, we do not believe that party activists will ignore electability, however deep their commitment to a set of ideological principles. The presidential nomination process is an example of coalition building, and we can therefore expect participants to base their decisions in part upon their estimates of likely outcomes. That our evidence shows 1980 party activists to be quite interested in selecting candidates with broad voter appeal suggests they realized that compromising some of their ideological interests in order to have a better chance at winning is preferable to maintaining strict ideological purity and suffering defeat. Moreover, as the experience of the Republicans in 1980 demonstrates, concern with electability need not result in the nomination of "me too" candidates. Moderation in the pursuit of victory is not always a virtue. Giving the voters a choice and not an echo is sometimes pragmatic strategy.

NOTES

1. They classified 23 percent of the 1968 Democratic delegates and 51 percent of the 1972 delegates as amateurs. Note that the questions Soule and McGrath used to classify delegates included more than the ideology-electability issue.

2. While we agree with DeFelice when he argues that the "amateur-professional" dimension in the literature confounds a number of concepts not necessarily related empirically, his operational indicator of the tension between ideological principle and electability is typically broad and abstract (DeFelice 1981, 798): "whether or not the respondent thinks that a candidate campaigning for office should be 'willing to change his position in order to secure the support needed to win the election; or refuse to change, even though his views are so unpopular that he will then be defeated.' "

3. The items we employ in Table 5.1 are very similar to those used by previous studies. For example, Soule and Clarke (1970) built an "amateur-professional index" which included the following Likert agree/disagree items (among others): "The principles of a candidate are just as important as winning or losing an election"; "I would object to a candidate who compromises on his basic values if that is necessary to win"; "Controversial positions should be avoided in a party

platform in order to insure party unity"; "Party platforms should be deliberately vague in order to appeal to the broadest spectrum of voters." These items have been used in a number of other studies (e.g., Roback 1975: 468; Hitlin and Jackson 1977) which have contributed to the literature arguing contemporary activists prefer ideological purity to compromising their principles even to nominate a winner.

4. The correlations (Pearson's r) between liberal-conservative identification and issue positions ranged from .32 to .66 with an average of .48.

5. All analyses of candidate preference will be restricted to the two major candidates in each party. In both parties, almost 90 percent of the activists supported one of the major contenders as their first choice for the party nomination. No other candidate in either party was the first choice of more than 2 percent of our respondents.

6. We have combined the five purism-pragmatism items in Table 5.1 into an additive index. We trichotomized the index into three groups of approximately equal size. Because the inter-item correlation (Pearson's r) among the items range from .07 to .49 with an average of .23, we replicated the analysis reported in Table 5.5 sorting each of the purism-pragmatism items separately. The results are identical to those reported in Table 5.5 with the effect of electability consistently outweighing the effect of ideology, and no systematic variation in the relative effects of the two variables with position taken on the individual purism-pragmatism items.

7. Among the Democrats, the dependent variable is the dichotomous candidate choice (prefer Carter, prefer Kennedy), while among Republicans, the dependent variable is preference for Reagan, or preference for Bush. The independent variables are the relative electability and ideological proximity measures for each candidate in the party. These are scored to produce a positive coefficient when the electability or ideology comparisons favor Carter among Democrats, or when they favor Reagan among Republicans. Because the dependent variable is dichotomous, we report a discriminant analysis rather than using ordinary least squares (although OLS yields identical substantive results). For an explanation of discriminant analysis and a comparison with OLS, see Aldrich and Cnudde (1975).

8. We perform path analysis with a dichotomous dependent variable because it is the most straightforward technique for assessing the relative causal effects (both direct and indirect) of the independent variables. Gillespie (1977) compares OLS with log-linear techniques when the dependent variable is dichotomous and argues that while log-linear techniques correct for some of the statistical problems associated with using OLS in this situation, these techniques do not permit the researcher to decompose the causal effects as we wish to do. Gillespie (1977; 109-10) suggests that OLS is the appropriate technique when this is the purpose of the analysis: "The researcher who uses dummy dependent-variable regression can

. . . multiply the regression slopes that represent the links in one or more causal chains in order to measure the indirect effects of an antecedent variable on another variable further down the causal chain." When the estimated OLS coefficients are not in the extremes (a range of between .2 and .8 is commonly cited), the estimates are very close to those provided by nonlinear techniques.

9. The 1972 study did not include a measure of ideological proximity; thus, we employ the position of the respondent on the ideological scale. The study did include proximity measures on four issues of the day: inflation, busing, Vietnam, and the rights of accused criminals. Analysis of proximity scores on these issues does not disturb the conclusions we present here. Indeed, with issue proximity *and* ideology controlled, the effects of electability on candidate choice remain very strong.

10. Replicating the path analysis in Table 5.6 for the Democrats in 1972 results in the following:

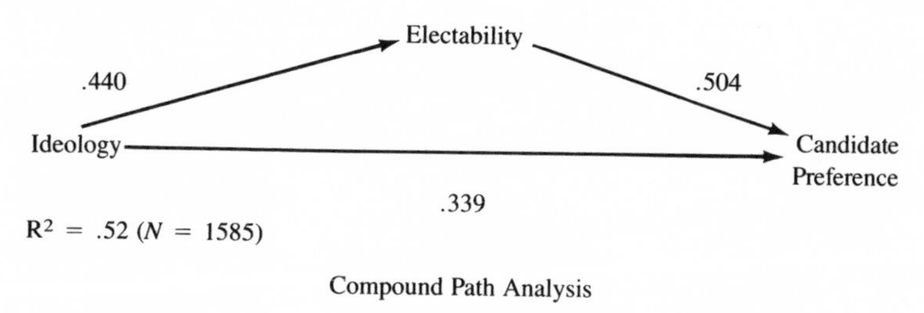

Compound Path Analysis

	Ideology	Electability
Direct effect	.339	.504
Indirect effect	.222	—
Total effect	.561	.504

Once again, the direct effect of electability on candidate preference outstrips the direct effect of ideology, but the total effect of ideology under the assumptions of this model does outweigh the total effect of electability. Whether the differences between the estimated effects of the independent variables in 1972 and in 1980 can be attributed to changes in the parties or to differences in the measures used in the two studies is impossible to tell. We do believe, however, that the results of our analysis of the 1972 Democratic Convention delegates portray them as considerably less attached to ideological purity—and more interested in supporting a winner—than the literature would have us believe.

REFERENCES

Abramowitz, Alan I., John J. McGlennon, and Ronald B. Rapoport. 1980. *Party Activists in Virginia*. Charlottesville, Virginia: Institute of Government.

Aldrich, John and Charles Cnudde. 1975. "Probing the Bounds of Conventional Wisdom: A Comparison of Regression, Probit, and Discriminant Analysis." *American Journal of Political Science* 19: 571- 608.

Coleman, James S. 1973. "Communication." *American Political Science Review* 67: 567-9.

DeFelice, E. Gene. 1981. "Separating Professionalism from Pragmatism: A Research Note on the Study of Political Parties." *American Journal of Political Science* 25: 796-807.

Downs, Anthony. 1957. *An Economic Theory of Democracy*. New York: Harper & Row.

Farah, Barbara G., M. Kent Jennings, and Warren E. Miller. 1981. "Convention Delegates: Reform and the Representation of Party Elites, 1972-1980." Presented to the Conference on Party Activists, Williamsburg, Virginia, October 1-3.

Gillespie, Michael W. 1977. "Log-Linear Techniques and the Regression Analysis of Dummy Dependent Variables." *Sociological Methods and Research* 6: 103-22.

Hitlin, Robert A. and John S. Jackson III. 1977. "On Amateur and Professional Politicians." *Journal of Politics* 39: 796-93.

Jackson, John S. III, Barbara Leavitt Brown, and David Bositis. 1982. "Herbert McClosky and Friends Revisited: 1980 Democratic and Republican Party Elites Compared to the Mass Public." *American Politics Quarterly* 10: 158-180.

Jackson, John S. III, Jesse C. Brown, and Barbara L. Brown. 1978. "Recruitment, Representation, and Political Values: The 1976 Democratic National Convention Delegates." *American Politics Quarterly* 6: 187-212.

Johnson, Donald B., and James R. Gibson. 1974. "The Divisive Primary Revisited: Party Activists in Iowa." *American Political Science Review* 68: 67-77.

Kirkpatrick, Jeane J. 1976. *The New Presidential Elite*. New York: Russell Sage.

Marshall, Thomas R. 1981. *Presidential Nominations in a Reform Age*. New York: Praeger.

McClosky, Herbert, Paul J. Hoffman, and Rosemary O'Hara. 1960. "Issue Conflict and Consensus among Party Leaders and Followers." *American Political Science Review* 54: 406-27.

Nexon, David. 1971. "Asymmetry in the Political System: Occasional Activists in the Republican and Democratic Parties, 1954-64." *American Political Science Review* 65: 716-30.

Polsby, Nelson W., and Aaron Wildavsky. 1980. *Presidential Elections: Strategies of American Electoral Politics*. New York: Scribner's.

Roback, Thomas H. 1975. "Amateurs and Professionals: Delegates to the 1972 Republican National Convention." *Journal of Politics* 37: 436-67.

Soule, John W., and James W. Clarke. 1970. "Amateurs and Professionals: A Study of Delegates to the 1968 Democratic National Convention." *American Political Science Review* 64: 888-98.

Soule, John W., and Wilma E. McGrath. 1975. "A Comparative Study of Presidential Nomination Conventions: The Democrats of 1968 and 1972." *American Journal of Political Science* 19: 501-17.

Verba, Sidney, and Norman H. Nie. 1972. *Participation in America: Political Democracy and Social Equality*. New York: Harper & Row.

Wilson, James Q. 1962. *The Amateur Democrat*. Chicago: University of Chicago Press.

PART THREE

Groups and Representation

6

Issue Group Activists at the Conventions

JOHN G. FRANCIS,
ROBERT C. BENEDICT

The rise of the new single issue groups has presented the Republican and Democratic parties with a novel challenge to their historic roles as broad-based coalition parties. Both parties now confront groups within their ranks that demand of party nominees a strict commitment to the position held by the group on a specified issue. We will examine the extent to which party delegates who are active in the new issue groups are distinguished from other delegates in their party commitment, issue positions, and ideological orientation. In short, have state party conventions been penetrated by new issue group activists, lacking any broader interest in or commitment to the party? We draw two conclusions from our analysis below: First, delegates in new issue groups are also active in other interest groups within their respective parties. This suggests that while delegates may belong to single issue groups, they may not have single issue political orientations. Second, delegates active in newer social issue groups can be distinguished from other delegates within their respective parties on certain measures of commitment, but nonetheless such delegates are clearly differentiated in their party orientation from delegates in the other party who are active in similar interest groups.

The two main American political parties, of course, are legally obligated to maintain open memberships and to maximize participation in the nominating process (Ranney 1975, 1978). Over the years both parties have come to enjoy the status of semistate agencies—that is, both the judicial and legislative branches have recognized that parties perform a critical role in the selection of the nation's leadership (Francis and Warr 1980). In return for this recognition, the parties have been obliged to remain relatively open to a large array of individuals and groups who opt to participate in the nominating process of either or both parties.

Over most of this century, economic issues have generated the principal cleavages between Republicans and Democrats (Sundquist 1972; Burnham and Chambers 1975). Well-established business and labor groups have long played important roles (albeit at sharply different levels) in both parties. In the past two decades, however, new issues have become salient—issues that are social and/or moral in nature. Along with the older established groups, issue groups such as the anti-abortionists, women's rights advocates, and environmentalists have sought to play important roles in American party politics.

There is some concern that the new social issue groups are inimical to the traditional conception of American parties (Commager 1980; Samuelson 1979). The new groups, it is argued, for the most part are committed to a very limited set of issues, have little interest in the broader range of concerns that make up national political parties, and are only willing to judge candidates or parties on the issue stance of concern to the group.[1] (Vinovskis 1979; Keller 1980; Crotty and Jacobson 1980; Weintraub 1980). In contrast, the older established economic groups such as labor or business are experienced in dealing with a range of diverse issues and have developed the art of compromise in working within the broad coalitions that are the two main political parties.

It might be presumed that the rise of a new issue group would have an equal chance of acceptance or rejection by each party in a two-party competitive system. But few issues are received with equal interest by the respective parties, nor is a new issue completely rejected by one party and fully accepted by the other. A party's commitment to a new issue area is, in part, dependent on the constellation of forces within the existing two parties. It may well be that a new social issue group in its relationship to the parties is quite similar to older, established groups when they started out; that is, an initial neutrality toward the system is followed by a gradually greater identification with one party rather than the other. An illustration is the environmentalist movement. When the environmentalists emerged as a major force in the late 1960s, they adopted a stance of strict party neutrality. Environmentalist issues were widely perceived as consumer issues requiring strong federal regulatory solutions. This perception of the problem made environmentalist concern understandable and appealing to many groups within the Democratic party who themselves favored strengthened federal regulatory intervention. It is increasingly apparent in the early 1980s that many environmentalist groups have decided to actively involve themselves in the Democratic party. Thus members in a new issue group are likely to be in the process of sorting out their group's relationship to the two main parties.

Of course, it is likely that political activists may belong to more than one interest group. Indeed, one way a new interest group may stand apart from, or be a part of, the broader coalitions that make up the two parties is the extent to which its members are also active in other groups. If, for example, activists in one group are also active in other organizations, then there is a greater chance they will share understanding of the various groups' concerns (Verba and Nie 1971). On the other hand, if the delegates who are active in one group are not noticeably active in any other groups, then the prospects for isolation from the party coalition are greater. We discuss below patterns of plural interest group membership and the implication for coalition-building within each party.

We examine three sets of questions concerning the relationships between interest groups and their political parties. First, what differences exist in terms of levels of support for the party among those who belong to an old or a new issue group? For example, are the activists in the new single issue groups less supportive of their political party than delegates who are not members of such groups? Second, what variations are evident in the issue positions of members of old or new groups? Would there be substantive differences between the issue positions of activists in a new single issue group and activists in the established economic groups? Finally, what is the extent of shared ideological orientation among members of the old or new groups? From answers to these questions we draw some tentative conclusions about the extent to which delegates with memberships in several groups enhance the integrative abilities of the political parties.

We test the following hypotheses in the exploration of activists' attitudes to their respective political parties:

Party support: Delegates who are active in new interest groups will be less likely to be supportive of the party than are delegates in the established economic interest groups.

Ideological Orientation: Delegates who are members of a new issue group will be ideologically distinct from other delegates at the convention.

Issue Orientation: Delegates who are active in new issue organizations will be distinct from other delegates at the convention on particular issue positions.

It is precisely because American political parties are so closely identified with the electoral system that a single issue group—indeed, any group wishing to influence the course of American politics—finds it less costly to devote some of its efforts to working within either or both parties. However, as the first hypothesis predicts, large numbers of delegates at a party convention who belong to a single issue group would increase the probability of greater fragmentation within the party. Less consensus on issues or candidates and less commitment to the party as an organization deserving of support in its own right would be expected. It is fairly apparent, for example, that a number of single issue groups have been increasingly active in the Democratic party in the past two decades. In one of the few empirical studies dealing with this subject Jeane Kirkpatrick surveyed delegates to the 1972 Democratic National Convention. The "interest group specialists," that is delegates who focused activity almost exclusively on the new social interest groups, were notable for their political style combining "high policy concern with little or no interest in party preservation or solidarity" (Kirkpatrick 1976; Polsby 1981). The first hypothesis, based upon the Kirkpatrick findings, predicts that the Democrats would be a party of policy divisions, that is, a party composed of a number of autonomous groups.

Moreover, the longer a group has enjoyed an association with a political party, the greater may be that group's strength of identification with that party. The economic groups have had, for the most part, long records of association with the two parties. What we are proposing is that there is a parallel between individual level socialization and party membership and group level socialization and party orientation. Some observers have stipulated that the longer an activist remains in the political party the greater the likelihood that there will be a shift in incentives (Wilson 1973, chapter 6). Initially some activists are activated by ideological considerations, but over time solidary and tangible rewards come to play larger parts in inducing activists to remain with a party (Roback 1980; Moe 1981, 1980). We suggest that interest groups' members also change in their orientation to the party over time. Group members come to establish social and political relationships with other activists in the party.

A network of relationships develops that socializes the new group members into a sympathetic appreciation of the problems of an electoral organization and its need to come up with viable candidates and issues capable of creating winning electoral coalitions (Kirkpatrick 1976). In turn, the party over time becomes more attuned to the demands of the group.

As grounding for the second hypothesis, we note that the new issue groups are likely to attract individuals of diverse backgrounds who are united only on the issue position held by the group (Kirkpatrick 1976, 224). These activists may come to the party from a range of ideological backgrounds. In contrast, party activists who are members of the older established economic groups or who are not active in groups at all are more likely to share broadly similar ideological orientations. Our data suggest that in terms of self-placement the Democrats are more likely to be found to the center-left while Republicans are to the center-right.

Finally, the third hypothesis is built on the assumption that the issues that confront social interest groups may be less susceptible to compromise than economic interests since they are more frequently presented in moral terms. For example, environmentalists may see the preservation of the public lands as a goal of incalculable value, of an order different from the bargaining and negotiation that takes place between business and labor groups. Similarly, if the anti-abortionists wish to secure the nomination and election of candidates who share the group's position on abortion, then group members would become politically active in the Democratic and Republican parties. If abortion is the only issue of concern to group members, then it is probable that no real pattern of issue compatibility will exist between delegate members of the anti-abortionist group and other delegates at the convention.

As described in the introductory chapter, the activists surveyed come largely from states located in the South and West. In most of these states political conventions are meaningful political activities. In these ideologically conservative regions the Republican party has enjoyed growing electoral success. Many of these states have seen major controversies during the last decade over such new issues as the environment, the Equal Rights Amendment, and abortion.

For the purposes of our analysis we examined the responses of delegates by party but not by state. Our justification for treating the eleven states as a whole is that it permitted us to explore the attitudes of delegates in a range of groups. If we had engaged in a state-by-state analysis, certain groups simply lacked sufficient representation in the Republican party to allow us to perform our analysis. By massing the delegates by party we were able to explore all groups in both political parties. We created two delegate subgroupings. The first is composed of delegates who are politically active in the new issue groups. We identified four such groups: opponents of abortion, advocates of women's rights, environmentalists, and civil rights activists. The last group, civil rights activists, presents some problems in classification. The civil rights groups may be illustrative of groups in transition. That is, they have a long record of association with the main political parties, principally the Democratic party, and have come to embrace a range of issues, many of which are economic in focus.

Our second category is composed of delegates who report that they are active in the traditional economic interest groups. We identified three such groups: labor unions, business organizations, and farm associations. We discuss educational groups as well as traditional economic groups, although we recognize that the category embraces both professional and civic-minded organizations. These economic groups, particularly labor in the Democratic party and business in the Republican party, have been important components of the national parties for the past fifty years.

Our analysis relies on what delegates themselves tell us about their political activities. Indicators of strength of partisan identification, degree of party support, campaign activity and ideological placement are all self-reported. We recognize that there may be a good deal of variance to the delegates' reports of their activity in various interest groups. Such activity could be interpreted as attendance at meetings or it could suggest that the delegate holds an active leadership role in the group. We also recognize that delegates were asked to respond to group categories rather than to particular groups such as, say, the Sierra Club. Categories such as conservation, ecology groups, woman's rights groups, or civil rights groups can embrace a variety of organizational possibilities.

With one exception, the data do not support our hypotheses. It does appear that social issue group delegates, particularly in the Democratic party, are less supportive of their party than are delegates who are not politically active in social issue groups. But single issue group delegates are not lacking in ideological relevance to their respective parties, although they may fall to one side of the party's ideological spectrum. Nor

Table 6.1. Delegates reporting interest group activity (percent)

	Democrats	Republicans
Economic Groups		
Labor unions	18.4 (1841)	2.8 (291)
Business organizations	15.4 (1557)	27.5 (2765)
Professional organizations	23.1 (2321)	23.5 (2381)
Farm organizations	12.6 (1291)	13.3 (1329)
Educational organizations	27.9 (2827)	14.4 (1474)
Social Groups		
Civil rights groups	19.6 (1990)	2.1 (227)
Environmentalists	15.8 (1566)	7.7 (779)
Women's rights groups	18.6 (1861)	4.2 (423)
Anti-abortionist groups	5.9 (596)	10.7 (1115)

are they divorced from the issue positions of their fellow delegates. We thus must reject the hypotheses predicting issue divergence and lack of ideological congruence between activists in the newer interest groups and their parties.

PATTERNS OF GROUP MEMBERSHIP

On the question of group membership, in Table 6.1 over 60 percent of all delegates surveyed claim to be active in groups outside their respective parties.

No one will be surprised to learn that interest groups do not enjoy equal representation in both parties. Democrats are involved in a wider, more diversified range of groups than the nearly 28 percent of the delegates professing activity in educational organizations; by contrast, Republican educationists come in at just under 15 percent. Some 18 percent of Democratic delegates identify themselves as labor activists—six times the representation of labor activists among Republicans. Just over half of all Republican delegates are active in either business (28.5 percent) or professional (23.5 percent) organizations—by far the largest groupings of Republican activists—but some 23 percent of Democrats identify themselves as involved in professional organizations, and 15 percent claim activity in business organizations. Farm organizations claim relatively

Table 6.2. Democratic activists in selected groups

	Labor union		Business organization		Farm organization		Educational organization		Women's rights group		Ecology group		Anti-Abortion group	
	%	*N*	%	*N*	%	*N*	%	*N*	%	*N*	%	*N*	%	*N*
Labor union	——		15.6	297	11.8	224	26.6	506	21.6	412	18.2	346	9.0	172
Business organization	18.5	297	——		20.6	331	26.6	427	17.9	288	16.8	269	8.6	137
Farm organization	16.4	224	24.2	331	——		32.7	447	15.7	214	22.4	307	11.8	161
Educational organization	17.2	506	14.5	427	15.2	447	——		25.7	757	19.1	564	6.7	199
Women's rights group	21.3	412	14.8	288	11.0	214	39.1	757	——		33.4	648	7.2	140
Ecology group	21.4	346	16.6	269	18.9	307	34.8	564	40.0	648	——		10.5	170
Anti-abortion group	27.3	172	21.8	137	25.6	161	31.6	199	22.3	140	26.9	170	——	

Note: Entries are percentages of groups reporting membership in other groups. For example, 15.6% of union members were in business organizations.

similar levels of involvement from delegates in both parties, 12.5 percent among Democrats and 13.3 percent among Republicans.

In the area of social issues, the events of the past twenty years have had more impact on group activities of Democratic delegates than on activities of Republican delegates, with one major exception, the abortion issue. Just under one-fifth of the Democrats report political activity in civil rights groups. Over 18 percent are active in women's rights groups. Somewhat below 16 percent are in the environmentalist movement. Such issue groups clearly constitute major forces in Democratic state conventions.

By contrast, the Republicans contain many fewer activists from these social issue groups. Just over 2 percent of Republican delegates are active in civil rights groups. Women's rights supporters constitute somewhat over 4 percent of the delegates. Next to the anti-abortionists, the environmentalists are the largest social group at nearly 8 percent. Significantly, the only issue category represented in double digits for the Republicans is the anti-abortion movement, which includes just over 10 percent of Republican delegates. In contrast, just under 6 percent of the Democrats report political activity in anti-abortion groups. This finding is surprising, for studies of the anti-abortion movement have described it as being successful in recruiting blue-collar Catholics, a group historically within the Democratic tradition. In another sense, however, the anti-abortionists are clearly conservative in their reaction against a change in social practice that was triggered by the Supreme Court decision legalizing abortion in Roe vs. Wade.

In analyzing the relationships between interest group activists and their parties, it must also be borne in mind that delegates who are active in one interest group tend to be active in others as well. In Tables 6.2 and 6.3 the pattern of plural or overlapping group membership is apparent in both the Republican and Democratic conventions. Read horizontally, the tables show the percent of activists of one type—for example, labor union activists—active in groups of other types such as business or farm organizations. In order to obviate the danger of overreporting, the categories selected in Tables 6.2 and 6.3 are ones that are less likely to have been confused with each other by the delegates. For example, the category of "civil rights groups" is not included in the analysis of overlapping group membership because members of women's rights groups might quite naturally have reported themselves as members of civil rights groups as well.

Table 6.3. Republican activists in selected groups

	Labor union		Business organization		Farm organization		Educational organization		Women's rights group		Ecology group		Anti-Abortion group	
	%	*N*	%	*N*	%	*N*	%	*N*	%	*N*	%	*N*	%	*N*
Labor union	——		28.7	87	14.9	45	24.5	74	8.4	26	13.3	41	18.6	57
Business organization	3.0	87	——		16.6	479	12.3	354	4.2	122	10.1	292	11.0	317
Farm organization	3.2	45	34.2	479	——		20.0	2.80	4.6	65	16.5	232	12.3	172
Educational organization	4.9	74	23.3	354	18.4	280	——		9.4	142	12.5	190	14.0	213
Women's rights group	5.7	26	27.3	122	14.5	65	31.7	142	——		19.1	86	24.7	110
Ecology group	4.9	41	35.6	292	28.2	232	23.1	190	10.4	86	——		13.3	109
Anti-abortion group	5.0	57	27.9	317	15.2	172	18.7	213	9.7	110	9.6	109	——	

In both parties, interest groups that attract the membership of large numbers of delegates appear to have a commanding position in serving as the center of a network of common issue concerns. A useful illustration is delegate membership in educational organizations in the Democratic party. In Table 6.2 between 26.6 percent and 39.1 percent of delegates in the other selected group categories also claim to be activists in educational organizations. This network of membership means that certain issues and interests in the area of education are likely to attract considerable attention among delegates at the several Democratic state conventions. In contrast, the network of the anti-abortionist groups among Democratic delegates is much more restricted. Only 6 percent of Democratic delegates claim to be active in anti-abortionist organizations. Those delegates are, themselves, active in many other interest groups. But their voice in the other organizations is not numerically strong, certainly in comparison to the educationists. The percentage of activists in the other types of organizations who are also active members of anti-abortionist organizations range from only 6.7 to 11.8 percent.

In the case of the Republican delegates, a different pattern of overlapping membership emerges. Active membership in business organizations appears to be the focal point for Republican delegates. In Table 6.3 between one-quarter and one-third of Republican delegates claiming to be active in the other selected groupings claim to be active in business organizations as well. The greater strength of the anti-abortionists in the Republican party is apparent as well in the pattern of overlapping membership. Between 11 and 24.7 percent of delegates claiming to be active in the other six groupings also claim activity in anti-abortion groups.

Of course, group membership is not necessarily equated with a specific issue central to the group leading the delegates to participate in the 1980 election campaign. Nonetheless, single issues apparently are an important source of motivation. Just under half of all Democratic delegates (48.2 percent) and nearly 60 percent of all Republican delegates (58.8 percent) claim that a single issue caused them to become involved in the 1980 campaign. An analysis of the issues by area, however, reveals that social issues are not the central motivators of delegates' participation in the 1980 elections. In Table 6.4, although the category of morality and conduct includes such issues as abortion and women's rights, overall the category attracted only 10 percent of delegates in both parties. The economy and government were the principal motivators of active participation in the 1980 elections.

Table 6.4. Issues motivating delegates to join the 1980 campaign (percent)

	Democrats	Republicans
Economic issues	21.3	33.0
Social welfare	9.1	2.8
Energy	6.9	2.5
Morality and conduct	11.2	10.4
Race	0.9	0
Defense	3.2	6.2
Government	26.1	28.2
Foreign relations	3.6	4.5
No issue	17.7	12.4
	100.0	100.0

If we turn to specific groups of delegates active in social issue groups, it is quite apparent that such groups are not composed of delegates motivated solely by the issue that is presumably central to the group's concern. Among Democrats active in women's rights groups, 62.8 percent claim to be participating in the 1980 election because of a specific issue, but only 18.9 percent of those delegates state that it is the women's rights issue. A similar pattern is found for Democrats active in anti-abortion groups: while 60.4 percent of such delegates claim to have become active in the election because of a specific issue, only 20 percent identify it as the abortion issue per se. A similar pattern holds for the Republican delegates. Republican activists in women's rights groups and anti-abortion groups claim by 62.3 percent and 66.4 percent respectively to have become active in 1980 in response to a specific issue. However, only 18.3 percent and 15.6 percent of the two groups of issue-motivated delegates attribute their activity to the women's rights or abortion issues respectively.

PARTY SUPPORT AND GROUP MEMBERSHIP

The heart of our concern is the extent to which delegates who are politically active in the new single issue groups are less party oriented than delegates in the more traditional economic or occupational organizations. Table 6.5 does reveal that delegates to both sets of state conventions are

Table 6.5. Delegates expressing strong partisan identification

	Democrats %	Republicans %
Economic groups		
Labor unions	81.5 (1406)	73.0 (197)
Business organizations	72.1 (1060)	79.1 (2342)
Professional organizations	74.5 (1615)	86.0 (1954)
Educational organizations	72.8 (1906)	79.1 (1097)
Farm organizations	75.9 (895)	88.2 (1281)
Social groups		
Civil rights groups	77.0 (1417)	66.4 (204)
Environmentalists	68.7 (1015)	82.5 (612)
Women's rights groups	75.1 (1313)	70.6 (287)
Anti-abortionist groups	69.0 (382)	81.2 (837)
All delegates	72.1 (6763)	84.5 (8136)

strong party identifiers. Republicans more so than Democrats express a strong sense of party affiliation; the figures are 80 percent and 70 percent respectively.

An examination of the groups in which Democratic delegates are active indicates that labor union activists, women's rights supporters, and civil rights group activists are among the strongest Democratic party identifiers. Labor union delegates lead all other groups in the strength of their identification, 81.5 percent. In contrast, the average for the party is 72.1 percent. The only two groups that fall below the party average are the environmentalists (68.7 percent) and the anti-abortionists (69.0 percent). All of the economic groups are either at the party average or just above.

In the Democratic party we found that delegates who are active in labor, civil rights, and women's rights groups are supportive of their party to an extent that is not apparent among Republican delegates active in those same groups. Republican activists supporting labor, civil rights, and women's groups are some ten percentage points below their fellow Republicans in expressing strong partisan affiliation. In contrast, Republican environmentalist and anti-abortionist activists are at 82.5 percent and 81.2 percent, just about the party average, in expressing a strong sense of identification. Business, professional, and farm groups are the three most strongly partisan of all the Republican groups.

Table 6.6. Support for party as motive for attending convention

	Democrats %	Republicans %
Economic groups		
Labor unions	70.6 (1300)	56.4 (170)
Business organizations	68.6 (1067)	67.8 (1893)
Professional organizations	62.9 (1460)	64.5 (1538)
Educational organizations	58.9 (1664)	61.3 (906)
Farm organizations	68.5 (885)	70.6 (950)
Social groups		
Civil rights groups	59.5 (1185)	54.5 (123)
Environmentalists	51.5 (799)	63.5 (505)
Women's rights groups	60.4 (1123)	59.9 (254)
Anti-abortionist groups	60.9 (363)	56.6 (617)
All delegates	61.9 (6281)	66.6 (6765)

Table 6.5 indicates that delegate groupings that are both large and influential within the party are more likely to contain strong party identifiers than groups with less successful records and smaller numbers of adherents in the party. Women's rights activists and labor unionists, for example, have not enjoyed much success in Republican state parties. In contrast, such groups have been important components of the Democratic party.

Reported strength of party affiliation is one measure of party commitment.[2] Another indicator that is more to the point in an analysis of the impact of interest group membership upon importance of party support is the motivation to attend caucuses. In Table 6.6, we see that Republicans are more inclined to believe that supporting the party was an important motivation than are Democrats. In the Democratic party, traditional economic groupings are more likely than newer social issue groups to emphasize support for the party. Both labor and business groups are over 9 and 8 percent higher, respectively, in assessing the importance of party support than the party delegates in general. In contrast, civil rights, women's rights and anti-abortionist groups are close to the party average. Environmentalists were much less motivated to participate by support for the party, falling 10 points below. In some sense the environmentalists are the least party-oriented of the Democratic groups; their group behavior most conforms to the prediction that single issue groups are not highly supportive of the party.

For the Republicans in Table 6.6, the pattern that was observed in regard to party affiliation by group activists is also apparent on the question of support for the party. Traditional economic groups are more likely to emphasize support for the party than are social issue groups. The single exception to this division between social and economic issues is Republican labor activists. Along with civil rights activists, they remain noticeably less motivated by support for their party. Republican anti-abortionists are next weakest in party motivation, remaining 10 percent below the average for Republican delegates.

Tables 6.5 and 6.6 provide some confirmation of our first hypothesis that social issue groups are less motivated by support for their respective political parties than are delegates in economic groups. Presumably, commitment to social issue groups can and does draw support away from the party. But any account of conflicting loyalties between group and party must be seen in the larger context of the success enjoyed by the group in the two parties. The more influential the interest group, the more its delegates were motivated by party loyalty.

IDEOLOGY AND PARTY MEMBERSHIP

In testing our second hypothesis—that is, the extent to which single issue group delegates are actually ideologically sympathetic to the party in which they are located—we examined the ideological self-placement of delegates in each party. The range for Republicans was from somewhat liberal, middle of the road, and somewhat conservative to very conservative. Democrats ranged from somewhat conservative to very liberal.

A survey of Table 6.7 shows three distinct ideological locations for the interest groups we have examined in the Democratic party. Economic organizations are skewed to the left of center. Among these groups, labor union activist delegates are the most liberal, while farm and business groups are the least liberal. The social issue groups, with the important exception of the anti-abortionists, are to the left of the economic groups and are therefore a strong liberal presence in the party conventions. There is a remarkable degree of ideological similarity among the women's rights groups, the civil rights activists, and the environmentalists. Members of each of these groups who claim to be middle of the road or somewhat

Table 6.7. Ideology of Democratic delegates in interest groups

	Ideological self-placement (%)			
Interest groups	Very liberal	Somewhat liberal	Moderate	Somewhat conservative
Economic				
Labor union	25.6 (465)	39.3 (713)	20.4 (369)	14.6 (265)
Business	15.0 (233)	32.1 (499)	23.5 (366)	29.3 (456)
Professional	21.9 (500)	39.6 (905)	21.1 (482)	17.5 (400)
Educational	19.5 (558)	43.2 (1233)	20.5 (584)	16.8 (479)
Farm	14.1 (193)	35.1 (464)	23.3 (307)	27.0 (356)
Social				
Civil rights	38.6 (766)	41.9 (832)	11.2 (223)	8.2 (163)
Environmentalist	37.1 (574)	39.3 (610)	12.0 (187)	11.6 (179)
Women's rights	35.0 (652)	44.2 (823)	12.4 (231)	8.3 (155)
Anti-abortionist	17.9 (107)	26.7 (159)	23.3 (139)	32.2 (192)
All Democrats	19.1 (1935)	39.4 (3987)	22.1 (2240)	19.4 (1970)

Note: Percentages are row percentages.

conservative do not exceed 25 percent. In contrast, among the Democratic economic groups, "right wings" range between 35 and 55 percent of their members.

The Democratic social issue groups appear in large part to be the left wing of the party. Their delegate members are on average more liberal than delegates in general attending the convention. Delegates active in the economic interest groups, by contrast, are at the party average. The anti-abortionist group is the most conservative in the party and stands out in comparison with other social groups. Nonetheless, the anti-abortionists are conservative Democrats, not all that ideologically distinct, for example, from Democrats who are active in farm groups. Thus, anti-abortionists are still ideologically more in tune with the Democrats than with the Republicans.

A survey of the distribution of Republican ideological positions by groups (Table 6.8) indicates, first, that there is more homogeneity within the Republican party than the Democratic party. The Republican delegates taken as a whole are overwhelmingly conservative, falling between somewhat and very conservative in ideological self-placement. Only just over

Table 6.8. Ideology of Republican delegates in interest groups

	Ideological self-placement (%)			
Interest groups	Somewhat liberal	Moderate	Somewhat conservative	Very conservative
Economic				
Labor union	7.9 (24)	11.4 (34)	46.1 (137)	34.5 (103)
Business	2.9 (81)	8.3 (235)	48.7 (1372)	40.1 (1128)
Professional	4.4 (103)	9.9 (236)	49.0 (1172)	36.7 (872)
Educational	6.2 (93)	12.6 (188)	52.8 (787)	28.4 (424)
Farm	3.4 (46)	9.2 (125)	50.3 (686)	37.1 (505)
Social				
Civil rights	16.0 (36)	16.0 (36)	47.4 (106)	20.5 (46)
Environmentalist	7.2 (58)	12.7 (102)	48.1 (384)	32.0 (255)
Women's rights	16.4 (70)	20.6 (88)	35.8 (154)	27.1 (116)
Anti-abortionist	1.6 (18)	3.5 (39)	35.0 (385)	59.9 (659)
All Republicans	3.8 (388)	9.0 (929)	46.6 (4802)	40.7 (4197)

Note: Percentages are row percentages.

13 percent of the delegates opt for either a somewhat liberal or moderate position. It should be recalled that membership in civil rights groups, women's groups, and labor unions is found only among a quite small subset of Republican delegates. Such groups are a good deal more moderate in their ideological placement than are the other much larger economic groups within the Republican party. As among Democrats, the most conservative group found in the Republican ranks is the anti-abortion group of delegates; only about 5 percent see themselves as somewhat liberal or moderate, whereas just short of 60 percent view themselves as very conservative.

The social issues groups we have selected have failed to take form as major organizational forces in the Republican party in the same way as they have for the Democrats. Civil rights, women's advocates, and environmental activists, are not potent forces in the Republican party. The great exception is the anti-abortion group, the largest social issue grouping among the Republican delegates. Ideologically it is the most conservative, and the least vigorously supportive of the party.

The configuration of ideological orientations on the one hand clearly

Table 6.9. Ideological Positions of Democratic group members

	Women's rights	Ecologist	Anti-abortionist	Labor	Business	All delegates
Economic issues						
Non-defense budget cuts	−23.6	−21.7	+0.3	−9.5	−2.4	−6.1
Wage and price controls	−7.6	−1.3	−8.3	−5.8	−2.9	−2.1
Reduce inflation even if it increases unemployment	−6.8	−9.9	−4.3	−15.1	+5.8	−2.6
Deregulate oil	−8.4	−14.2	−5.8	−17.5	−8.0	−5.1
More rapid development of nuclear power	−28.1	−46.0	−10.4	−7.4	+4.7	−11.8
Social issues						
Equal Rights Amendment	−87.5	−65.3	+3.7	−28.4	−29.9	−40.0
Anti-Abortion Amendment	−57.0	−47.0	+55.6	−16.3	−16.1	−21.0
Affirmative action	−39.6	−27.4	+6.5	−22.9	−12.8	−16.9
Foreign and defense issues						
Reinstituting the draft	−17.4	−24.3	+24.2	+7.4	+22.1	+5.0
Ratification of Salt II	−23.0	−19.0	+1.9	−5.4	−2.3	−8.5
Increased U.S. military presence in the Middle East	−9.7	−14.5	+7.8	+9.3	+17.1	+3.5

Note: Each entry is the percent strongly agreeing minus the percent strongly disagreeing with the issue.

distinguishes the several social and economic issue groups within the respective parties. On the other hand, clear cut ideological divisions exist between the two parties and their respective sets of social and economic groups.

Our second hypothesis, which predicts that members of new issue groups would not show ideological congruence with their party, is thus unsupported. We can further explore the relative congruence between members of new interest groups and their parties by testing a third hypothesis, that members of the newer groups are less likely to share issue positions with others in their party.

ISSUE POSITIONS AND GROUP MEMBERSHIP

There are sharp differences between the two parties on a whole range of issues, particularly questions of social policy. The most outstanding difference is that Republicans are strongly unified on nearly every issue. Republicans have clear-cut, definite positions on most of the questions asked. In contrast, the Democrats exhibit very little unity on economic, defense, or foreign policy issues. The only area that reveals some issue consensus on the part of Democrats is that of social policy.

It is a seeming paradox that the Democratic party, transformed into a majority party nearly forty years ago by the economic crisis of the 1930s, now seems to lack any sense of agreement on economic policy. In contrast, the Republicans (at least in the summer of 1980) exuded a great deal of confidence in their prescriptions for economic policy.

Our study of issue positions is reported in tables 6.9 and 6.10. We employed a measure on policy position agreement that is used in Kirkpatrick (Kirkpatrick 1976, chapter 9). We have examined eleven issues: five in the area of economic policy, three social issues and three foreign and defense questions. Each score reported in the tables is the result of subtracting delegates who were strongly in favor of an issue position from those who were strongly opposed. A positive score should be interpreted as indicative of a conservative ideological position. A negative score should be understood as favoring a liberal position. An example is the proposed constitutional amendment to prohibit abortions except when the mother's life is endangered. A conservative position is interpreted to mean the delegate favors the amendment. If a + 100 score is calculated for Republican delegates on this issue, then all Republicans

Table 6.10. Ideological Positions of Republican group members

	Women's rights	Ecologist	Anti-abortionist	Labor	Business	All delegates
Economic issues						
Non-defense budget cuts	+28.8	+34.5	+47.9	+26.0	+43.7	+38.1
Wage and price controls	+28.0	+37.2	+44.7	+32.7	+49.3	+40.3
Reduce inflation even if it increases unemployment	+13.8	+18.2	+19.5	+12.1	+23.3	+21.0
Deregulate oil	+25.6	+35.3	+40.2	+24.2	+45.1	+37.5
More rapid development of nuclear power	+16.5	+23.8	+37.3	+29.8	+40.2	+32.9
Social issues						
Equal Rights Amendment	−24.6	+19.3	+79.8	+32.2	+36.6	+38.5
Anti-Abortion Amendment	−20.5	+9.6	+77.2	+6.8	−3.6	+18.2
Affirmative action	+2.3	+23.2	+29.7	+28.5	+26.9	+24.5
Foreign and defense issues						
Reinstituting the draft	+16.0	+24.3	+22.7	+30.9	+32.0	+28.5
Ratification of Salt II	+38.5	+46.5	+68.2	+60.6	+45.6	+54.9
Increased U.S. military presence in the Middle East	+14.8	+17.3	+20.1	+24.5	+25.7	+22.1

Note: Each entry is the percent strongly agreeing minus the percent strongly disagreeing with the issue.

strongly favor such a constitutional amendment. A weakness in this scoring device is that a very low score could reflect either a deeply divided party or a party with only a limited interest in the issue at hand.

Before examining the scores on issues by delegates active in interest groups, we will examine the respective issue stances of Republicans and Democrats in general in order to establish a comparative context for the analysis of the social and economic groups. First, for Democrats, it is apparent in Table 6.10 that none of the economic issues elicits consensus.

No clear-cut Democratic position emerges on such issues as the desirability of nondefense budget cuts, deregulation of oil, or wage and price controls. The lack of Democratic party unity on these issues may reflect the set of states available in the survey. But such disharmony is clearly not to be found among the Republicans drawn from the same states.

On economic issues, the Republicans hold very strong views. In Table 6.10 there are remarkably high levels of support to deregulate oil, cut the budget, oppose wage and price controls, and fight inflation even at the expense of increased unemployment. Many of these proposals have, of course, been realized by the Reagan administration. On social issues, Republicans exhibit somewhat less unity, particularly if opposition to the Equal Rights Amendment is set aside. Some divisions do exist among the Republican delegates on abortion and affirmative action, but these divisions are not large.

It is only on social issues that the Democrats reveal much party unity. The new social issues that made their way into the Democratic party in the 1960s and the 1970s have clearly won for themselves a base of support extending beyond the delegates who are politically active in the new single issue groups. There is widespread support for the Equal Rights Amendment among Democrats. Indeed, it is the issue beyond all others that generates a party consensus. On two other highly divisive issues, we find the Democrats exhibiting more agreement in support of affirmative action and in opposition to a constitutional amendment outlawing abortion than on all economic and foreign policy issues.

Foreign policy and defense issues fail to generate much unity or commitment among Democrats. There is little support among Democrats for ratification of SALT II even though the Carter administration had invested considerable time and political capital in the treaty. The issues of reinstituting the draft and increasing U.S. military presence in the Middle

East do not elicit much commitment from Democratic delegates. In contrast, it is in opposition to the SALT II ratification that the highest issue agreement is reached among Republican delegates.

The Republican party consistently reveals consensus on the topical issues of the day. Such consensus may easily flow not only from the greater ideological unity of the Republican delegates, but from the underlying demographic homogeneity found in the Republican party. The Democrats are a far more diverse party, but as we have seen, it does not appear to be the social issues that are promoting divisions within the Democratic ranks.

To test our third hypothesis further, we have examined in more detail the policy attitudes of three single issue groups operating within each party—the anti-abortionists, advocates of women's rights, and environmentalists.[3] Our concern is to examine, first, how much the respective groups have in common that transcends party lines and, second, the extent to which delegates who are members of such groups indeed possess but a single interest. That is, do these delegates hold a general set of issue positions that places them within a well-defined segment of their respective political party or are these delegates in the party to realize their group's goals alone?

In the case of the anti-abortionists and women's rights groups, our survey included specific questions that capture the presumed central concerns of the group. These questions concerned the possible passage of the Equal Rights Amendment and an anti-abortion amendment to the Constitution. The question of more rapid development of nuclear power is not perhaps as central to environmentalists as the two issues described above. Nonetheless, it is an issue of deep concern to many environmentalist organizations in the nation and clearly distinguishes the Democratic activists with ecological concerns from other Democrats at the conventions.

What observations can be made concerning single issue group politics and political party delegates on the basis of Tables 6.9 and 6.10? For certain issues central to the groups concerned, feminists and anti-abortionists are clearly linked regardless of party. But this linkage in the case of women's rights group activists is one of direction rather than one of intensity. The score for Democratic feminists on support for the Equal Rights Amendment is −87.0; for Republican feminists it is −24.6. The scores for their respective parties are: Democrats, −40; Republicans,

+38. Republican feminists are certainly outside their party on this issue and are closer to Democratic delegates, but they are still quite distant from Democratic women's rights group activists. On the broader range of issues, it is apparent that Republican feminists are on the left of their party, particularly on social policy issues, but their liberalism does not place them in the same ideological camp as women's rights group activists in the Democratic party. What the two groups of activists share is that they are on the left of their respective parties, but the distance between the two groups is far greater than the distance between each group and their fellow party delegates.

Similarly, there is little congruity between Republican and Democratic environmentalists. This incongruity is quite apparent in attitudes toward the development of nuclear power. The support score for more rapid development of nuclear power is +23.8 for the Republican activists in environmentalist organizations. In contrast, the opposition among Democratic environmentalists is high for a score of −46.0. Thus Democratic environmentalists are firmly on the left and are remarkably similar in their issue positions to the supporters of women's rights. Both feminists and environmentalists reveal a great deal of unity on social issues, particularly on the issue of nuclear power. Both groups are far more likely to oppose domestic budget cuts than are Democrats in general. The two groups are much more supportive of SALT II and far more in opposition to the draft than Democrats in general. The congruence in attitudes among members of these groups is not surprising in light of their overlapping memberships, as 49 percent of Democrats claiming to be active in ecology groups are also active in women's rights groups (see Table 6.3).

Republican environmentalists are for the most part very similar in the positions they hold to Republican delegates in general. It is only on the issues of equal rights and abortion that the environmentalists are less supportive of conservative positions. But on economic issues, there is virtually no difference between environmentalist Republican delegates and the rest of the party. Indeed, no particular sets of issue concerns appear to differentiate Republican environmentalists from the mainstream of Republican delegates.

It is with the anti-abortionists, the best known single interest group, that we find sharp differences in issue orientation from others in the party. Anti-abortionists are conservative, particularly on social issues, but also on foreign policy concerns as well. They cluster on the right in both parties. But as for the other sets of social issues groups, there remain substantial partisan differences between the two groups of anti-abortionists. A good illustration is SALT II ratification, where Republican anti-abortionists vigorously oppose Senate consent. Democratic anti-abortionists lack such unity. On economic questions, the Democratic anti-abortionists are very similar to Democrats in general in that no strong pattern of issue positions is observable. Perhaps the most telling difference is on the Equal Rights Amendment: here the Republican anti-abortionists are even more opposed to the ERA than they are in favor of an anti-abortion amendment, albeit only slightly. The same pattern is not duplicated for Democratic anti-abortionists who are too divided to have a unified vigorous stance one way or the other on the issue.

In short, the Democratic anti-abortionists are conservative Democrats. They are very distant from the ideological orientation held by Democratic environmentalists and women's rights advocates, but they are removed from the Republican party as well. If pressed they might find the Republicans more sympathetic on social issues and some defense issues, but still great gaps would remain that would ideologically separate them on many issues from their fellow anti-abortionists in the Republican party.

We have also examined the issue positions of two economic groups, business and labor, in the two parties. (See Tables 6.9 and 6.10.) There are some clear parallels with the pattern we found for the social issue groups. Both Republican and Democratic delegates who were active in business groups were consistently more conservative on economic issues than all the other groups described in this analysis as well as in comparison to the over-all averages of delegates in their respective parties. But it is also clear that Republican business delegates are consistently more conservative on economic issues than are Democratic delegates. The differences between the two sets of business group delegates are far greater than the differences between labor and business delegates within each of the two parties.

What is apparent in comparing labor and business group delegates within the Republican conventions is the remarkable unity on social issues. The only social question that generates any difference between the two Republican groups is the anti-abortion amendment where Republican business group activists express slight opposition. There are clear-cut differences between labor and business delegates on economic issues, with Republican business activists more conservative, but the differences are ones of magnitude.

Differences between labor and business activists in the Democratic Party are confined to economic issue areas. An illustration is that there is more support among Democratic business activists than labor activists for an anti-inflation policy that could cost jobs. On social issues a remarkable similarity between labor and business activists exists on the ERA and opposition to the anti-abortion amendment. There is some difference on support for affirmative action programs with labor activists being much more supportive. On foreign policy questions, Democratic labor activists and especially business activists are somewhat more conservative than Democratic delegates in general.

On the basis of our investigation, it is reasonable to conclude that in spite of the activities of interest groups, the political parties are still decidedly identifiable bodies possessing a high degree of loyalty and varying degrees of ideological unity.

The Democrats are the more deeply divided party. There are divisions between liberals and moderates and little unity is manifested on a range of topical issues. Party support is lower than that found in the Republican party. Democrats, confronted with a large number of diverse and active interest groups, may simply be much less of a definable political entity than Republicans. Where there is some semblance of commitment and consensus in the Democratic party, however, it is in the area of social issues. Here, deeply controversial issue positions have achieved a level of delegate support not reflected in either economic or foreign policy issues. In reference to the Democratic party the first hypothesis is partially confirmed, as support for the party is stronger among the older established economic groups. These economic groups are also more in the mainstream of the party ideologically—more so than most of the single issue groups who occupy a liberal position in the party.

In the Republican party the need to modify the hypothesis is more evident. The position a group enjoys in the party clearly influences the group's level of party support. Many of the newer social groups, as well as labor, have not enjoyed much support among Republicans. In turn, such groups are the least supportive of the party. In addition to sheer numbers, it is likely that multiple group memberships enhance the group's opportunity to have its issue position disseminated throughout the party. The greater the number of delegates who are members of business groups, the greater the ease of generating probusiness sympathies. The greater the extent of plural membership, the greater the likelihood of mutual appreciation of issue concerns and of coalitions built on such common concerns.

It is the anti-abortionist movement that presents the most obvious test for hypotheses concerning the extent of party loyalty found in a single issue group. Like nearly all other groups, the group has had a differential impact on the two parties. It has much less representation among Democratic delegates than the other social issue groups. It is a movement that is ideologically on the right of the Democratic party, but still anti-abortionist delegates have more in common with other Democrats than they do with Republican anti-abortionists. The Republican anti-abortionist movement among Republican delegates is relatively large and ideologically consistently to the right of any other group in the party. Like the other social issue groups in the Republican party, it is less willing to support the party than are delegates in general. The anti-abortionist movement is very much still in the process of establishing itself and, if the examples of social issues in the Democratic party give us guidance, we would predict that the anti-abortionists would gain in influence in the Republican party and diminish in strength among the Democrats. Social issues seem to follow a zero-sum course of partisan distribution not unlike the issue itself. If one party supports the issue, then the other party ultimately will not. In contrast, economic groups with the exception of labor have a good deal more flexibility in surviving in and accommodating to both parties. The challenge to parties is not the rise of single issue groups, but sorting out the process by which issue groups find their respective ideological homes.

NOTES

1. Discussion of single issue groups is not new to American politics. The abolitionists and the suffragettes are examples of powerful nineteenth-century movements. In the current debate more attention has focused on the effective communication strategies of the New Right social issues groups.

2. A subjective measure of party support (question 5 in the appendix) has been selected rather than objective measures such as attendance at party functions or activities undertaken in behalf of party candidates. The subjective approach is justified on the basis that the delegates surveyed form an elite within the party and are capable of making such judgments.

3. These groups were chosen because they have arisen in the past ten to fifteen years.

REFERENCES

Burnham, Walter D. and William Chambers. 1975. *The American Party Systems*. New York: Oxford.

Commager, Henry S. 1980. "Single Interest Politics: The Mugging of American Democracy." *Current* 228: 3-5.

Crotty, William and Gary Jacobson. 1980. *American Parties in Decline*. Boston: Little, Brown.

Francis, John and P. Warr. 1980. "Courts and Parties: Some Problems in Institutional Discipline." Paper presented at Western Political Science Organization Meeting.

Keller, Bill. 1980. "Lobbying for Christ: Evangelical Conservatives Move from Pews to Polls, But Can They Sway Congress." *Congressional Quarterly* 38: 2627-2634.

Kirkpatrick, Jeane. 1976. *The New Presidential Elite*. New York: Russell Sage Foundation.

Polsby, Nelson. 1981. "Coalitions and Faction in American Politics: An Institutional View." In *Party Coalitions in the 1980's,* edited by Seymour M. Lipset. San Francisco: Institute for Contemporary Studies.

Moe, Terry. 1980. *The Organization of Interests*. Chicago: University of Chicago Press.

______. 1981. "Toward a Broader View of Interest Groups." *Journal of Politics* 43: 531-543.

Ranney, Austin. 1975. *Curing the Mischiefs of Faction: Party Reform in America*. Berkeley: University of California Press.

______. 1978. "The Political Parties: Reform and Decline." In *The New American Political System,* edited by Anthony King. Washington, D.C.: American Enterprise Institute.

Roback, Thomas. 1980. "Motivation for Activism Among Republican National Convention Delegates: Continuity and Changes, 1972-1976. *Journal of Politics* 42: 181-201.

Samuelson, Robert. 1979. "Fragmentation and Uncertainty Litter the Political Landscape: The Rise of Single-Interest Groups and the Decline of Political Parties." *National Journal* 11: 1726-1736.

Sundquist, James. 1972. *Dynamics of the Party System*. Washington, D.C.: Brookings Institution.

Verba, Sidney and Norman Nie. 1971. *Participation in America*. New York: Harper and Row.

Vinovskis, Maris. 1979. "Politics of Abortion in the House of Representatives in 1976." *Michigan Law Review* 77: 1790-1827.

Weintraub, Bernard. 1980. "Million Dollar Drive Aims to Oust 5 Liberal Senators." *New York Times* March 24, p. B6.

Wilson, James Q. 1973. *Political Organizations*. New York: Basic Books.

7

Migration and Activist Politics

LAURENCE W. MORELAND,
ROBERT P. STEED, TOD A. BAKER

That population movements have important implications for the political life of the nation has long been recognized by students of American politics. Early work by Arthur Holcombe (1933) demonstrated that the historic regional politics of the nineteenth century was giving way to urban-rural conflicts. And later works by Lou Harris (1954), Samuel Lubell (1952; 1956), Campbell, Converse, Miller, and Stokes (1960), Richard Scammon and Ben Wattenberg (1970), and Kevin Phillips (1969) have argued that population shifts in combination with social and economic changes have resulted in profound modifications of the American party system.

In their landmark study, Campbell et al. (1960, 232-233) identified three kinds of political effects as potential consequences of population movement. First, there is the impact on the political composition of the areas from which movers leave and into which they move. Second, there is the impact on the mover of the move itself, which may in turn reflect other factors promoting political change (such as a dramatically improved financial condition). And, third, there is the impact on the mover of the new environment into which he moves. In 1960 when Campbell and associates were writing, they identified one out of every seven persons as residing in a region other than the one in which he grew up, and an even larger proportion was found to have changed their places of residence in terms of a move from an urban area to a suburban one or from a rural area to an urban one. In the intervening twenty years, more recent census data continue to demonstrate the high mobility of the United States population (Bureau of the Census 1983, Table 1).

This chapter seeks to examine one aspect of the first potential consequence of population movement, the impact on the political environment of the area into which the migrant moves. A number of studies have sought to assess the impact of in-migration on the aggregate political environment, that is, on mass voting behavior. For example, it has been shown that a substantial part of Republican voting in the South has been due to the migration into the traditional Democratic South of persons who strongly identified with the Republican party (Campbell 1977; Lyons and Durant 1980; Nie, Verba, and Petrocik 1976). Much less studied, however, has been the impact of population movement on political elites, that is, the extent to which political elites may be composed of relatively recent arrivals and the extent to which those recent arrivals may be different from longer-term residents.[1]

In this chapter we seek to examine at least some of the ways in which recent migrants may have affected local political environments. The focus of the chapter is on state party elites—those party activists who so often play an important role in choosing party candidates, who take issue positions through the adoption of platforms or resolutions, who perform much of the work of the party, and who in general help to shape the image each party presents to the electorate. As Samuel Eldersveld (1964, 180-181) has written about party activists, "The party, in one sense, is what it believes—its attitudes and perspectives, at all echelons. And what the party leaders believe may certainly determine in large part the image it communicates to the public, and the success with which it mobilizes public support."

As a beginning toward understanding the impact of population movements on state party elites, we will compare relatively recent residents (that is, migrants or movers) with longer-term residents and natives. The analysis will focus on the impact of migration on four areas: general demographic background, selected aspects of past political activity, ideological and issue positions, and attitudes toward 1980 presidential candidates. Democratic and Republican delegates will be analyzed separately.

With regard to length of residence, the respondents have been divided into three groups. The first group consists of the migrants or movers who are relatively recent residents of the states in which they are currently politically active; these are persons who have resided in their states of current residence ten years or less. They have been designated as short-term residents (STRs). A second group has been designated as medium-term residents (MTRs); these are persons who have lived in the state of

Table 7.1. Length of residence: party activists and general population (percent)

	Democrats[a]			Republicans[a]			General population[b]
State	STR	MTR	LTR	STR	MTR	LTR	Recent in-migrants
Arizona	31.6	23.0	45.4	31.1	25.9	43.0	24.4
Colorado	24.1	19.0	56.9	21.6	24.1	34.3	21.0
Iowa	12.2	12.1	75.8	11.3	9.3	79.4	8.0
Maine	25.5	13.9	60.6	14.4	13.5	72.1	10.9
Missouri	6.1	8.9	85.0	10.4	12.2	77.4	9.5
No. Dakota	8.7	10.3	81.1	5.3	8.5	86.2	12.8
Oklahoma	9.8	11.8	78.4	17.7	16.5	65.8	13.9
So. Carolina	13.0	13.2	73.8	22.7	21.4	55.9	11.6
Texas	12.9	11.8	75.3	14.0	17.9	68.1	11.3
Utah	19.8	13.4	66.8	20.4	13.3	66.4	16.3
Virginia	15.3	18.4	66.2	22.1	21.5	56.5	14.2

[a]Data for these columns, and all following tables, were derived from the eleven-state survey of party activists. For Tables 7.1-7.7 and 7.9 the following key is used:
STR = short-term residents (resident in state for 10 years or less)
MTR = medium-term residents (residents in state for 10-20 years)
LTR = long-term residents (resident in state for more than 20 years)

[b]The figure in this column represents the percentage of the population in each state resident in 1980 but not resident in 1975. The Bureau of the Census does not collect ten-year statistics. Source: Bureau of the Census, *1980 Census of Population, Vol. I: Characteristics of the Population* (Washington, D.C.: Department of Commerce, 1983).

their current residence from ten to twenty years. The third group consists of natives and long-term residents (LTRs); these are persons who have resided in the state of their current political activity for twenty years or more. In the data which follow, 17.3 percent of the total number of respondents were STRs (of these, 47.0 percent were Democrats and 53.0 percent were Republicans), and 66.9 percent of the respondents were LTRs (of these, 51.2 percent were Democrats and 48.8 percent were Republicans).

Table 7.1 shows the percentages of political activists falling in each of the three length-of-residence categories on a state-by-state basis as well as the percentage of the general population who are recent migrants. Arizona, perhaps the most notable state reflecting sunbelt growth, had the highest percentages of relatively recent residents for both Democratic

(31.6 percent) and Republican (31.1 percent) activists. The states with the smallest percentages of STRs among their political activists were Missouri for the Democrats (6.1 percent) and North Dakota (5.3 percent) for the Republicans.

DEMOGRAPHIC AND POLITICAL BACKGROUNDS

Campbell et al. (1960, 233) found that interregional movers had higher educations and incomes than the natives of the areas they left. That result described, not political activists, but the general mass of citizenry who chose to move their places of residence. The data from the eleven-state survey of state political activists reveals similar findings, when migrants are compared with other political activists of the states to which they have moved.

For the Democrats, 69.5 percent of the STRs were college graduates compared with 57.4 percent of the MTRs and 45.6 percent of the LTRs. Similarly, among the Republicans, 62.0 percent of the STRs were college graduates as compared with 55.3 percent of the MTRs and 51.8 percent of the LTRs.

Despite their better educations, however, the STR political activists earned no better incomes than their less well educated associates who were longer-term residents (table 7.2). Indeed, for both parties medium-term residents and long-term residents were both slightly more concentrated at the higher income levels than the short-term residents. We may speculate that these shorter-term residents were more likely to be concentrated in high-education/medium-income occupations (such as elementary and secondary school teaching).

In addition, table 7.2 indicates that those political activists who were relatively recent migrants (STRs) were considerably younger than longer-term residents (both MTRs and LTRs) among both Democrats and Republicans alike. Over half (54.3 percent) of the Democratic STRs were between eighteen and thirty-four years of age (as compared with 29.6 percent of the LTRs) and about two-fifths (39.6 percent) of the Republican STRs were between eighteen and thirty-four (as compared with 21.5 percent of the Republican LTRs). For both parties medium-term residents tended to be older than short-term residents but younger than long-term residents.

There were fewer differences with regard to the sex of the political

Table 7.2. Characteristics of party activists

	Democrats %			Republicans %		
	STR	MTR	LTR	STR	MTR	LTR
Age group						
18-34	54.3	41.4	29.6	39.6	28.3	21.5
35-54	37.2	49.4	42.7	41.9	51.4	45.8
55+	8.5	9.2	27.8	18.5	20.2	32.7
	100.0%	100.0%	100.1%	100.0%	99.9%	100.0%
N	(1385)	(1239)	(5816)	(1443)	(1443)	(5536)
Sex						
Female	50.0	52.0	49.3	38.5	41.3	39.8
Male	50.0	48.0	50.7	61.5	58.7	60.2
	100.0%	100.0%	100.0%	100.0%	100.0%	100.0%
N	(1381)	(1238)	(5835)	(1560)	(1454)	(5555)
Race						
White	91.9	91.7	88.3	98.0	98.1	98.2
Black	4.4	5.6	8.5	0.8	0.6	0.8
Hispanic	2.5	1.7	2.0	0.5	0.6	0.2
Other	1.2	1.0	1.2	0.8	0.7	0.7
	100.0%	100.0%	100.0%	100.1%	100.0%	99.9%
N	(1365)	(1223)	(5745)	(1551)	(1438)	(5516)
Educational level						
Some high school or less	1.6	2.0	5.6	1.0	2.4	3.3
High school graduate	5.7	12.2	17.6	6.5	10.7	12.6
Some college	23.3	28.3	28.1	30.5	31.5	32.3
College graduate	24.5	18.4	19.1	27.7	24.3	26.0
Post-college	45.0	39.0	29.5	34.3	31.0	25.8
	100.1%	99.9%	99.9%	100.0%	99.9%	100.0%
N	(1370)	(1218)	(5683)	(1519)	(1434)	(5440)
Income level						
$0-14,999	21.0	15.7	20.1	13.3	11.6	13.5
$15,000-24,999	30.3	27.0	31.9	25.7	22.2	25.4
$25,000-34,999	23.4	26.0	23.1	24.8	24.6	24.2
$35,000-44,999	12.8	15.4	12.3	16.1	15.1	14.6
$45,000-59,999	6.5	8.7	6.4	10.6	12.5	9.6
$60,000+	6.0	7.3	6.2	9.5	14.1	12.7
	100.0%	100.1%	100.0%	100.0%	100.1%	100.0%
N	(1347)	(1185)	(5507)	(1486)	(1357)	(5144)

Table 7.3. Party activists as delegates to state or national conventions

Past experience as a delegate	Democrats %			Republicans %		
	STR	MTR	LTR	STR	MTR	LTR
Yes	31.3	40.3	51.8	35.7	50.2	56.2
No	68.7	59.7	48.2	64.3	49.8	43.8
	100.0%	100.0%	100.0%	100.0%	100.0%	100.0%
N	(1189)	(1159)	(5542)	(1520)	(1430)	(5472)

activists. Among the Democrats, about half of all activists were female, regardless of length of residence; of the Republicans, about 40 percent were female, regardless of length of residence.

With regard to race, Republican STRs were overwhelmingly white (98.0 percent), as were longer-term residents (98.1 percent for MTRs and 98.2 percent for LTRs). For the Democrats, short-term residents tended to be slightly more white and less black than longer-term residents.

In short, then, although the subgroups were similar with regard to sex, race, and income, there were some systematic background differences among them with regard to age and education.

It is to be expected, although by no means certain, that those who have only comparatively recently moved into a state would have less extensive histories of party activism than longer-term residents. Research has suggested that those who have recently moved into a community are less likely to be integrated into community life than longer-term residents (Milbrath and Goel 1977, 113). A sampling of the data at least partially confirms this expectation. For example, only about a third of the STRs for both Democrats and Republicans alike had previously served as delegates to state or national party conventions, as compared (for both parties) with more than half of the LTRs who had such experience (Table 7.3).

Similarly, these shorter-term residents had been somewhat less active generally in political campaigns (Table 7.4). Fewer than one-half of the STRs of either party had been active in all or most political campaigns. These differing levels of political activity may be related to the age differentials among the three subgroups since (as noted above) the short-term residents tended to be significantly younger than longer-term residents. However, when we do control for age, correlations are not affected

Table 7.4. Campaign activity of party activists

	Democrats %			Republicans %		
Active in—	STR	MTR	LTR	STR	MTR	LTR
All campaigns	21.0	29.9	31.8	25.2	32.1	31.5
Most campaigns	22.3	24.0	28.0	22.2	24.9	27.5
A few campaigns	36.0	29.9	27.7	30.5	28.8	27.9
None	20.7	16.1	12.5	22.2	14.2	13.0
	100.0%	99.9%	100.0%	100.1%	100.0%	99.9%
N	(1411)	(1256)	(5906)	(1570)	(1460)	(5610)

Table 7.5. Organizational activity of party activists

	Democrats %			Republicans %		
Politically active in—	STR	MTR	LTR	STR	MTR	LTR
Labor unions	14.4	13.7	18.5	3.8	3.1	2.5
Educational organizations	25.3	26.5	27.5	15.1	13.9	14.3
Other professional org.	26.5	21.6	20.3	25.0	22.3	23.1
Business organizations	13.8	10.4	15.1	23.8	23.3	27.6
Church groups	22.9	25.8	29.3	40.0	36.6	37.5
Women's rights groups	25.1	21.6	16.6	5.8	4.4	4.1
Civil rights groups	25.9	21.9	17.7	2.6	2.4	2.2
Ecology groups	22.3	17.0	12.7	7.2	7.4	7.6
Public interest groups	25.4	23.6	22.6	15.0	17.8	17.6
Anti-abortion groups	4.4	5.9	6.0	13.9	11.9	10.2
Farm organizations	6.7	6.1	15.1	5.9	7.1	15.3
Other issue groups	19.8	21.5	16.4	18.6	18.7	16.3
Column averages	19.4	18.0	18.2	14.7	14.1	14.9

for either party (Pearson product moment correlations decline only from .43 to .37 for Democrats and from .38 to .33 for Republicans).

With regard to having switched parties, the data show that Democratic short-term residents were more likely than longer-term residents to have changed their party affiliation or identification. Almost a third (31.4 percent) of the Democratic STRs had switched parties, as compared with somewhat smaller proportions of longer-term residents (26.7 percent for MTRs and 20.6 percent for LTRs). For the Republicans, however, short-term residents were no more likely to have switched parties than longer-term residents (the range was only from 27.6 percent of MTRs to 28.8 percent of LTRs).

With regard to organizational membership, short-term residents were as politically active as longer-term residents (table 7.5).

In some new issue groups (ecology groups, civil rights groups, and women's rights groups), Democratic STRs were more active than longer-term activists. Longer-term Democratic activists are more active in church and farm groups. Republican STRs were slightly more active than longer-term activists in anti-abortion groups, but trailed their longer-term colleagues in farm and business groups. The column averages in table 7.5 indicate that, in general, there are few differences between long and short term residents in either party in level of interest group activity. On the other hand, for all residence groups there is a modest difference between the two parties, with Democrats showing higher levels of organizational activity.

Thus, while the STRs may bring more education and youth to each of the parties, they have been less active in their parties; however, in terms of interest groups, the STRs were just as likely as MTRs and LTRs to be politically active.

IDEOLOGY AND ISSUES

While the involvement of STRs affects the make-up of the parties with regard to personal and political backgrounds, factors which may be important in the skill and vigor of party activity, an equally critical question concerns the philosophical and attitudinal component of their party activity. Some of the most interesting perspectives with regard to political activists who are short-term residents and those activists who are longer-term residents appear in the areas of political philosophy and issues of the 1980 campaign. Table 7.6 indicates that among Republicans there was little difference on political philosophy regardless of length of residence in the state. Both short-term residents and longer-term residents were concentrated on the conservative end of the political spectrum with 86.9 percent of the STRs, 89.1 percent of the MTRs, and 87.1 percent of the LTRs all describing themselves as conservative in some degree. This consistency is yet another reflection of the ideological homogeneity that tends to characterize the Republican party.

Table 7.6. Political philosophy of party activists

	Democrats %			Republicans %		
Philosophy	STR	MTR	LTR	STR	MTR	LTR
Very liberal	28.7	22.6	15.5	0.8	0.6	0.7
Somewhat liberal	44.3	44.0	38.8	2.8	2.7	3.0
Middle-of-the-road	16.6	19.0	23.8	9.6	7.6	9.2
Somewhat conservative	8.9	13.4	18.6	44.4	47.5	45.5
Very conservative	1.4	1.0	3.3	42.5	41.6	41.6
	99.9%	100.0%	100.0%	100.1%	100.0%	100.0%
N	(1365)	(1214)	(5706)	(1557)	(1446)	(5547)

The data on the thirteen specific issue questions were highly consistent with the activists' own self-placement on the political spectrum. The differences between short-term Republican residents and longer-term Republican residents were at most 1 or 2 percent.

Among Democrats, however, there were decided differences among the activists both in terms of self-placement on the ideological continuum and in responses to specific issues. A substantially larger proportion of the short-term residents as contrasted with longer-term residents considered themselves to be liberal in some degree. Almost three-fourths of the Democratic STRs described themselves as liberal (73.0 percent), while 66.6 percent of the MTRs and only 54.3 percent of the LTRs did so. For the eleven states in this study, the liberal (majority) wing of the Democratic party has been disproportionately represented by relatively new resident activists. (These differences were reflected as well on the specific issues. See Table 7.7.) The average difference between STR and LTRs is 11.1 percent, with newer residents being at least slightly more liberal on all issues. Differences are particularly great on "new politics" issues (average difference of 14.4 percent), but less on economic issues (average difference of 5.9 percent). For Republicans, on the other hand, there were no clear or consistent differences between more and less recent immigrants.

These differences among Democratic activists between short-term residents and longer-term residents help to explain some of the greater heterogeneity of the Democratic party as compared with the Republican party. For the Democrats, then, but not for the Republicans, the short-term residents brought to their political activism more strongly liberal lean-

Table 7.7. Support index on issues

Issue	Democrats %			Republicans %		
	STR	MTR	LTR	STR	MTR	LTR
New issues						
ERA	84.0	81.3	71.3	23.2	22.7	23.3
Anti-abortion amendment	21.0	28.0	37.6	52.2	50.3	53.4
Nuclear power	30.0	38.8	48.0	83.8	81.8	82.7
Affirmative action	76.4	74.7	65.8	25.9	26.5	27.4
Economic issues						
National health insurance	71.0	68.0	63.2	8.5	8.2	8.4
Deregulation oil/gas	46.5	47.4	48.0	82.9	83.7	80.8
Spending cuts to balance budget	34.1	38.2	46.4	80.7	82.3	80.9
Anti-inflation measures	39.7	41.9	46.6	70.8	73.3	73.0
Wage-price controls	52.9	54.8	53.9	18.9	21.0	23.9
Defense issues						
Increased spending	32.5	40.1	52.6	92.0	93.6	92.2
Salt II	69.6	67.1	64.3	13.5	12.9	15.3
Draft registration	48.2	53.9	66.5	78.0	78.5	77.8
U.S. Military in Middle East	44.2	50.7	58.0	78.5	78.3	75.3
Minimum *N*s	1148	1100	5136	1507	1403	5444
Maximum *N*s	1410	1250	5777	1568	1462	5560

Note: The index combines the "strongly favor" and "mildly favor" categories, and adds to that percentage half of the "not sure" category.

ings, and thus were in a position to affect in a measurable way the ideological stance of the party.

As noted above in the passage on demographic backgrounds, the Democratic STRs did not substantially differ from their longer-term party counterparts except with regard to age and education. Thus it may well be that the relative youth of the Democratic STRs together with their better educations accounted for their greater liberality rather than their relatively recent residence in the states of their political activity. To refine the data further, in order to consider this possibility, partial correlations were utilized to control for age and education among the Democratic activists (controls were not utilized for the Republican activists inasmuch as the homogeneity of the Republican data leaves almost no differences requiring further explanation). As Table 7.8 shows, controls for both education

Table 7.8. Partial correlations of residence length with ideological positions

Questionnaire item	Zero-order correlations	First-order partials controlling for age	First-order partials controlling for education	Second-order partials controlling for age and ed.
Ideology	.17*	.14	.15	.12
ERA	.13	.11	.11	.09
Anti-abortion	−.14	−.12	−.11	−.09
Nuclear power	−.16	−.11	−.15	−.10
Affirmative action	.11	.09	.09	.09
Health insurance	.09	.07	.07	.08
Deregulation oil/gas	−.03	−.01	−.02	−.02
Spending cuts	−.13	−.09	−.10	−.08
Anti-inflation	−.08	−.03	−.06	−.04
Wage-price controls	.00	.01	.01	.03
Defense spending	−.18	−.14	−.16	−.12
Salt II	.07	.07	.05	.05
Draft registration	−.15	−.12	−.14	−.10
Military in Middle East	−.11	−.10	−.11	−.09

Note: Correlations are reported for the Democratic delegates only; see the text for explanation. For complete wording of questionnaire items see the appendix.

and age only reduce the correlation between length of residence and ideology from .17 to .12. For the thirteen issues, controlling for age and for education eliminates some differences among the three groups with regard to ideology and issue position, but it certainly does not eliminate differences. (Partials run on a state-by-state basis indicated no significant variations from this pattern.) Thus the data suggest that, while the Democratic STRs brought a liberalizing element to the Democratic party, that impact may be both a direct and an indirect result of their migration status. In other words, recent movers (STRs) tended to be younger and better educated, characteristics which seemingly help to account for their greater political liberality.

ATTITUDES TOWARD CANDIDATES

The choice of delegates to the party's national presidential nominating convention is one of the most important tasks of a state party convention

Table 7.9. Evaluation of candidates by length of residence.

	Democrats			Republicans		
Candidate	STR	MTR	LTR	STR	MTR	LTR
Carter	2.86	2.52	2.21	4.67	4.70	4.72
Kennedy	2.78	2.98	3.12	4.88	4.87	4.92
Brown	3.48	3.63	3.82	4.64	4.63	4.68
Reagan	4.61	4.59	4.52	1.47	1.40	1.41
Bush	3.70	3.67	3.83	2.43	2.42	2.28
Anderson	2.73	2.90	3.27	3.87	3.98	3.89
Minimum *N*	1286	1117	4709	1328	1235	4649
Maximum *N*	1398	1246	5793	1565	1460	5562

Note: Mean evaluation of candidate on a scale running from 1 (very favorable) to 5 (very unfavorable).

in caucus-convention states. These choices reflect the delegates' attitudes toward the various presidential candidates (see Table 7.9). The attitudes of the party activists in the eleven states under study here reflected very closely their ideological self-placement on the political spectrum.

Republicans, regardless of the length of their residence in a given state, were remarkably homogeneous in their attitudes toward presidential candidates. The Republican delegates were uniformly unfavorable toward Democratic candidates, but showed consistently favorable mean evaluations of Ronald Reagan (1.47 for STRs, 1.40 for MTRs, and 1.41 for LTRs); they were much cooler toward George Bush (ratings of 2.43 for STRs, 2.42 for MTRs, 2.28 for LTRs), and cooler still toward John Anderson (3.87 of STRs, 3.98 of MTRs, and 3.89 of LTRs). Consistent with their conservatism, and regardless of length of residence, Republicans overwhelmingly preferred the most conservative candidate.

Democrats, however, were much more diverse in their preferences, and, in addition, there were clear differences between short-term residents and longer-term residents. While Democrats were rather uniformly unfavorable toward Reagan and Bush, STR Democratic activists were somewhat more favorable toward those candidates generally regarded as liberal, such as Ted Kennedy (who had favorability ratings of 2.78, 2.98, and 3.12 by STRs, MTRs, and LTRs, respectively), and Jerry Brown, who, while not strongly favored by any of the subgroups, nevertheless fared better among STRs (3.48 on the scale) than among MTRs (3.63) and LTRs (3.82).

Similarly, John Anderson, the maverick of 1980 presidential politics,

Table 7.10. Partial correlations of residence length with candidate orientations

Candidate	Zero-order correlations	First-order partials controlling for age	First-order partials controlling for education	Second-order partials controlling for age and ed.
Carter	−.17	−.13	−.16	−.12
Kennedy	.09	.05	.07	.05
Brown	.11	.07	.10	.07
Reagan	−.04	−.04	−.04	−.03
Bush	.05	.04	.02	.03
Anderson	.16	.13	.13	.11

Note: Partial correlations are reported for Democratic delegates only; see the text for an explanation.

was more favorably regarded by STRs (2.73) than by MTRs (2.90) and LTRs (3.27). Anderson's apparent liberalism in the context of the 1980 campaign made him more popular among Democratic STRs than any other subgroup, Democratic or Republican.

Finally, consistent with their greater approval of Kennedy, Democratic STRs were dramatically less supportive of Jimmy Carter than Democratic MTRs or LTRs (2.86 for STRs, 2.52 for MTRs, 2.21 for LTRs). These scale scores reflect sharp percentage differences: the percentage of STRs very favorable toward Carter was little more than half of the percentage of LTRs very favorable toward Carter, and the percentage of STRs very unfavorable toward Carter (22.7 percent) was almost twice the percentage of LTRs very unfavorable (13.0 percent).

As in the case of ideology and issues, the introduction of age and education controls results in reductions in zero-order correlations between length of residence and candidate preference. (See Table 7.10.) Once again, among Democratic STRs the impact of shorter-term residents is at least partly an indirect one; the age and education of these activists who move apparently had much to do with their patterns of candidate support.

The data on attitudes of activists toward presidential candidates rather closely mirror the data on the activists' ideological predispositions. Republicans, regardless of length of residence, were impressively consistent and homogeneous in their attitudes toward the presidential candidates. Democrats, on the other hand, were much more likely to be divided in their preferences, and short-term residents were more favorable toward candidates generally thought of as liberal or moderately liberal.

The mobility of the American electorate in the twentieth century together with other important socioeconomic developments has had a profound and far-reaching impact on the American party system; it has eroded old loyalties without necessarily creating new ones (see, e.g., Ladd with Hadley 1975). The fact of population mobility has not been limited to the mass elecorate but has affected party elites as well, as a substantial portion of party activists are new immigrants to the state party systems in which they have become active.

The research reported in this chapter indicates that, for both parties, party activists who were relatively short-term residents in the states of their party activity tended to be younger and substantially better educated than the longer-term residents they joined. Partly because of their youth, these short-term resident activists brought less political experience to their politics, although their current levels of organizational activity were at least as high as those of longer-term residents.

Perhaps the most interesting finding of this research is that short-term residents who were Democratic activists were likely to bring greater liberalism to their politics than longer-term residents. In that respect, these Democratic movers probably tended to strengthen the liberal wing of the Democratic party in those states to which they chose to move. The introduction of age and education controls does not necessarily diminish the significance of these findings. Such controls do suggest that length of residence, standing alone, is not a complete explanation of greater liberalism among Democratic STRs. But this merely means that the impact of these short-term residents flows in part indirectly from their mover status. In other words, among Democratic STRs, movers tended to be younger and better educated, and these characteristics in turn correlate with greater political liberalism. The fact that these activists moved relatively recently into the states of their political activity did not, in itself, explain their liberal political leanings, but the characteristics that frequently accompanied these moves (relative youth and better educations) do seem to suggest an explanation for the differences in political philosophy and issue position. Thus the relationship between length-of-residence and political attitude exists.[2]

Republican movers, on the other hand, varied little in ideology or in their attitudes toward 1980 campaign issues as compared with longer-term residents, and therefore their presence among party activists had little or no effect on changing the ideological stance of the party. This is not to say these short-term residents had no impact on Republican politics, because they clearly confirmed and strengthened the ideological unity of the party.

Finally, these short-term residents held views of the 1980 presidential candidates in ways consistent with their ideological and issue preferences. Republican movers, in preferring Reagan and disdaining other candidates, differed little from their associates who were longer-term residents. Democratic movers, however, were more favorable toward candidates such as Kennedy, Brown, and Anderson, all generally identified with liberal or moderately liberal politics, but this again was apparently a reflection of their age and education levels.

The data analyzed here suggest that attention to in-migrants helps to clarify patterns of party activity. Population shifts may affect party organizations and images as much as they affect aggregate voting patterns. Further refinements in analyzing the impact of population redistribution among party activists should serve to further an understanding of the dynamics of political activism.

NOTES

1. What work has been done with regard to elites and population has only peripherally considered this relationship. See e.g., Patterson (1963).

2. Unfortunately, the data collected for this study do not provide sufficient basis to determine if the STRs migrated from more liberal party systems to less liberal ones, and therefore that possibility cannot be ruled out.

In an effort to clarify this point, the state of childhood for the STRs was examined to determine if those data would help to resolve the matter. These childhood states were widely scattered with no apparent explanatory pattern.

REFERENCES

Campbell, Angus, Philip Converse, Warren Miller, and Donald Stokes. 1960. *The American Voter.* New York: John Wiley and Sons.

Campbell, Bruce A. 1977. "Patterns of Change in the Partisan Loyalties of Native Southerners: 1952-1972." *Journal of Politics* 39 (August): 730-761.

Eldersveld, Samuel J. 1964. *Political Parties*. Chicago: Rand McNally.
Harris, Louis. 1954. *Is There a Republican Majority?* New York: Harper and Brothers.
Holcombe, Arthur N. 1933. *The New Party Politics*. New York: Norton.
Ladd, Everett C., with Charles D. Hadley. 1975. *Transformations of the American Party System*. New York: Norton.
Lubell, Samuel. 1952. *The Future of American Politics*. New York: Harper and Brothers.
______. 1956. *The Revolt of the Moderates*. New York: Harper and Brothers.
Lyons, William and Robert F. Durant. 1980. "Assessing the Impact of Immigration on a State Political System." *Social Science Quarterly* 61 (December): 473-84.
Milbrath, Lester and M. L. Goel. 1977. *Political Participation*, 2nd ed. Chicago: Rand McNally.
Nie, Norman, Sidney Verba, and John Petrocik. 1976. *The Changing American Voter.* Cambridge: Harvard University Press.
Patterson, Samuel C. 1963. "Characteristics of Party Leaders." *Western Political Quarterly* 16 (June): 332-352.
Phillips, Kevin P. 1969. *The Emerging Republican Majority.* Garden City, New York: Doubleday.
Scammon, Richard and Ben J. Wattenberg. 1970. *The Real Majority.* New York: Coward, McCann, and Geoghegan.

PART FOUR

Issues and Ideology

8

Elite Attitudinal Constraint

RONALD B. RAPOPORT

The issue of attitudinal constraint levels among mass publics has been a major focus of substantive and methodological research in political behavior over the past twenty years (for a sampling see Butler and Stokes 1971; Bishop, Oldendick, and Tuchfarber 1978; Converse 1964; 1975; Field and Anderson 1969; and Nie, Verba, and Petrocik 1978). Articles concerned with the interpretation of averaged correlations among a set of issues as well as the empirical questions of what factors are associated with high or low levels of constraint are commonly found in a wide range of political journals. A corresponding interest in the constraint levels of elites has been much less explored (for a rare example, see Welch and Peters 1981).

This paper will examine determinants of elite constraint in order to address three questions:

What is the effect of education on attitudinal constraint among politically involved individuals?

What are the effects of type and degree of party activity and political motivations on constraint levels?

To what degree do the zero order effects of education and political activity and motivations disappear, once we control for other variables?

The most influential study of elite constraint is probably that of Converse (1964). He compared constraint levels of 1958 Congressional candidates with those of a national sample of eligible voters, and found large differences between the two. Over a set of seven issue responses and party, the average tau-c intercorrelations were .36 for elites, and .15 for the mass sample. More recently Bishop and Frankovic (1981) replicated the 1958 study for 1978 with similar results. They used nine issue questions and party, and found average correlations (gammas) for elites of .62, and for the mass sample of .16. In both cases, however, the investigators took the elite sample as a general comparison group, and therefore did not look at factors increasing or decreasing constraint within it. In fact, Converse viewed the specific type of elite sample used as irrelevant for his purposes. He argued that the contrasts with mass samples were to be expected, "if the elite had been a set of newspaper editors, political writers, or another group that takes an interest in politics" (1964, 229). However, in one of the very few attempts to look at differences within an elite, Welch and Peters (1981) did find subgroup differences in attitudinal constraint among state legislators.

Congressional candidate and state legislative samples are theoretically and substantively a particularly interesting group in that they help explain "the character of the interaction between citizen and government" (Converse 1975, 87). The large gap between mass and elites is instructive in this regard and the stability of findings over a twenty year period is particularly striking. In dealing with the question of what factors may cause increased levels of constraint among masses as well as elites, elites are also potentially a useful group to study. Elite samples provide us with large numbers of highly involved, highly politicized respondents, and allow us to study groups which may be present only at trace levels in mass samples, and to test theoretically interesting and important hypotheses. For example, in a 2000-person national sample the number of respondents having run for even local office is too small to analyze, let alone to divide into subgroups. Use of elite samples can allow us, however, to control for high levels of involvement while examining independent effects of other variables and vice versa. But "elite sample" is an imprecise term. Congressmen differ from mass samples not only in level of involvement, but also in terms of education, occupation, and income, and the presence of all these at once. This means that it may be difficult to separate out which of these differences or groups of differences is responsible for the higher level of constraint among elites.

What is relevant about this data set, for our purposes, is that in all cases the convention played an active role in nominations. This fact increases the likelihood that there would be competition for state delegate slots, and therefore that our respondents would be highly involved in politics.

Using state convention delegates rather than national convention delegates or Congressional candidates provides a sample more varied in length of involvement, types of involvement, age, and education, than we might find for those more elite samples.

Substantively, state convention delegates are important political actors. They are potential campaign activists, and a rather broad based group; they have the ability to influence office holders and their selection. They are, then, in their own right, an important, if academically neglected group, and the ways that they structure issues and the factors influencing the degree of this structuring are important. Finally, subgroup differences in structuring, by activists, may have important implications for the political system.[1]

The thirteen issues were analyzed using factor analysis with a varimax rotation. Only items which loaded at least .40 on a factor were included as part of that factor, and items were included only with the factor on which they loaded highest. The three factors are: Strong America, Traditional Domestic Issues, and New Issues. Strong America issues include: increases in defense spending, institution of draft registration, U.S. military presence in the Middle East, and commitment to nuclear power. Traditional Domestic issues include: affirmative action programs for minorities, national health insurance, wage and price controls, and oil and gas deregulation. New Issues include: ERA, a constitutional amendment to prohibit abortions, and SALT II.[2]

Because we are interested in relative positions on issues, and because support of (or opposition to) the issues involved demand varying levels of liberalism or conservatism, and consequently have differing variances, we will use average gammas as our measure of interattitude constraint. The advantage of gamma over product moment correlation or variance explained is that it is much less affected by variance differences in the variables (Bruner 1976). Missing data are deleted pairwise rather than listwise.

BACKGROUND AND HYPOTHESES

Since Converse's article, interest has focussed on at least two different methodologies of looking at structuring of attitudes: first by using open-ended questions to ascertain the degree to which common ideas, like liberalism-conservatism, relate to a variety of more immediate political concerns (e.g., candidates, issues, and parties); and secondly by using issue intercorrelations to deduce psychological interrelatedness. The first technique is one with which we can be confident that the respondent is aware of how issues do relate to each other. This is true since the respondent is given the opportunity to explicitly state the connection. In the intercorrelation technique no such conscious link can be uncovered. It is rather inferred from empirical relationships.[3]

In looking at political ideology in both of these ways, the search for correlates has focussed on two categories: those relating to general cognitive skills, such as education and cognitive level, and those relating to specifically political experiences, such as campaign involvement and psychological involvement in politics. The reasoning for each set is clear. Without the skills needed to integrate political information, political exposure is futile. But without political information there is no substance on which to bring skill to bear. The crucial questions are: what is the minimum degree of each that is required for high levels of constraint, and to what degree can each set of skills substitute for the other?

Given the large difference in the two approaches used, it is therefore not surprising that the two measures do not show the same relationship with certain independent variables. However, since both techniques were designed to tell us something about the degree to which an individual's attitudes on one issue affect or constrain other issue positions, it would give us more confidence in both measures if such anomalies could be reconciled. Although both measures are correlated with political involvement, the same cannot be said for education. "Levels of conceptualization", has consistently been found to relate strongly to education. This holds for studies done in the U.S. (Klingeman and Wright 1974; Converse 1964) and in Europe (Klingeman 1979; Butler and Stokes 1971). The U.S. data covers almost two decades and holds up well even when political involvement is controlled.[4] This relationship is not surprising. Education presumably increases the abilities to think abstractly and deductively, and these are very important in developing high levels of conceptualization. Neither is it surprising that political involvement plays an important independent role in developing high levels of conceptualization, since one must be motivated in order to use skills which one possesses.

More perplexing are the correlates, and lack of correlates, of attitude intercorrelation among mass samples. Although involvement has consistently been found to be related to constraint (Bowles and Richardson 1969; Converse 1964; Nie, Verba, and Petrocik 1978; Pierce and Hagner 1980), education has not (Bennett, Oldendick, Tuchfarber, and Bishop 1979; Converse 1975; Nie et al. 1978). Nie et al. (1978), comparing those with at least some college with those having less than a high school diploma, found consistent but weak education effects for every presidential year between 1956 and 1972 (the only Congressional election at which they looked, 1958, showed the same results).

However the existence of even a small relationship is challenged by Bennett et al. Using more precise education categories for presidential election years from 1956 to 1976, they found that, "only in 1956 does a linear trend emerge . . . [and] . . . in only 2 years . . . [are] the college educated . . . substantially more consistent than the least educated" (1979, 59). The reason for this "nonfinding" is rather clear. People can develop constraint either by deduction and linking, or by taking over the consistent attitudes of a friend, acquaintance, or political figure (see Campbell et al. 1960, and Converse 1975 on "ideology by proxy").

The first process is enhanced by both education and by political involvement. The role of education is clear, but as Abelson argues (1959, 344), "pressure toward consistency only operates when the issue is salient; that is, when thought about." Political involvement brings with it salience. However, insofar as constraint is caused by taking over the attitudes of a politically more involved person, it is only involvement that comes into play. It is the involved, and not necessarily the educated, respondent who will elicit and pay attention to cues and therefore be able to act on them. The result of these concurrent processes of constraint formation is that, among mass samples, not only is involvement more strongly related to constraint than is education, but education is only weakly related.

This might lead us to attribute differences between mass and elite constraint levels to differences in involvement. However, it is also possible that education is effective in raising constraint only after one has reached a fairly high level of involvement so that the two factors are hierarchically arranged. With a mass sample such hypothesis would be difficult if not impossible to test given the problem of declining cell size. Among elites, however, this should be much less true. While involvement should continue to have a strong impact, the fact that all respondents have a substantially higher proportion of members in the "high involvement category" will restrict the sample variance on involvement, and diminish its effect, while allowing education's effect among the highly involved to be fully explored. That is, since everyone in an elite sample is politically involved, those individuals whom we find in a mass public with high education, but low involvement (who would diminish the effect of educa-

Table 8.1. Constraint in three issue Areas, by education

Education	Strong America issues	Traditional domestic	New issues	All issues
HS graduate or less	.41 (2479)	.34 (2292)	.28 (2448)	.25 (2403)
Some college	.48 (4721)	.45 (4615)	.40 (4687)	.35 (4635)
College graduate	.54 (8734)	.52 (8316)	.50 (8716)	.43 (8584)

Note: In this and succeeding tables, constraint measures are average gamma correlations among pairs of issues in each issue domain; unweighted *N*s are in parentheses.

tion on constraint), will not be present, with the result of an increased effect of education.

The only attempt to measure constraint among elites for different educational groups is that of Welch and Peters (1981). They found a substantial effect of education on social issues (using issues similar to our New Issues), but no difference on economic-welfare issues (roughly equivalent to our Traditional Domestic Issues). However, their analysis is hampered by small Ns (they report data on only eighty-two respondents with fourteen years of education or less), which made controls for involvement or other variables impossible.

EDUCATION AND POLITICAL INVOLVEMENT

Our first cut at the data provides support for our hypotheses.[5] In all three attitude spheres, as Table 8.1 shows, we find differences between respondents with a high school diploma or less, and those with a college degree of between .13 and .22 (i.e., differences between average gammas), and of .18 across all thirteen issues. Given the high level of involvement of all respondents in our sample, our findings seem to establish, at the very least, the effect of education among the most involved sector of the electorate, and it certainly lays to rest any idea that involvement can, by itself, totally substitute for generalized intellectual skills in the development of consistent ideologies.[6]

In looking at elites, the concept of involvement is much less easily operationalized. Clearly anyone attending a local caucus, let alone a state convention, would be considered very high in involvement relative to the electorate. Certainly some important differences do exist among these delegates—in terms of length of previous involvement and in terms of type of previous involvement. In addition, delegates differ as well in terms of motivation for involvement. But how should we expect these to relate to constraint differences?

To the degree that constraint is psychological and sociological, rather than strictly logical, it is at least partly a function of learning which attitudes should go with which attitudes. Will foreign policy hawks also be domestic liberals, or will they be domestic conservatives? There is no logical connection between these issues unless certain premises are accpeted such as: "interventionism in the economy and foreign interventionism are both attempts of government to ameliorate the conditions of the downtrodden." Or "the more money spent on arms the less money spent on domestic programs." The first of these premises may have been more commonly accepted in the early 1960s, and the latter in the 1970s. (See Erikson, Luttbeg, and Tedin 1980, 71, for a similar example based on Vietnam war attitudes.) But neither is true of logical necessity. Premises are learned through interaction with the politics of the time. This explains the relationship between involvement and constraint among mass samples. Once the premises are learned, the ability to derive consistent issue positions from them is dependent on general cognitive skills. Clearly the more one is involved in politics, the greater the opportunity one has to learn. This might lead us to expect that length and extent of participation should be related to level of constraint. But it is also possible that the learning of general political premises requires sufficiently low levels of involvement such as would be possessed by even those of our delegates only briefly involved in politics.

We have three measures of extent of involvement: number of years active, number of campaigns in which one has been involved, and type of campaign activity engaged in. When we examine constraint levels by the number of campaigns involved in, we find only a weak trend in the expected direction for Traditional Domestic Issues and inconsistent results for the other two issue areas (Table 8.2). Since Traditional Domestic Issues are the longest standing of the three issue areas, the finding of greatest effect of involvement is not surprising. However, when we look at the relation between length of involvement and constraint, the results are surprising. Rather than finding modest support for our hypothesis, as we

Table 8.2. Constraint in three issue areas, by experience

	Strong America issues	Traditional domestic	New issues	All issues
Active in campaigns				
All	.49 (4900)	.49 (4707)	.42 (4866)	.37 (4820)
Most	.52 (4270)	.49 (4107)	.46 (4251)	.40 (4204)
Some	.50 (4762)	.45 (4484)	.44 (4755)	.36 (4663)
None	.49 (2423)	.41 (2245)	.45 (2417)	.35 (2360)
Years active				
0-5	.52 (6606)	.47 (6116)	.47 (6487)	.38 (6368)
5-10	.54 (3635)	.48 (3484)	.51 (3623)	.42 (3580)
10-20	.49 (3483)	.49 (3333)	.44 (3467)	.38 (3423)
20+	.43 (2856)	.43 (2723)	.31 (2830)	.30 (2795)
Types of activities				
Important	.51 (4122)	.49 (3966)	.44 (4104)	.39 (12241)
Unimportant	.50 (12494)	.46 (11817)	.43 (12437)	.40 (4057)

did with number of campaigns, we find the opposite relationship. Those active over the longest period of time were the least constrained, and those involved over the shortest period of time were the most constrained.

Such an unexpected finding suggests a possible spurious relationship. Both involvement variables are related to motivational variables such as reason for attending the convention and pragmatism, as well as to education. In all three cases the relationship is rather mild (gamma 〈.20), and approximately the same for each. The strongest relationship is with age. Clearly the younger respondents have had less opportunity to get involved in a large number of campaigns (gamma = .23) and, to an even greater extent, are unlikely to have been active for as long a time as older respondents (gamma = .51). So there is a possibility of age acting as a spurious variable in the case of length of involvement, and as a suppressor variable in the case of number of campaigns involved. When we do control for age, the negative relationship between time involved and constraint is eliminated, but no relationship between constraint and either years or campaigns involved in shows up (data not shown).

It is possible of course that it is neither length of time nor number of campaigns involved in, but type of involvement in the campaigns. To this end, we asked respondents which sorts of jobs they had held in campaigns. We counted respondents who had managed a campaign, written speeches, or planned strategy as having had important campaign jobs and respondents who had had no positions or who had done clerical work, canvassing, coffees, or fundraising as having fulfilled unimportant jobs. By this criterion, approximately one in four respondents (27 percent) had held important positions. Unlike the other involvement variables, this one was unrelated to age (gamma = .006). However, the difference in constraint between those who had held important campaign positions and those who had not was consistently small (see Table 8.2). What seems to be clear is that involvement is important in developing high levels of constraint, but only up to a point. Therefore, in mass samples, where very few respondents go beyond that point, we find strong involvement effects. In elite samples, where all respondents are quite involved, we find only very small effects.

MOTIVATIONAL EFFECTS ON CONSTRAINT

Besides general cognitive skills (education) and extent of contact with politics (amount or type of involvement), we should also expect to find that motivations to attend conventions that derive from specific interest in ideological purity and ideological content of politics would produce higher levels of constraint. This derives from the role of thinking about the topic has on decreasing dissonance (Abelson 1959).

Although we do not have a direct measure of general ideological orientation to politics, respondents were asked to indicate how important a variety of influences were in their decision to become involved in politics in 1980. These influences included issues, candidates, party, meeting people, furthering career, civic duty, excitement of campaign, and public visibility of delegate. A factor analysis of these influences revealed two factors, the first consisting of issues and candidate influences, and the second consisting of all other influences except for party and civic duty which did not load strongly on either factor. The items loading strongly on each factor were combined in a simple additive scale. Respondents were then divided into high and low on each scale. The first scale we labelled Ideology and the second Personalism.[7] Respondents were also asked if their participation was motivated by a particular issue.

Finally we asked a battery of questions designed to measure purism versus pragmatism. Purists focus more strongly on ideology in politics, while pragmatists focus more strongly on electability (Soule and Clark,

Table 8.3. Constraint in three issue areas, by motivation

	Strong America issues	Traditional domestic	New issues	All issues
Pragmatism				
High	.43 (2187)	.41 (2122)	.38 (2181)	.33 (2902)
2	.47 (4246)	.43 (4049)	.36 (4237)	.32 (5526)
3	.53 (5623)	.48 (5351)	.47 (5603)	.40 (4178)
Low	.57 (2960)	.57 (2804)	.58 (2952)	.48 (2166)
Ideology				
High	.51 (10223)	.50 (9736)	.45 (10153)	.39 (10029)
Low	.50 (5221)	.42 (4942)	.41 (5223)	.35 (5128)
Personalism				
High	.49 (2538)	.35 (2419)	.38 (2527)	.30 (2495)
Low	.51 (11566)	.50 (11009)	.48 (11537)	.40 (11368)
Single issue				
Yes	.54 (8088)	.49 (7708)	.49 (8048)	.41 (7941)
No	.47 (7654)	.46 (7252)	.39 (7641)	.37 (7511)

1970). The pragmatism/purism questions were combined to form an additive scale. The scale was divided to produce smaller ("purer") groups at each extreme (19 percent and 17 percent of the sample respectively) with the remainder in the two middle categories.

Although it is likely that ideological constraint for delegates did not develop over the course of the 1980 campaign alone, one would expect, in general, that a person's reasons for involvement in 1980 would not be atypical of his general motivations for political participation. Therefore, respondents high on the Ideology scale, those low on the Personalism scale, and those motivated by single issues would be expected to have the most ideological orientations and therefore show the highest levels of constraint. The Pragmatism scale measures a general orientation to politics, and we should expect, therefore, that the most purist, i.e., those who want to further ideology even at the expense of electoral success, would be more constrained than the less purist, more pragmatic respondents.

As Table 8.3 shows, we find general support for our hypotheses using all four measures of ideological salience. Although the Ideology Index shows the weakest discrimination, this is attributable to the fact that fully two-thirds of our respondents indicated that both issues and candidates were "very important," putting them into our "High Ideology" category.

Ideological salience measures have almost exactly the same effect on all three issue areas. This is not surprising since the reasons for increased constraint here, i.e., salience, should apply equally to all three areas.

The greatest and most consistent effect of motivational variables is for pragmatism. In fact the effects of pragmatism on all three issue areas are almost as strong as those of education. Although it is reasonable that those individuals who emphasize ideology in choosing a candidate would be more likely to be concerned with ideological consistency and constraint, it is a particularly interesting finding in light of Stone and Abramowitz's conclusion, in chapter 5, that both purists and pragmatists relied much more heavily on electability than on ideological proximity. This may suggest that even though pragmatism questions seem to address the degree to which one wants a candidate to embody issue concerns, it may be behaviorally more relevant to issue choice than to candidate choice. In other words, if we had asked respondents about their voting on platform planks, we might have found that the purist would be more likely to follow his ideological predilections, while the pragmatist might be more willing to compromise. This is of course only speculation, but it is plausible considering the stress that standard pragmatism questions put on the issue component of candidate choice.

We find, then, that at the zero order level, education has the greatest effect on constraint in all three issue areas. Motivation variables show consistent, and in the case of pragmatism, strong effects as well. Only involvement shows no zero order effect.

THE INDEPENDENT EFFECT OF EDUCATION

Our most interesting findings relate to education. The fact that, among an involved elite sample, education has such a strong effect on constraint implies that cognitive variables do have an important role to play among those for whom politics is salient. This also explains the failure to find education effects among mass samples. However in looking at the zero order relationship only, we are not able to determine the degree to which education's effects are due to the spurious effects of involvement and motivation.

Looking, however, at the effect of education within categories of our control variables does allow us to control for the spuriousness possibility. When we do so, by looking at education's effect on constraint, across the

Table 8.4. Domestic constraint by education and motivation

	HS graduate or less	Some college	College graduate
Pragmatism			
High	.36 (249)	.37 (487)	.48 (1298)
2	.29 (613)	.40 (1159)	.46 (2112)
3	.34 (696)	.47 (1568)	.53 (2883)
Low	.47 (366)	.56 (875)	.52 (1451)
Ideology			
High	.37 (1566)	.47 (2995)	.56 (4770)
Low	.28 (450)	.42 (1210)	.45 (3092)
Personalism			
High	.27 (384)	.36 (776)	.39 (1149)
Low	.36 (1354)	.49 (3039)	.54 (6193)
Single issue			
Yes	.41 (1043)	.46 (2271)	.53 (4059)
No	.28 (1066)	.45 (2001)	.51 (3902)

20 categories of our 7 control variables (the motivational and experience variables), we find that the average differences in constraint between college graduates and respondents with a high school degree or less, within categories, is almost exactly the same as for the sample as a whole (see Tables 8.4 and 8.5). For Traditional Domestic, Strong America and New Issues, the zero order effects of education on constraint (differences between high and low education groups) were .18, .13 and .22 respectively. Across categories of our control variables, they average .17, .12, and .22 respectively. In addition, across the 20 categories, for the three issue areas (60 comparisons) there is but a single case in which the highest education group does not show the highest level of constraint (and this by only .01). Similarly, there is only one case in which high school educated respondents show higher constraint levels than respondents with some college (by .02). Clearly, the effect of education is undiminished by controls. This stable effect of education across subgroups implies that higher levels of education can make up for motivational effects, and also raises the question of whether motivational effects can overcome educational deficiencies, so that for instance, highly motivated delegates, with only a high school degree, will show greater constraint than less motivated college graduataes. (Our analysis here will focus on Traditional Domestic

Table 8.5. Domestic constraint by education and experience

	HS graduate or less	Some college	College graduate
Active in campaigns			
All	.33 (651)	.46 (1364)	.52 (2476)
Most	.39 (568)	.48 (1150)	.52 (2271)
Some	.34 (628)	.47 (1284)	.54 (2384)
None	.32 (396)	.42 (636)	.49 (1159)
Years active			
0-5	.37 (751)	.48 (1825)	.55 (3335)
5-10	.39 (418)	.46 (926)	.53 (2009)
10-20	.32 (471)	.45 (908)	.49 (1804)
20+	.27 (621)	.39 (815)	.48 (1125)
Types of activities			
Important	.33 (370)	.45 (1017)	.54 (2382)
Unimportant	.35 (1922)	.46 (3498)	.52 (5932)

Issues, although the results for Strong America, New Issues, and all issues combined are similar in all cases.)

In *The American Voter,* Campbell et al. (1960) examined the potential of involvement to overcome education differences in levels of conceptualization. They found only small compensatory effects. Here, however, we find that both education and motivation can make up, at least partly for deficiencies in the other, and neither totally dominates the other. Respondents low in constraint motivation (i.e., high on Personalism and pragmatism, low on Ideology, and nonsingle issue delegates) were able to overcome this disadvantage if they were high in education. For example, nonsingle issue college graduates, showed levels of constraint higher than single issue respondents with some college. Education's effect was equally strong in raising college graduates with the highest level of pragmatism to levels of constraint above those of the least pragmatic delegates with some college.

Motivation variables also play an important role in partially overcoming educational deficiencies. For example, low education delegates, lowest in pragmatism equal or surpass college graduates from each of the two highest pragmatism levels. Respondents high on our Ideology scale, with only some college, show higher constraint than college graduates low on Ideology. Viewed from another perspective, what this clearly implies is that both educational and motivational effects remain, after controlling for the other, and that, for the most part, the two effects are independent of one another.

The role of involvement is much less clear. Given our earlier finding that length of campaign involvement, extent of involvement, and types of involvement had only very limited effects on constraint, it is not unexpected that we find only a small ability of experience to make up for education. With a single exception, no low education group, regardless of years of involvement or type of campaign involvement, shows greater constraint than any middle education group, and no middle education group shows greater constraint than any high education group.

We do, however, continue to find strong effects of education as an important compensatory variable. For example, college graduates with no important campaign responsibilities, were more constrained than respondents with important campaign responsibility, but with only some college education. Similarly, college educated respondents at any level of years of activity, were more constrained than noncollege graduates at any level of activity. The same basic relationship holds for number of campaigns in which respondent has been involved.

To summarize, then, for both motivational and involvement variables, we find that concurrent controls for education and other variables diminished the zero order effect of each variable only slightly. Education effects remain strong and consistent throughout.

The findings here are important in showing that education does have an important role to play in explaining interattitudinal constraint. Previous negative findings about the role of education on constraint were foreordained by the use of mass samples. Our findings here show that education does increase constraint substantially, but apparently only among respondents with at least a reasonably high level of political involvement. Since a mass sample has few such individuals, failure to find effects is unsurprising. Among a sample of activists, such as used here, however, education accounts for large increases in constraint, increases greater than those caused by length or type of involvement, or by type of motivation. Even controls for motivation and involvement leave education's impact almost entirely intact.

On a more general level, our findings indicate a consistently high level of attitudinal constraint among political elites, in spite of substantial variation in constraint levels. Even in times of substantial instability in partisanship, and voting behavior, there remains a clear and consistent structuring of political attitudes. Although this structuring is particularly strong once we divide attitudes into different issue areas, there is still a high level of constraint across issues areas. To the degree that elites set agendas, and serve as cue givers to masses, there is no reason to expect declines in the levels of constraint at the mass level.

NOTES

1. Both Democrats and Republicans were weighted to a total N of 10,000, giving us a resulting N of 20,000. Using convention representation weights both state population and party strength within states. Alternatives of weighting by population alone, or equally weighting each state party group are less promising since the theoretical universe is either less clear or less interesting. (Although analyses weighting each state party equally produced almost identical results.)

2. Rao's canonical factor analysis with varimax rotation yielded three factors for the thirteen issue questions. Eleven of the thirteen issues loaded at least .40 on one of the three factors, and were included as part of that issue group. Spending cuts to balance the budget and stronger action to reduce inflation, even if it meant increased unemployment, did not load on any of the three factors. They were included, however, in the "All Issues" computations throughout the paper. The factor loadings were as follows (eigenvalues for the three factors were 12.56, 2.37, and 2.04 respectively):

	Factor 1	Factor 2	Factor 3
ERA	.385	−.209	.700
Amendment prohibiting abortion	.002	.148	−.504
Increase in defense spending	−.395	.624	−.429
National health insurance	.710	−.253	.328
Nuclear power	−.347	.536	−.274
Spending cuts to balance budget	−.388	.342	−.297
Affirmative action	.505	−.223	.405
Deregulation of oil and gas	−.534	.312	−.062
Wage and price controls	.662	−.075	.061
Strong action to reduce inflation	−.349	.381	−.111
Reinstitution of draft registration	−.136	.612	−.116
SALT II Treaty	.461	−.250	.496
Increase American presence in Middle East	−.097	.609	−.190

3. The uses of constraint measures to assess ideology have come under attack from a variety of scholars (Balch 1981; Bennett 1975; Brown 1970; Coveyou and Piereson 1977; Lane, 1973; Luttbeg 1968; Marcus, Tabb, and Sullivan 1974).

Correlational measures have been criticized on three different grounds: first, that they assume that all individuals have attitudes on the relevant issues and the issue positions are unidimensionally related for everyone; second, that correlations across a group of individuals may imply little or nothing about structuring of attitudes by individuals; and third, that items sampled are not important to the individual and to the political system. The first and third of these are much less applicable for our sample. The issues about which we asked were widely discussed in 1980, and anyone active in party politics during that year would be conversant with these issues and have a common understanding of them. Empirical support is provided by the fact that a single factor did account for 80 percent of the common variance across the thirteen issues, and the average correlation between the self-placement liberal conservative five point scale and the individual issue items was .52 (gamma) with a range between .34 and .71. Furthermore, we do look at factors separately. Concerning the problem of inferring individual structuring from group correlations, this is much less a problem when the individuals in question share a common perspective on politics. This too is to be expected among a group who have been exposed to common political experiences and events, as these 1980 delegates have. Also, statistical artifacts (e.g., a few outliers, extreme consensus on certain issues) that might artificially inflate or decrease correlations (Balch 1981) are not present in our data.

4. In the 1956 (Campbell et al. 1960) and 1973 (Klingeman and Wright 1974) surveys in the U. S., low interest college educated respondents were higher in levels of conceptualization than high interest high school educated respondents.

5. Our education categories are a bit different from those employed by Nie et al. (1978) (who used less than high school degree and college educated as their two categories) and from Bennett et al. (1979), who used O-8 years, 9-11 years, high school grad, some college, and college graduate. Given our elite sample we use high school graduate or less, some college, and college graduate as our break points.

6. It is of course possible that it is party and not education which is having the observed effect on constraint. Republicans are less likely to have only a high school education, and if they showed higher levels of constraint, their preponderance in the higher education groups, even though small, could be responsible for the effect we find. However, equiweighting Democrats and Republicans within each education category did not alter the results at all (only two of the nine average gammas changed by as much as .01).

7. Rao's canonical factor analysis with varimax rotation yielded two factors for the sample, when we analyzed all eight motives (with eigenvalues of 8.3 and 2.2 respectively):

	Factor 1	Factor 2
Support party	.230	.267
Help political career	.522	−.066

Excitement of campaign	.750	.015
Meet other people	.652	.217
Support a candidate	.007	.567
Work for issues	−.104	.597
Visibility	.671	.048
Civic responsibility	.218	.254

Our scale for Ideological motivation divided our sample into those who said that both candidate and issue considerations were "very important" reasons for their participation in 1980 (about two-thirds of our sample) and those for whom at least one of these motivations was not "very important." The Personalism scale was constructed from the four personal motivation items. If a motivation was cited as "very important", respondents were assigned a score of 1, if "somewhat important", a score of 2, "not very important," a score of 3, and "not important at all," a score of 4. Respondents with a combined score of 8 were placed in the high Personalism category (i.e., those for whom, on average, personal motivations were at least "somewhat important"), and the rest were placed in the low Personalism category.

REFERENCES

Abelson, Robert 1959. "Modes of Resolution of Belief Dilemmas." *Conflict Resolution* 3: 343-352.

Balch, George I. 1981. "Statistical Manipulation in the Study of Issue Consistency: Aggregation Problems of Correlation." *Micropolitics* 1: 45-70.

Bennett, Lance W. 1975. *The Political Mind and the Political Environment.* Boston: D. C. Heath.

Bennett, Stephen E., Robert W. Oldendick, Alfred J. Tuchfarber, and Bishop, George. 1979. "Education and Mass Belief Systems: An Extension and Some New Questions." *Political Behavior* 1: 53-72.

Bishop, George and Kathleen A. Frankovic. 1981. "Ideological Consensus and Constraint among Party Leaders and Followers in the 1978 Election." *Micropolitics* 1: 87-111.

Bishop, George, Robert W. Oldendick, and Alfred J. Tuchfarber. 1978. "Change in the Structure of American Political Attitudes: The Nagging Question of Question Wording." *American Journal of Political Science* 22: 250-269.

Bowles, Roy T. and James Richardson. 1969. "Sources of Consistency of Public Opinion." *American Journal of Sociology* 74: 676-684.

Brown, Steven. 1970. "Consistency and the Persistence of Ideology: Some Experimental Results." *Public Opinion Quarterly* 34: 60-68.

Bruner, Jere. 1976. "What's the Question to That Answer: Measures and Marginals in Crosstabulation." *American Journal of Political Science* 20: 781-804.

Butler, David, and Donald Stokes. 1971. *Political Change in Britain*. 2nd ed. New York St. Martin's Press.

Campbell, Angus, Philip Converse, Warren Miller, and Donald Stokes. 1960. *The American Voter.* New York: John Wiley and Sons.

Cobb, Roger W. and Charles D. Elder. 1975. *Participation in America: The Dynamics of Agenda-Building*. Baltimore: Johns Hopkins University Press.

Converse, Philip. 1964. "The Nature of Belief Systems in Mass Publics." In *Ideology and Discontent,* edited by David Apter. New York: Free Press, pp. 206-261.

———. 1975. "Public Opinion and Voting Behavior." In *Handbook of Political Science,* (volume 4), edited by Nelson W. Polsby and Fred I. Greenstein. Reading, Mass: Addison-Wesley.

Coveyou, Michael R. and James Piereson. 1977. "Ideological Perceptions and Political Judgement: Some Problems of Concept and Measurement." *Political Methodology* 4: 77-102.

Erikson, Robert S., Norman R. Luttbeg, and Kent L. Tedin. 1980. *American Public Opinion: Its Origins, Content, and Impact.* (2nd ed.). New York: Wiley.

Field, John O. and Ronald E. Anderson. 1969. "Ideology in the Public's Conceptualization of the 1964 Election." *Public Opinion Quarterly* 33: 380-398.

Klingeman, Hans. 1979. "Measuring Ideological Conceptualizations." In *Political Action,* edited by Samuel Barnes and Max Kaase. Beverly Hills, Calif.: Sage, 215-254.

——— and William Wright. 1974. "Levels of Conceptualization in the American and German Mass Publics." Paper presented at Workshop on Political Cognition, University of Georgia, Athens, Georgia.

Lane, Robert E. 1973. "Patterns of Political Belief." In *Handbook of Political Psychology,* edited by Jeanne Knutson. San Francisco: Jossey-Bass.

Luttbeg, Norman R. 1968. "The Structure of Beliefs Among Leaders and the Public." *Public Opinion Quarterly* 32: 398-409.

Marcus, George, David Tabb, and John L. Sullivan. 1974. "The Application of Individual Differences Scaling to the Measurement of Political Ideologies." *American Journal of Political Science* 16: 25-42.

Nie, Norman, Sidney Verba, and John Petrocik. 1978. *The Changing American Voter.* 2nd ed. Cambridge, Mass.: Harvard University Press.

Pierce, John C. and Paul R. Hagner. 1980. "Changes in the Public's Political Thinking: The Watershed Years, 1956-1968." In *The Electorate Reconsidered,* edited by John C. Pierce and John L. Sullivan. Beverly Hills, Calif.: Sage.

Soule, John and James Clarke. 1970. "Amateurs and Professionals: A Study of Delegates to the 1968 Democratic National Convention." *American Political Science Review* 64: 888-899.

Stone, Walter J. and Alan I. Abramowitz. 1982 "Activist Support for Presidential Candidates: Ideology and Electability in 1980." Paper presented at Annual Meeting of the Midwest Political Science Association.

Welch, Susan and John G. Peters. 1981. "Elite Attitudes on Economic- Welfare & Social Issues. *Polity* 14: 160-177.

9

Issue Constellations in 1980

JEFFREY L. BRUDNEY,
JEAN G. MCDONALD

According to Malcolm Jewell and David Olson, state party organizations exhibit many patterns of factionalism. Jewell and Olson (1982, 52) define factions as "any sign of disagreement within a political party . . . any divergence of opinion." Based on the varying issue stances of groupings or factions present in the parties at the 1980 state presidential nominating conventions, this chapter examines such "divergence of opinion" within, rather than between, state parties.

"Ideology is not supposed to have much importance in American political life," Dwaine Marvick (1980, 72) once wrote in describing contemporary politics. Yet, as Marvick was aware, research on party activists from the precinct to the presidential level has demonstrated consistently that they possess rather sophisticated ideological belief systems. Opinions on "issues of the day" are well-developed within the ranks of the party leadership; attitudes and beliefs demonstrate constraint and fit into more general schemata or ideologies (Conover and Feldman 1980). This level of ideology contrasts with that found among rank and file party identifiers, who tend to have less well-defined belief systems (for example, Marvick 1980; Montjoy et al. 1980; Dunn 1975; Flinn and Wirt 1971; McCloskey et al. 1960). Not only is ideology salient to party elites, but also, historically, the two parties have professed very different ideological orientations, with the Republicans decidedly more conservative than the Democrats.

While prior research has established these findings, important questions remain. For instance, are activists in each party monolithic in attitudes, as is usually presumed, or is diversity in opinion tolerated? If attitudinal heterogeneity is prevalent, what varieties of political opinion are countenanced among party activists? Are these differences related to party roles, candidate preferences, and/or ideological self-identification? Do the viewpoints of party activists demonstrate a unidimensional structure (especially along a liberal-conservative continuum), or do they conform to a more complex multi-dimensional pattern?

Samuel Eldersveld (1964) addressed the issue of attitudinal diversity within the parties in his classic study of local party organization in Wayne County, Michigan. In this fluid, pragmatic party system, Eldersveld found differing ideological orientations among party leaders. He related these differences to several factors, including position in the party hierarchy. Eldersveld concluded that ideological differences were accepted among the party leaders, although they became socialized to the basic orientation of their party: "Contrasting viewpoints could be tolerated within the parties because of their loose knit structures; slack was common in the local party organizations. . . . The party gladly embraces, and freely associates with, a most ideologically conglomerate set of political supporters and activists" (Eldersveld 1964, 218).

Like Eldersveld, Edmond Costantini (1971) identified position in the party hierarchy as an important source of differing perspectives and ideological viewpoints within the parties. Costantini argued that top party leadership would have a more moderate policy orientation than lower-level party elites. He reasoned that those at the top would be most concerned with gaining electoral victory and appealing to a broad base of popular support; party activists at lower levels would participate primarily because of ideological predispositions, and thus could be expected to deviate from the superstructure of the party by holding more extreme views. Although Costantini's study was limited by the exclusion of Republicans, it did substantiate his basic hypothesis that the party substructure was more extreme in attitudes than top leadership. He concluded that "the leadership-follower dichotomy adopted by McCloskey [1960] may conceal significant aspects of the complex pattern of clash and counterpoint within a political party" (Costantini 1971, 289). Although Eldersveld (1964) did not find that lower-level party leaders were necessarily more extreme in their views than top leadership, both studies reported ideological diversity among activists according to their position in the party hierarchy.

A second grouping within the party which may be related to the issue orientation of its leadership, especially in a presidential election year, is candidate preference. According to Jeane Kirkpatrick (1976), candidate factions differed considerably in their political attitudes at the 1972 presidential nominating conventions. On the one hand, two of the Democratic candidate factions—those supporting McGovern and Wallace—were highly ideological. In contrast, the Humphrey and Muskie factions were ideologically diverse, as could be observed in their disparate stands on the issues; the personality of the candidate and the loyalty he evoked were the coalescing factors in these factions. Kirkpatrick (1976, 264-268) contended that the Democratic party did not conform to the stereotype of a group of "like-minded men," but neither did it appear to be an association exclusively for the electorally-minded; the party was both. On the other hand, the Republican party displayed much less factionalism than the Democrats. Kirkpatrick argued that consensus was much higher among Republicans (although they were not monolithic), hence differences in political attitudes were less sharp.

Other researchers have also found the Republican party to be less diverse and more united in opinion than the Democrats. As a result of the internal and external constituencies facing the party, the Republicans have been able to survive (although only barely at times) with a more limited popular appeal but a more unified issue orientation. Barton and Parsons (1977), for example, characterized Republicans as having the most structured belief system of any of several groupings of party elites; they constituted a relatively homogeneous group with a high degree of consensus on the issues. A diverse lot, Democrats evidenced both less structured belief systems and much less consensus than the Republicans.

Marvick's (1980) research on party activists points to a third source of attitudinal diversity within the parties: ideological predisposition. In his studies of Los Angeles party committee members over time, Marvick found that ideological diversity was tolerated within the parties. Year after year, for example, moderate Republicans held distinctly different opinions on the issues than conservative members of their party. Similarly, moderate Democrats diverged from their liberal counterparts. These groupings were accepted within the party structure and apparently were not disciplined or ousted for their deviance. In sum, the parties may include varying ideological factions which may affect political attitudes and policy outlooks.

Recent research has addressed the related issue of the dimensionality of belief systems. Increasingly, the literature has recognized that political attitudes are dynamic and multidimensional, if not always consistent (for example, Herzon 1980; Conover and Feldman 1981, 1980; Stimson 1975). Herzon's (1980) work, in particular, suggests the multidimensionality of belief systems among elite groups. In his sample of Philadelphia lawyers, Herzon found a lack of consensus on ideological viewpoints. He was able to identify the "themes underlying the respondents' positions on the issues and . . . reveal the ideological dimensions that structure their political thinking" (Herzon 1980, 247). While attorneys with different backgrounds may demonstrate less agreement than activists in a common political party organization, nevertheless one would expect structured, viable ideologies to characterize both groups. The multidimensional belief system found among the attorneys suggests that a similarly complex structure may be prevalent among party leaders.

Based on this research, groupings or factions within the parties resulting from position in the party hierarchy, candidate preference, and ideological predisposition may lead to differing issue positions and political beliefs, thus belying the conception of monolithic party systems. The literature also suggests that these differences will be more pronounced among Democrats than Republicans. Finally, the belief systems underlying the views of party leadership are more likely to display a multidimensional than a unidimensional structure. The following hypotheses summarize these findings for purposes of empirical test:

• Republican party leaders will exhibit less diversity in opinion than will Democratic party leaders.

• Upper levels of party leadership will differ in issue orientation from those at lower levels; not only may upper-level leaders be concerned with a different set of issues, but also they may be less extreme in their views than the party substructure.

• Factions based on candidate preference will exhibit different issue stances within the same party.

• Issue positions within the parties will differ according to ideology (liberal-conservative), but moderates across the two parties will also differ.

• Intraparty factions or groupings can be expected to demonstrate multidimensional issue structures underlying their political attitudes.

These hypotheses are examined empirically based on a very large sample of over 17,000 political activists who served as delegates to the 1980 conventions of the Democratic or Republican party in their state. Although only a subset of the United States is represented in this sample, the collection of states seems sufficiently diverse (politically, geographically, economically, etc.) to approximate a broad cross-section of state party activists.

Among the questions put to the state convention delegates were thirteen items soliciting their opinions on important issues of public

Table 9.1. Issue positions by party

	Democrats			Republicans			
Issue	Mean	Std. dev.	*N*	Mean	Std. dev.	*N*	Diff. std. dev.*
Equal Rights Amendment	2.06	1.37	8489	3.96	1.34	8641	.03
Amendment banning abortion	3.56	1.55	8414	2.85	1.60	8606	−.05
Increase defense spending	3.09	1.41	8398	1.56	0.87	8637	.54
National health insurance	2.54	1.34	7428	4.50	0.88	8217	.46
Nuclear power	3.27	1.37	8364	2.02	1.05	8591	.32
Spending cuts/balance budget	3.22	1.31	8286	2.00	1.25	8581	.06
Affirmative action programs	2.45	1.20	8296	3.71	1.11	8486	.09
Deregulation of oil and gas	3.10	1.31	8183	1.99	1.09	8482	.22
Wage and price controls	2.90	1.33	8228	3.96	1.23	8506	.10
Reduce inflation	3.13	1.21	8191	2.35	1.11	8345	.10
Draft registration	2.73	1.46	8294	2.16	1.21	8524	.25
Ratification of SALT II	2.57	1.20	8100	4.26	1.05	8431	.15
U.S. military in Middle East	2.88	1.24	8281	2.25	1.05	8490	.19

*Standard deviation for Democrats minus standard deviation for Republicans.

policy: the Equal Rights Amendment, a constitutional amendment prohibiting abortions unless the life of the mother is endangered, increases in defense spending at the expense of domestic programs, national health insurance, nuclear power, cuts in nondefense spending to balance the federal budget, affirmative action programs, deregulation of oil and gas prices, wage and price controls, action to reduce inflation even if unemployment results, reinstitution of draft registration, ratification of the SALT II Treaty, and increasing America's military presence in the Middle East. The full text of the items may be found in the appendix (Question 19). For each item, delegates were asked to place themselves on a five-point scale, ranging from "strongly favor" (1) to "strongly oppose" (5).

ISSUE POSITIONS

The first hypothesis proposed that Republican party activists will display greater homogeneity in opinion than will their counterparts in the Democratic party. Table 9.1 presents data to evaluate this hypothesis. The table includes the mean and standard deviation of responses on the thirteen issues for both Democrats and Republicans, as well as the difference between the standard deviations for each item (standard deviation for Democrats—standard deviation for Republicans).

Table 9.1 supports the hypothesis. With the exception of the abortion issue, Republican delegates consistently display less variation in opinion than do Democratic delegates, as assessed by the respective standard deviations. Even with respect to abortion, the differences in standard deviations is not large. For two of the issues, defense spending and national health insurance, the Republicans are markedly more unified in opinion than the Democrats (differences in standard deviation are .54 and .46, respectively), and for four others, nuclear power (difference = .32), draft registration (.25), deregulation of oil and gas (.22), and a U.S. military presence in the Middle East (.19), they are considerably more monolithic. Although the remaining six issues reveal somewhat smaller differences in the variability of issue positions between Democrats and Republicans (.15 or less), Republicans are consistently more similar in opinion. The latter are also consistently conservative, while the Democrats are moderate to liberal.

According to the second hypothesis, upper levels of party leadership can be expected to differ in issue orientation from those in the lower echelon, i.e., the party substructure. Because of the difficulty of ranking party offices hierarchically, especially across states, in this research a basic distinction is made between delegates who hold public office (upper level leaders) and those who do not (lower level leaders). Table 9.2 reports the results of analyses of variance comparing mean scores on the issues across these two groups for each party.

Certainly among Republican delegates, the hypothesis does not receive empirical support: The largest difference in mean scores observed between public officeholders and nonofficeholders is only .15 (nuclear power), and for only one other issue (action to reduce inflation at the expense of unemployment) is the difference greater than .10. Apparently, Costantini's (1971) findings documenting issue differences between the leadership and the substructure of the Democratic party may not be generalizable to the Republican party. Whether holders of public office or not, Republicans were consistently conservative on the issues and exhibited remarkable consensus of opinion.

Not so for the Democratic party. Democratic officeholders differed by as much as .51 (nuclear power) from the party substructure. Comparable differences are observed on the issues of defense spending (.43), draft

Table 9.2. Issue positions among public officeholders and nonofficeholders

Issue	Officeholders			Nonofficeholders				
	Mean	Std. dev.	*N*	Mean	Std. dev.	*N*	Diff. means	Eta/Eta²
				Democratic delegates				
Equal Rights Amendment	2.40	1.49	976	2.02	1.34	7513	.38	.09/.008**
Amendment banning abortion	3.36	1.54	967	3.59	1.55	7447	−.23	.05/.002**
Increase defense spending	2.71	1.41	973	3.14	1.40	7425	−.43	.10/.009**
National health insurance	2.67	1.38	925	2.52	1.33	6503	.15	.04/.001**
Nuclear power	2.82	1.30	955	3.33	1.36	7409	−.51	.12/.014**
Spending cuts/balance budget	3.02	1.35	957	3.24	1.30	7329	−.22	.06/.003**
Affirmative action programs	2.55	1.25	951	2.43	1.19	7345	.12	.03/.001*
Deregulation of oil and gas	2.95	1.34	938	3.12	1.30	7245	−.17	.04/.002**
Wage and price controls	2.79	1.38	949	2.91	1.32	7279	−.12	.03/.001*
Reduce inflation	2.98	1.24	943	3.16	1.20	7248	−.18	.05/.002**
Draft registration	2.37	1.31	946	2.77	1.47	7348	−.40	.09/.008**
Ratification of SALT II	2.63	1.18	931	2.56	1.20	7169	.07	.02/.000
U.S. military in Middle East	2.57	1.18	952	2.92	1.24	7329	−.35	.09/.008**
				Republican delegates				
Equal Rights Amendment	3.98	1.28	993	3.96	1.35	7648	.02	.01/.000
Amendment banning abortion	2.79	1.55	981	2.86	1.61	7625	−.07	.01/.000
Increase defense spending	1.54	0.82	989	1.57	0.87	7648	−.03	.01/.000
National Health Insurance	4.52	0.83	958	4.50	0.88	7259	.02	.00/.000
Nuclear power	1.88	0.97	991	2.03	1.06	7600	−.15	.05/.002**
Spending cuts/balance budget	1.97	1.26	984	2.00	1.25	7597	−.03	.01/.000
Affirmative action programs	3.75	1.09	974	3.70	1.11	7512	.05	.01/.000
Deregulation of oil and gas	2.03	1.10	973	1.98	1.09	7509	.05	.02/.000
Wage and price controls	3.96	1.24	978	3.96	1.23	7528	.00	.00/.000
Reduce inflation	2.24	1.11	954	2.37	1.11	7391	−.13	.04/.001**
Draft registration	2.10	1.19	982	2.17	1.22	7542	−.07	.02/.000
Ratification of SALT II	4.24	1.05	970	4.26	1.05	7461	−.02	.00/.000
U.S. military in Middle East	2.22	1.04	974	2.25	1.05	7516	−.03	.01/.000

*Difference in means statistically significant at the .01 level.

**Difference in means statistically significant at the .001 level.

registration (.40), the Equal Rights Amendment (.38), and a U.S. military presence in the Middle East (.35). However, the remaining eight issues show less than a one-quarter point difference between officeholders and nonofficeholders. Although for all but one issue (ratification of the SALT II Treaty) the differences between the mean issue positions of the two groups achieves statistical significance (largely due to sample size), the eta^2 statistics assessing explained variation are quite small, only once surpassing even 1 percent (nuclear power). Thus, while the hypothesis is substantiated for hierarchical groupings within the Democratic party, the evidence is not overwhelming.

Analysis of the Democratic delegates also shows that with the exception of a single issue (mandatory wage and price controls), officeholders maintained a more conservative orientation than did the party substructure. Thus, as Costantini (1971) found, within the Democratic party the substructure appears more extreme than top leadership.

As suggested by the third hypothesis, issue differences across candidate factions are more substantial for both parties. Democratic delegates pledged to incumbent Jimmy Carter saw the issues in a far different light than did those pledged to challenger Edward Kennedy. As could be expected, Kennedy delegates were far more liberal than Carter supporters. As a group, Kennedy delegates were more opposed to reinstituting draft registration (by 1.27 points on a 5-point scale), more supportive of a national health insurance program (by 1.17), more opposed to increased defense spending (by .97), and more supportive of mandatory wage and price controls (by .92). Carter delegates were more supportive of the development of nuclear power (by .83), deregulation of oil and gas prices (by .76), a U.S. military presence in the Middle East (by .74), cuts in nondefense spending to balance the budget (by .72), and action to reduce inflation (by .69). On eleven of the thirteen issues, the mean scores for Carter and Kennedy supporters differ by more than half a point. Were it not for the fact that some of the liberal Democratic delegates had endorsed Carter as a candidate because he seemed more likely to win—despite their preference for Kennedy's views—the differences on the issues between these candidate factions would have been even greater (see chapter 5).

As was the case with respect to the comparison of officeholders and nonofficeholders (see Table 9.2), candidate factions in the Republican party display greater similarity in issue positions than do the candidate followings in the Democratic party (Table 9.3). As a group, state conven-

Table 9.3. Issue positions among candidate factions

	Democratic delegates							
	Carter delegates			Kennedy delegates				
Issue	Mean	Std. dev.	*N*	Mean	Std. dev.	*N*	Diff. means	Eta/Eta²
Equal Rights Amendment	2.17	1.40	4484	1.60	1.06	1686	.57	.19/.04**
Amendment banning abortion	3.57	1.52	4444	3.80	1.51	1678	−.23	.07/.01**
Increase defense spending	2.79	1.35	4436	3.76	1.32	1679	−.97	.31/.09**
National health insurance	2.85	1.34	4015	1.68	0.92	1363	1.17	.38/.14**
Nuclear power	3.03	1.32	4411	3.86	1.26	1676	−.83	.27/.07**
Spending cuts/balance budget	3.01	1.28	4383	3.73	1.24	1660	−.72	.25/.06**
Affirmative action programs	2.56	1.21	4403	2.05	1.10	1667	.51	.19/.04**
Deregulation of oil and gas	2.87	1.25	4336	3.63	1.32	1653	−.76	.26/.07**
Wage and price controls	3.15	1.30	4352	2.23	1.19	1665	.92	.31/.09**
Reduce inflation	2.94	1.15	4338	3.63	1.21	1656	−.69	.26/.07**
Draft registration	2.30	1.26	4391	3.57	1.47	1647	−1.27	.40/.16**
Ratification of SALT II	2.58	1.18	4296	2.40	1.20	1634	.18	.07/.01**
U.S. military in Middle East	2.61	1.15	4390	3.35	1.28	1663	−.74	.27/.07**
	Republican delegates							
	Reagan delegates			Non-Reagan delegates				
Issue	Mean	Std. dev.	*N*	Mean	Std. dev.	*N*	Diff. means	Eta/Eta²
Equal Rights Amendment	4.21	1.15	3160	3.38	1.50	1236	.83	.29/.08**
Amendment banning abortion	2.67	1.57	3131	3.31	1.54	1230	−.64	.18/.03**
Increase defense spending	1.38	0.74	3159	1.80	1.03	1235	−.42	.22/.05**
National health insurance	4.51	0.90	3092	4.47	0.87	1139	.04	.02/.00
Nuclear power	1.90	1.03	3132	2.17	1.10	1232	−.27	.11/.01**
Spending cuts/balance budget	1.90	1.28	3127	2.17	1.28	1228	−.27	.09/.01**
Affirmative action programs	3.83	1.10	3097	3.54	1.12	1217	.29	.12/.01**
Deregulation of oil and gas	1.93	1.13	3102	1.92	1.06	1222	.01	.01/.00
Wage and price controls	3.93	1.29	3108	3.90	1.22	1226	.03	.01/.00
Reduce inflation	2.28	1.13	3050	2.38	1.07	1194	−.10	.04/.00*
Draft registration	1.97	1.14	3116	2.19	1.19	1226	−.22	.09/.01**
Ratification of SALT II	4.42	0.96	3079	4.00	1.15	1213	.42	.18/.03**
U.S. military in Middle East	2.08	1.04	3107	2.38	1.05	1220	−.30	.13/.02**

*Difference in means statistically significant at the .01 level.

**Difference in means statistically significant at the .001 level.

tion delegates committed to Ronald Reagan have nearly identical positions in support of deregulation of oil and gas prices and action to reduce inflation even if unemployment should increase, and in opposition to wage and price controls and national health insurance as those not pledged to Reagan (the only other sizable candidate faction). These groups do differ substantially on a number of issues, however. For example, Reagan delegates were more opposed to the Equal Rights Amendment (by .83) and to the SALT II Treaty (by .42) and more in favor of an amendment prohibiting abortions except when the mother's life is endangered (by .64) and increases in defense spending (by .42). On the remaining issues, the differences between Reagan delegates and supporters of other candidates range between .22 and .30. While the issue positions taken by candidate factions among Republicans are closer than those found in the Democratic party, on most issues a clear (albeit smaller) difference is discernible.

Tables 9.4 and 9.5 allow examination of the fourth hypothesis concerning the issue positions of ideological factions with the parties. Delegates classified themselves on an ideological dimension ranging from very liberal to very conservative. Table 9.4 contrasts the views on the thirteen issues of "very" and "somewhat" liberal Democratic delegates with those of party moderates; the table also presents a comparison of the opinions of "very" and "somewhat" conservative delegates with moderates in the Republican party.

As anticipated, large differences on the issues separate the ideological factions within the same party. Democratic moderates are far more conservative than party liberals, and Republican moderates are far more liberal than party conservatives. The differences are especially marked among the Democrats: On nine of the thirteen issues, the means for liberals and moderates differ by more than one-half point, the largest disagreements occurring on defense spending (1.00), draft registration (.95), the Equal Rights Amendment (.87), and national health insurance (.84). Had very liberal Democratic delegates alone been compared with the combined group of those who considered themselves somewhat liberal or moderate, the differences in issue positions would have been even greater than those displayed in Table 9.4.

Republican conservatives and moderates also demonstrate sizable differences on the issues, but they are generally smaller than those found between Democratic ideological factions. On six issues (compared with

Table 9.4. Issue positions among party ideological factions

Issue	Democratic delegates							
	Very/somewhat Liberal			Moderate				
	Mean	Std. dev.	*N*	Mean	Std. dev.	*N*	Diff. means	Eta/Eta²
Equal Rights Amendment	1.60	1.05	4842	2.47	1.40	1778	−.87	.32/.10
Amendment banning abortion	3.90	1.43	4792	3.26	1.53	1773	.64	.19/.04
Increase defense spending	3.59	1.30	4790	2.59	1.24	1768	1.00	.33/.11
National health insurance	2.12	1.15	4264	2.96	1.30	1560	−.84	.30/.09
Nuclear power	3.63	1.30	4788	2.86	1.25	1754	.77	.26/.07
Spending cuts/balance budget	3.56	1.22	4747	2.89	1.22	1740	.67	.24/.06
Affirmative action programs	2.11	1.06	4776	2.80	1.15	1738	−.69	.27/.07
Deregulation of oil and gas	3.27	1.30	4673	2.95	1.25	1736	.32	.11/.01
Wage and price controls	2.76	1.29	4701	3.10	1.32	1733	.34	.12/.01
Reduce registration	3.35	1.18	4689	2.89	1.15	1724	.46	.17/.03
Draft registration	3.14	1.48	4739	2.19	1.20	1734	.95	.28/.08
Ratification of SALT II	2.32	1.12	4657	2.79	1.14	1702	−.47	.18/.03
U.S. military in Middle East	3.16	1.23	4737	2.53	1.07	1731	.63	.23/.05

Issue	Republican delegates							
	Very/somewhat conservative			Moderate				
	Mean	Std. dev.	*N*	Mean	Std. dev.	*N*	Diff. means	Eta/Eta²
Equal Rights Amendment	4.14	1.21	7399	2.81	1.49	759	1.33	.30/.09
Amendment banning abortion	2.73	1.59	7360	3.64	1.43	759	−.91	.16/.03
Increase defense spending	1.47	0.76	7397	2.08	1.09	755	−.61	.22/.05
National health insurance	4.57	0.82	7104	4.13	1.06	676	.44	.14/.02
Nuclear power	1.95	1.01	7349	2.39	1.11	760	−.44	.13/.02
Spending cuts/balance budget	1.92	1.23	7355	2.43	1.23	751	−.51	.12/.01
Affirmative action programs	3.79	1.07	7263	3.29	1.12	753	.50	.14/.02
Deregulation of oil and gas	1.93	1.07	7253	2.33	1.13	749	−.40	.11/.01
Wage and price controls	4.03	1.21	7276	3.58	1.27	750	.45	.11/.01
Reduce inflation	2.31	1.11	7130	2.56	1.09	749	−.25	.07/.01
Draft registration	2.12	1.20	7287	2.28	1.22	755	−.16	.04/.00
Ratification of SALT II	4.37	0.97	7220	3.66	1.14	740	.71	.20/.04
U.S. military in Middle East	2.20	1.03	7267	2.46	1.08	746	−.26	.07/.01

Note: All differences in means statistically significant at the .001 level.

Table 9.5. Issue positions among moderates in each party

Issue	Democrats Mean	Democrats Std. dev.	Democrats *N*	Republicans Mean	Republicans Std. dev.	Republicans *N*	Diff. means	Eta/Eta^2
Equal Rights Amendments	2.47	1.40	1778	2.81	1.49	759	.33	.11/.01*
Amendment banning abortion	3.26	1.53	1773	3.64	1.43	759	−.38	.11/.01*
Increase defense spending	2.59	1.24	1768	2.08	1.09	755	.51	.19/.04*
National health insurance	2.96	1.30	1560	4.13	1.06	676	−1.17	.40/.16*
Nuclear power	2.86	1.25	1754	2.39	1.11	760	.47	.18/.03*
Spending cuts/balance budget	2.89	1.22	1740	2.43	1.23	751	.46	.17/.03*
Affirmative action programs	2.80	1.15	1738	3.29	1.12	753	−.49	.19/.04*
Deregulation of oil and gas	2.95	1.25	1736	2.33	1.13	749	.62	.23/.05*
Wage and price controls	3.10	1.32	1733	3.58	1.27	750	−.48	.17/.03*
Reduce inflation	2.89	1.15	1724	2.56	1.09	749	.33	.13/.02*
Draft registration	2.19	1.20	1734	2.28	1.22	755	−.09	.03/.00
Ratification of SALT II	2.79	1.14	1702	3.66	1.14	740	−.87	.33/.11*
U.S. military in Middle East	2.53	1.07	1731	2.46	1.08	746	.07	.03/.00

*Difference in means statistically significant at the .001 level.

nine for the Democrats), for example, the means for Republican conservatives and moderates diverge by one-half point or better; differences on ten issues surpass a criterion of .40 (compared to eleven for the Democrats). In addition, the largest difference in issue positions in Table 9.4 is observed for the Republican factions with respect to the ERA (1.33), and opinions on the amendment banning abortion reveal the fourth largest difference (.91).

Table 9.5 compares the issue positions of Democratic moderates with those of moderates in the Republican party. The differences in means observed are not as pronounced as those based on the analysis of intraparty ideological factions (Table 9.4). Only four of the issues—national health insurance (1.17), ratification of the SALT II Treaty (.87), deregulation of oil and gas prices (.62), and increases in defense spending (.51)—show a difference in means greater than one-half point, and just seven issues exhibit mean differences larger than .40. As expected, the Democrats are consistently more liberal than the Republicans, but the abortion amendment presents an anomaly: Moderate Democrats are more suppor-

Table 9.6. Factor analysis of all delegates ($N = 13{,}595$)

Issue	Government interference	Defense/ security	Moral/ ethical	Commun- ality (h^2)
Equal Rights Amendments	.36	−.21	.74	.73
Amendment banning abortion	−.03	.13	−.50	.27
Increase defense spending	−.36	.64	−.44	.74
National health insurance	.70	−.23	.35	.66
Nuclear power	−.32	.53	−.30	.47
Spending cuts/balance budget	−.38	.34	−.30	.35
Affirmative action programs	.47	−.24	.38	.42
Deregulation of oil and gas	−.54	.28	−.08	.38
Wage and price controls	.65	−.06	.09	.43
Reduce inflation	−.34	.38	−.09	.26
Draft registration	−.11	.61	−.10	.39
Ratification of SALT II	.46	−.26	.50	.53
U.S. military in Middle East	−.10	.62	−.18	.43
Percent total variance	41.0	9.5	8.4	59.0
Percent common variance	80.1	11.6	8.4	100.0
Eigenvalue	5.33	1.24	1.10	

tive (by .38) of an amendment banning abortion unless the life of the mother is endangered than are moderate Republicans. (Democrats are also slightly more in favor of draft registration, but the difference in means is only .09). In sum, the evidence regarding the similarity of moderate factions across the parties is mixed. Although clear differences in ideology demarcate their views, with respect to (absolute) proximity of issue positions, moderates in the two parties may sometimes have more in common with each other than with the dominant ideological faction in their respective parties.

ATTITUDE DIFFERENCES

In order to test the final hypothesis and examine the dimensional structure underlying the policy attitudes of the state party activists, factor analyses were performed on the thirteen issues for the entire sample as well as each of the subgroups identified above. Table 9.6 presents the results of the factor analysis for all delegates.

Three coherent dimensions emerge in this factor analysis. The first is defined by high loadings of national health insurance (.70), wage and price controls (.65), deregulation of oil and gas prices (– .54), affirmative action programs (.47), ratification of the SALT II Treaty (.46) and the relatively more modest loadings of the Equal Rights Amendment (.36), increases in defense spending (– .36), cuts in nondefense spending to balance the federal budget (– .38), and action to reduce inflation (– .34). These items evince a common concern among delegates with "government interference" in several critical spheres—social (the ERA, affirmative action, national health insurance, defense spending at the expense of domestic programs), economic (spending cuts to balance the budget, deregulation of oil and gas, wage and price controls, steps to combat inflation), and international (SALT II). The direction (i.e., signs) of the loadings suggest that the dimension captures the notion of federal intervention in the affairs of the nation: Opposition to the Equal Rights Amendment, affirmative action programs, national health insurance, wage and price controls, and the SALT II Treaty is accompanied by support for deregulation of oil and gas, as well as increases in defense spending, cuts in non-defense spending, and reducing inflation at the expense of social programs and unemployment. The dimension can be interpreted as placing delegates along a continuum of support or opposition to "government interference" in important issue areas. This dimension might also be characterized as an emerging concept of liberalism-conservatism.

The second dimension is labelled "defense/security," and with good reason: Increases in defense spending (.64), a U.S. military presence in the Middle East (.62), and reinstitution of draft registration (.61) all load heavily on this dimension. The development of nuclear power (.53) is also associated strongly with this dimension. Apparently, delegates envisage nuclear power as an alternative to U.S. resource dependence on the volatile Middle East and thus an aspect of the security of the nation. It is interesting to note that ratification of the SALT II Treaty loads in the opposite direction from the other items, but with only small magnitude (– .26). Delegates do not seem to conceive of the treaty as part of defense strategy or as a viable alternative to a strong military.

The third dimension defines a "moral/ethical" orientation. Its major tenets—the Equal Rights Amendment (.75), SALT II (.50), a constitutional amendment prohibiting abortions (– .50), increases in defense spending at the cost of social programs (– .44), affirmative action programs (.38), and national health insurance (.35)—require delegates to

Table 9.7. Factor analysis of Democratic and Republican delegates

Issue	Democratic delegates (N = 6,392)			
	Defense/ security	Moral/ ethical	Government interference	Commun- ality (h^2)
Equal Right Amendment	−.18	.69	.10	.52
Amendment banning abortion	.19	−.39	.13	.21
Increase defense spending	.68	−.44	−.11	.68
National health insurance	−.19	.34	.63	.55
Nuclear power	.55	−.29	−.08	.40
Spending cuts/balance budget	.40	−.29	−.21	.28
Affirmative action programs	−.15	.47	.34	.36
Deregulation of oil and gas	.35	.08	−.33	.24
Wage and price controls	−.05	.01	.54	.29
Reduce inflation	.41	−.07	−.23	.23
Draft registration	.63	−.25	−.12	.48
Ratification of SALT II	−.18	.43	.12	.23
U.S. military in Middle East	.63	−.22	.01	.44
Percent total variance	31.7	10.6	9.5	51.7
Percent common variance	72.6	15.3	12.0	100.0
Eigenvalue	4.12	1.38	1.23	

Issue	Republicans delegates (N = 7,203)			
	Government interference	Defense/ security	Moral/ ethical	Commun- ality (h^2)
Equal Rights Amendment	.22	−.11	.70	.56
Amendment banning abortion	.04	−.02	−.52	.27
Increase defense spending	−.19	.58	−.32	.48
National health insurance	.50	−.04	.19	.29
Nuclear power	−.19	.43	−.14	.24
Spending cuts/balance budget	−.20	.19	−.15	.10
Affirmative action programs	.30	−.15	.22	.16
Deregulation of oil and gas	−.48	.19	.02	.27
Wage and price controls	.68	.01	.03	.47
Reduce inflation	−.17	.31	.04	.12
Draft registration	.04	.49	.04	.25
Ratification of SALT II	.36	−.22	.42	.35
U.S. military in Middle East	−.02	.52	−.09	.27
Percent total variance	23.0	11.4	10.2	44.6
Percent common variance	61.2	21.0	17.8	100.0
Eigenvalue	2.99	1.49	1.33	

make difficult moral choices on pressing matters of national and international policy. Opposition to the ERA, affirmative action, national health insurance, and SALT II lie at one end of the scale, and support for increases in defense spending and an amendment banning abortion fall at the other.

With few exceptions, these general dimensions are found in the factor analyses performed for each major subgroup. However, the analyses reveal important differences across subgroups both in the scope of the dimensions (i.e., constituent items) and in the emphasis placed upon them.

Republican delegates demonstrate a dimensional structure comparable to that shown in table 9.6 (Republicans constitute 53 percent of the sample, Democrats the remaining 47 percent). Table 9.7 reveals that government interference is again the first dimension, identified by high loadings of wage and price controls (.68), national health insurance (.50), deregulation of oil and gas (−.48), and to a lesser extent, ratification of SALT II (.36) and affirmative action programs (.30). The defense/security dimension shows high loadings only for defense spending (.58), U.S. military presence in the Middle East (.52), draft registration (.49), and nuclear power (.43). The moral/ethical choice dimension is characterized by the loadings of the Equal Rights Amendment (.70), the abortion amendment (−.52), the SALT II Treaty (.42), and to a lesser degree, defense spending (−.32).

For Democratic delegates, defense/security emerges as the first dimension, followed by the moral/ethical choice dimension, with government interference last (see Table 9.7). The government interference dimension is much less prominent in the dimensional structure of Democrats than Republicans, accounting for just 9.5 percent of total space variation compared with 23.0 percent for Republicans. Surprisingly, a greater number of issues seem to take on moral overtones for Democrats than Republicans. In addition to the items which load high on this dimension for Republican delegates, significant loadings are found for the Democratic delegates on the ethical dimension for national health insurance (.34), nuclear power (−.29), cuts in nondefense spending (−.29), and U.S. military presence in the Middle East (−.22).

Because an overwhelming number (88 percent) of Republican delegates who indicated that they were pledged to a candidate were supporters of Ronald Reagan, the factor analysis based on these Reagan delegates

Table 9.8. Factor analysis of Carter and Kennedy delegates

Issue	Defense/ security	Moral/ ethical	Government interference	Commun- ality (h^2)
	Carter delegates (N = 3,462)			
Equal Rights Amendment	−.22	.66	−.08	.49
Amendment banning abortion	.17	−.28	.23	.16
Increase defense spending	.69	−.42	−.01	.65
National health insurance	−.12	.43	.51	.45
Nuclear power	.53	−.20	−.02	.33
Spending cuts/balance budget	.36	−.30	−.12	.23
Affirmative action programs	−.16	.53	.25	.37
Deregulation of oil and gas	.28	.07	−.32	.19
Wage and price controls	.03	.04	.54	.29
Reduce inflation	.34	−.10	−.19	.16
Draft registration	.58	−.18	−.03	.37
Ratification of SALT II	−.16	.42	.04	.20
U.S. military in Middle East	.60	−.16	.09	.40
Percent total variance	27.2	11.3	9.6	48.1
Percent common variance	68.2	18.9	12.9	100.0
Eigenvalue	3.54	1.47	1.25	

Issue	Liberal-Conservative/ Ideology	Economic/ budget	Government interference	Commun- ality (h^2)
	Kennedy delegates (N = 1,222)			
Equal Rights Amendment	−.45	.14	.34	.34
Amendment banning abortion	.46	−.04	−.09	.22
Increase defense spending	.73	.29	−.09	.63
National health insurance	−.17	−.19	.60	.43
Nuclear power	.59	.22	−.07	.41
Spending cuts/balance budget	.39	.30	−.12	.26
Affirmative action programs	−.32	.01	.45	.30
Deregulation of oil and gas	.06	.53	−.09	.29
Wage and price controls	.05	−.11	.34	.13
Reduce inflation	.19	.48	−.12	.28
Draft registration	.62	.26	−.10	.46
Ratification of SALT II	−.43	−.03	.26	.26
U.S. military in Middle East	.59	.25	.03	.41
Percent total variance	29.3	10.1	9.9	49.3
Percent common variance	72.6	14.5	12.9	100.0
Eigenvalue	3.81	1.31	1.28	

resembles very closely that for all Republican delegates (see Table 9.7). For the same reason, the dimensional structure for Democratic delegates pledged to Jimmy Carter is very close to that for all Democrats (72 percent of those delegates indicating a candidate pledge were committed to Carter). However, interesting differences distinguish Carter delegates from those pledged to Edward Kennedy. The factor analyses performed for these subgroups are presented in Table 9.8.

The most arresting aspect of Table 9.8 is the first dimension found for the Kennedy delegates. In contrast to the results for Carter delegates and all Democrats, this dimension reveals a pervasive ideological orientation which links social and military issues in a coherent framework—for the Equal Rights Amendment (−.45), affirmative action programs (−.32), and SALT II (−.43), and against the amendment prohibiting abortions (.46), cuts in nondefense spending (.39), as well as nuclear power (.59), the draft (.62), U.S. military presence in the Middle East (.59), and increases in defense spending (.73). As opposed to the Carter supporters, these delegates apparently do not conceive of defense/military as a separate issue or dimension but as part of an integrated liberal-conservative ideology. The Kennedy delegates also identify an explicitly economic/budget dimension, characterized by high loadings of deregulation of oil and gas prices (.53), action against inflation (.48), cuts in nondefense spending (.30), and increases in defense spending (.29). The single point of overlap between Carter and Kennedy delegates is the government interference dimension which appears for both groups, but even here differences are evident: Although national health insurance and wage and price controls are found in this dimension in the two subgroups, the factor analysis for Kennedy delegates also places the ERA (.34), affirmative action (.45), and the SALT II Treaty (.26) in this dimension, while the analysis based on Carter supporters adds deregulation of oil and gas prices (−.32). There was good reason, then, for the bitterness and controversy which surrounded the primary contest between Carter and Kennedy: Supporters of the two candidates saw the major issues from disparate perspectives.

The parties demonstrate intriguing differences between those holding public office and the rank and file. Nonofficeholders in each party visualize the issues in terms of the three dimensions found in Table 9.6: government interference, defense/security, and moral/ethical choice. However, Democrats again conceive the ethical dimension more comprehensively (i.e., with more constituent issues), and the defense/security dimension is the first factor for them, accounting for the most variance; government interference emerges first for the Republicans.

The dimensional structures underlying the policy attitudes of officeholders in each party are more complex. Factor analyses demonstrated that for both Democratic and Republican officeholders who served as convention delegates, the thirteen issues must be understood in more than three dimensions—four for the Democrats and five for the Republicans. The Democrats have as their first two dimensions the now familiar defense/security and moral/ethical factors found for most of the subgroups examined. However, like the Kennedy delegates (see Table 9.8), they also identify an economic/budget dimension characterized by the high loadings of deregulation of oil and gas prices (.64), cuts in nondefense spending to balance the federal budget (.43), action to reduce inflation (.38), and increases in defense spending (.25). Moreover, the final dimension is a pale reflection of the government interference continuum exhibited by all delegates as well as by Democratic delegates: For example, national health insurance, the keystone to this dimension for other subgroups, has a loading of just .24. Wage and price controls demonstrates the highest loading on the dimension, .53.

For Republican officeholders, the moral/ethical dimension is the first and most important, and defense/security is the second. The third dimension, government interference, is muted, with appreciable loadings for only wage and price controls (.57), deregulation of oil and gas (−.57), and national health insurance (.43). The abortion item, which loads heavily on no other factor, constitutes the fourth dimension with a loading of (.68); the Equal Rights Amendment (−.32) displays the next largest loading, implying a more broadly conceived women's rights dimension. The final dimension is concerned with economic/budget issues. Like the economic dimension found for Democratic officeholders, it is distinguished by the loadings of deregulation of oil and gas prices (.43), action to reduce inflation (.42), spending cuts to balance the budget (.32), and increases in defense spending (.27). In sum, although their policy attitudes diverge dramatically, the complexity of the attitudinal structures displayed by officeholders of both parties and the similarities found between structures suggest that these two groups may be closer to one another in their conception of major issues (but not in issue positions) than to the rank and file of their respective parties.

In contrast, members of the same party claiming different ideological predispositions (i.e., liberalism-conservatism) demonstrate more similar attitudinal frameworks. Factor analyses based on Democratic delegates who classify themselves as "liberal" as opposed to those who identify as "moderate" or "conservative" both show defense/security as the first dimension, with comparable, high loadings for defense spending, draft registration, U.S. military presence in the Middle East, and development of nuclear power. The moral/ethical dimension constitutes the second factor for the two groups, identified by significant loadings for the Equal Rights Amendment, increases in defense spending, and ratification of the SALT II Treaty. Yet, moderate/conservative Democrats also consider affirmative action programs (.51) and national health insurance (.45) part of this dimension, and the constitutional amendment prohibiting abortions falls in the dimension for liberal Democrats. Although a few discrepancies arise, the loadings for a core of critical variables identify the last two dimensions for both factions as economic/budget and government interference.

Liberal/moderate Republican delegates and conservative Republicans also conceive of the issues in comparable dimensions. For each group, defense/security (defense spending, draft registration, U.S. military presence in the Middle East, and nuclear power) constitutes the first dimension. The two factions also envisage a strong abortion/women's rights dimension, defined by high loadings for a constitutional amendment banning abortions and the Equal Rights Amendment. Liberal/moderate Republicans and their conservative counterparts identify a common government interference dimension, consisting of the ERA (loadings of .30/.43, respectively), defense spending (−.24/−.21), national health insurance (.29/.49), affirmative action (.49/.41), and ratification of SALT II (.41/.47). Finally, for both groups an economic/budget dimension emerges with deregulation of oil and gas prices, wage and price controls, and national health insurance the key components. With respect to dimensional structure, these analyses suggest that moderates have more in common in the conception of issues with the more partisan faction of their own party than with moderates in the other party.

In this chapter we have examined the content and structure of issue orientations of delegates to the 1980 state party conventions, with particular emphasis on issue constellations, or groupings, within the parties.

Issue constellations exist but are more evident and divisive within the Democratic than within the Republican party. They appear to be tolerated within the parties, perhaps even encouraged by them. Although these data cannot establish whether sanctions are brought to bear against party factions, the study does reveal substantial diversity of opinion among party leadership.

As hypothesized, Republican delegates were more homogeneous in opinion than Democrats. For Democrats, a wider range of issue positions may reflect a variety of delegate perspectives, including the attraction of a candidate, position in the party hierarchy, or ideological standing. For Republicans, ideology showed the strongest association with issue orientations.

Data analysis provided little evidence for the hypothesis that public officeholders within the Republican party adhere to different beliefs than nonofficeholders. Within the Democratic party, however, hierarchial differences were more marked and in the expected direction—i.e., public officeholders were more moderate or conservative in opinion than the more liberal substructure.

Candidate factions in both parties differed in opinion from fellow activists. Although the data available cannot answer the question of causal precedence governing candidate support and issue position, candidate factions displayed prominent intraparty differences in the content of belief systems. Again, these differences were more pronounced within the Democratic party. Kennedy delegates held quite different opinions than did Carter delegates; the latter were more moderate or divided in opinion than were the highly cohesive, ideological Kennedy supporters. Among Republicans, delegates who favored Reagan and those who did not were distinguished by less sharp differences on the issues.

Ideological groupings within the parties also demonstrated differences in the content of their beliefs. As anticipated, moderate Republicans held different opinions than conservative Republicans; moderate Democrats expressed more moderate views on the issues than did their more liberal counterparts. Nevertheless, moderates across parties did not always closely resemble one another. While in some instances the moderate factions were closer to each other than to the more extreme wing of their respective party, when ideological viewpoint and attitude structure are considered, overall, the groups resembled other delegates in their party more than moderates in the other party.

Factor analyses performed on the thirteen issues substantiated the hypothesis of a multidimensional structure underlying the attitudes of the party leadership. Three coherent dimensions emerged which characterized the entire sample of delegates as well as each of the party subgroups examined: These consisted of government interference, defense/security, and moral/ethical choice. An economic/budget dimension also characterized some of the subgroups (for example, officeholders in each party), and an abortion/women's rights dimension appeared less frequently, only among Republican delegates.

The factor analyses suggest that Democratic and Republican delegates conceived the issues in comparable dimensions, but that the dimensions differed in salience or priority across the two parties. Similarly, while ideological and candidate groupings within the parties viewed the issues from similar dimensional frameworks, important differences again arose. For example, Democratic delegates pledged to Edward Kennedy demonstrated the most comprehensive ideological dimension of any subgroup examined. The structure and content of their attitudes varied dramatically from that of delegates pledged to Jimmy Carter. These findings help to explain why the struggle between these two candidates and their followers was so intense: They saw the issues differently.

Officeholders in each party displayed complex attitudinal structures with four dimensions in common: defense/security, moral/ethical choice, economic/budget, and government interference. Delegates not holding office in the two parties also revealed a similar dimensional structure, consisting of government interference, defense/security, and moral/ethical choice. Thus, in both parties public officeholders may view the political landscape in a different and more complex fashion than the party substructure. The demands of holding office and appealing to a broad constituency may result in a more complicated political world for public officials.

This research shows that delegates to the 1980 Democratic and Republican party conventions in the caucus states differed in issue positions and attitude structures. These cleavages were reinforcing in the sense that groupings which differed in issue positions varied as well in the structure of their beliefs. Generally, the differences were related to position in the party hierarchy, candidate preference, and ideological perspective. In sum, the parties appear more a collection of similar views than a monolithic front.

NOTES

1. The factor analysis used was a principal factor with interaction (PA2), with a varimax rotation. Because of the difference in method of factor analysis, and a difference in weighting, the results differ slightly from those reported in chapter 8.

REFERENCES

Apter, David L. ed. 1964. *Ideology and Discontent*. Glencoe, Ill: Free Press.

Barton, A., and Parson, R. W. 1977. "Measuring Belief System Structure." *Public Opinion Quarterly*. 41:159-180.

Conover, Pamela J., and Feldman, Stanley. 1981. "The Origins and Meaning of Liberal/Conservative Self-Identifications." *American Journal of Political Science*. 25:617-645.

Conover, Pamela J., and Feldman, Stanley. 1980. "Belief System Organization in an American Electorate: An Alternate Approach." In *The Electorate Reconsidered*, edited by John Pierce and John L. Sullivan. Beverly Hills, CA: Sage Publications.

Costantini, Edward. 1971. "Intraparty Attitude Conflict: Democratic Party Leadership in California." In *A Comparative Study of Party Organization*, edited by William E. Wright. Columbus, OH: Charles E. Merrill.

Dunn, Delmar. 1975. "Policy Preference of Party Contributors and Voters." *Social Science Quarterly*. 55:983-990.

Eldersveld, Samuel J. 1964. *Political Parties: A Behavioral Analysis*. New York: Rand McNally.

Flinn, Thomas A., and Wirt, Frederick M. 1971. "Local Party Leaders: Groups of Like-Minded Men. In *Comparative Study of Party Organization*, edited by William E. Wright. Columbus, OH: Charles E. Merrill. pp. 225-246.

Herzon, Frederick D. 1980. Ideology, Constraint and Public Opinion: The Case of Lawyers. *American Journal of Political Science*. 24:233-258.

Jewell, Malcolm, and Olson, David. 1982. *American State Political Parties and Elections*. Homewood, IL: Dorsey Press.

Kirkpatrick, Jeane J. 1976. *The New Presidential Elite: Men and Women in National Politics*. New York: Russell Sage Foundation.

Marcus, George E., Tabb, D., and Sullivan, John L. 1974. The Application of Individual Differences Scaling to the Measurement of Political Ideologies. *American Journal of Political Science*, 18: 405-420.

Marvick, Dwane. 1980. Party Organizational Personnel and Electoral Democracy in Los Angeles, 1973-1978. In *The Party Symbol: Readings on Political Parties*, edited by William Crott. San Francisco: W. H. Freeman.

McCloskey, Herbert Hoffman, Paul J. and O'Hara, Rosemary. 1960. Issue Conflict and Consensus Among Party Leaders and Followers. *American Political Science Review*. 54: 406-427.

Montjoy, Robert S., Shafer, William, and Weber, Ronald. Policy Preferences of Pary Elites and Masses: Conflict or Consensus? *American Politics Quarterly*. 8: 319-343.

Nie, Norman H., Verba, Sidney, and Petrocik, John R. 1976. *The Changing American Voter.* Cambridge, MA: Harvard University Press.

Stimson, James A., 1975. Belief Systems: Constraint, Complexity, and the 1972 Election. *American Journal of Political Science*. 19: 393:417.

10

The Permeability of Parties

ROBERT W. KWEIT, MARY GRISEZ KWEIT

American political parties have traditionally been major links between the electorate and political officials. The primary way in which parties have performed that linkage function has been by making the electoral process more understandable to the voting public. While the public now may be less receptive to party cues than in the past, parties continue to try to simplify and guide the electoral choice of voters by reducing the number of alternatives, defining those alternatives, and providing stable symbols.

As a byproduct of performing such electoral functions, parties assumed various social roles which augment the electoral linkage. As Clinton Rossiter (1960) argued, "the parties serve a useful social purpose in acting as buffers and adjusters between individuals and society, especially as the latter intrudes into the lives of ordinary persons in the shape of impersonal political authority."

Because of the crucial role parties play in linking citizens to political authorities, the legitimacy of our representative government depends to a large extent on the degree to which the party system is open to infiltration and manipulation by new social forces. While it is clear, given the candidacies of George Wallace in 1968 and John Anderson in 1980, that a two-party system is not inevitable, it is also clear that at the present time no third party structure provides any meaningful competition to the dominance of the Democratic and Republican parties. This means that the openness of the party system is in essence equivalent to the openness of the two major parties.[1] It is the purpose of this study to examine one aspect of the openness of parties: the extent to which state party conventions are permeable to involvement by those representing social groups or issue positions which differ from those of the traditional coalition bases of the party.

In their quest for electoral majority, parties have traditionally attempted to have an inclusive rather than an exclusive membership. From the time that party workers literally met the boats full of immigrants at the docks, parties have devoted considerable efforts to ensure that the party-in-the-electorate achieves maximum size. Yet, while the party leaders sought inclusiveness in the party-in-the-electorate, they were never as eager to seek the same goal for the party leadership itself, or so it often seemed. An indicator of the extent to which the permeability of party leadership is considered important is the degree to which that leadership has been the focus of efforts by reformers to open its functions to more widespread involvement by the mass membership.

We have, in the last decade and a half, experienced the most recent of efforts to reform the parties. The reforms focused primarily on ensuring representativeness in the process of choosing delegates to the national conventions. Most agree that the primary impetus for this period of reform was the turbulent Democratic National Convention of 1968. Prior to that convention, an ad hoc committee of the Democratic party investigated complaints concerning the convention and concluded that "state systems for selecting delegates to the National Convention display considerably less fidelity to basic Democratic principles than a nation which claims to govern itself can safely tolerate." (Congressional Record 1968, E.9172). The charge made was basically that closed and unrepresentative groups of party regulars in the states were choosing convention delegates, thus limiting in significant ways which presidential candidates could be nominated. In the aftermath of this, a party commission chaired by George McGovern and Donald Fraser was created to right the wrongs which had become painfully clear in 1968. Austin Ranney (1974, 44), one of the members of that commission, identified the goals of that commission as follows:

> The prime objective . . . was not to make the party more combat-ready for November, but rather to ensure a more *representative* . . . national convention. More representative of whom? Not necessarily of all elements of the New Deal coalition, but rather of certain demographic groups—women, youth, minority groups—the commissions believed had been discriminated against by the traditional overstocking of conventions with middle-aged white males. Certainly *not* the representation of party notables or regulars or contributors, but rather of people who in 1972 were active on behalf of particular presidential aspirants. In Polsby's and Wildavsky's cate-

gories, the reforms were intended to maximize the representation of "purists," not of "professionals."

In this statement Ranney initially identifies the goal as one of assuring that the nomination process would be open to all demographic groups, and the force of the reforms which were adopted was aimed at providing what Pitkin (1967) refers to as "descriptive representation." The means by which this was to be achieved was a requirement that state parties insure that blacks, women, and young people be represented in the national convention delegations in proportion to their number in the population. Yet, as the last part of Ranney's statement implies, there was also concern about ensuring that varying viewpoints be guaranteed representation—"substantive representation" in Pitkin's terms.

Thus the major focus of these reforms was to increase the permeability of national conventions. The reforms have since been revised by the Mikulski and Winograd Commissions, yet the goals remained. As Keefe (1980, 4) concludes, the subsequent reform commissions "further refined party rules to increase intraparty democracy. The broad thrust of the 1969-1978 reforms was to increase popular participation in the presidential nominating process while at the same time diluting the power of party professionals." These reforms were intended as Democratic reforms, but the Republicans have in many cases also been affected because Democrat controlled state houses often made the reforms state law.

There seems to be widespread agreement that the reforms had a definite effect on the national conventions, although not entirely what was intended. As Jeane Kirkpatrick (1976) has thoroughly documented, a "new presidential elite" has come to dominate the national conventions. This elite included more minorities, women, and young people than had been present before and fewer of the traditional white, Anglo-Saxon, male party regulars. Thus the conventions became permeable by new groups, but it should be noted that they were not necessarily any more representative of the mass of party identifiers than were prereform delegates. She found the new delegates tended to have a much higher socioeconomic status and, especially among the Democrats, to hold issue positions that differed greatly from those of the party mass.

The effect of these reforms on the states is less well documented. *Cousins* v. *Wigoda* made it clear that the national parties had the legal right to determine the processes states use to choose delegates to the national conventions. It is also clear that since 1968, the number of presidential primaries has increased precipitately. The primaries have been the major focus of research on the effect of the reforms at the state level. Some have argued the increase was directly due to the reform (Wayne 1980, 86). Others contest this (Bode and Casey 1980, 16-18). More relevant to the topic of this paper has been research to determine the extent to which the voters in these primaries are representative of the general electorate. While the primary electorate has generally been seen as a small and atypical subset of the general electorate, Rubin (1980) has argued that the size of the primary electorate jumped in the postreform period. In addition, his analysis and that by Kritzer (1980) indicated that the primary electorate differs from the general electorate only in terms of level of partisanship and interest in politics, not in terms of demographics or issue concerns. This would seem to indicate primary states are highly permeable to new forces.

The evidence seems to indicate that the reforms have in fact altered the participation in national conventions and may have broadened the participation in state primaries. What has received less attention from researchers has been what has been going on in those states which did not jump on the primary bandwagon and which are still using the caucus-convention method for choosing delegates to the national conventions. This research will use the data on state party convention delegates in such states to assess the extent to which the conventions in those states are open to involvement by new groups in the party which differ in significant ways from those delegates who may be seen as more traditional party activists.[2]

In this chapter we investigate continuity and change among these convention delegates by a cohort analysis. Three types of new party activists were identified: (1) those who have recently become active in party politics; (2) those who have recently switched parties; and (3) those who are young and are thus of necessity new activists. Because of the potential important effect of the reforms of the last decade on the composition of the convention delegates, the years 1971-1980 were used to delineate the first cohort in each of these three groupings.

The years 1961-1970 delineated the second cohort in each grouping. This cohort was chosen for two reasons. In the first place it permits a clear comparison of pre- and postreform periods. This will provide evidence on the effect of the reforms on the permeability of these state conventions. Secondly, this period was one of extraordinary turbulence, when many new social forces were demanding increased access to the political process. Those delegates who became politically active, or who switched parties, or who came of political age during that time may well bear some imprint of that period that makes them distinct. If so, their presence in the state convention in 1980 would indicate both the permeability of the party and some continuing impact of that period on current politics. In addition, if such differences are found among those who became active during that period, this may be evidence that even before the reforms, parties were open to the activity of those who differed from traditional activists. Of course, no definitive judgment can be made on this point since it is impossible to know if they also differed at the time they became active.

The years before 1961 delineated the third cohort in each grouping. When examining the party switchers, those who have never switched parties constituted a fourth comparison group. Those active for more than twenty years, or those over forty years of age, or those who have never switched parties are considered to represent the mainstream of the party and the new activists were compared with these groups to determine if the conventions are permeable by activists who differ in significant ways from the mainstream.

There is one caveat to be made about this analysis. Like any cohort analysis, the cohorts are examined at one point in time, yet longitudinal inferences are often made which the data cannot directly support. For example, if the 1960s cohorts are found to differ from the other delegates, the data do not directly indicate the differences arose from the experiences in the 1960s. This is, however, not a major problem for the analysis. The question addressed here is not what is the origin of differences which are found, but rather whether the conventions in caucus-convention states are permeable by groups which differ from the traditional party activists.

Specifically, we will examine the extent of differences among the cohorts in each of the three groups of new party activists in both parties. Since the movement of new activists into the party is a primary form of party rejuvenation, it is to be expected that the attitudes of newer activists will differ from those of older activists.

There are three types of differences which will be examined here: demographic characteristics, organizational memberships, and issue positions. Demographic characteristics and organizational memberships determine the coalitional bases of the parties. Changes in this coalitional base are important because parties aim their appeals primarily at those who are believed to be their traditional supporters; this means that the involvement of new party activists with different demographic or organizational characteristics will potentially have long-range effects on the party platform and therefore on what the party attempts to achieve in government (Pomper and Lederman 1980, 146-47). This is the reason permeability of the parties is important. The linkage between party positions and the involvement of new activists who differ significantly in their issue positions is even more direct.

Initial investigations of the cohorts on the basis of these three types of differences indicated amazing similarity between the age cohorts and the length of activity cohorts. Suspecting that the similarity may be due to a large overlap between these cohorts, correlations between the cohorts were computed. Among the Democrats, the correlation was .72 and among the Republicans it was .70, confirming the overlap. Thus to avoid repetition, information on only the length of activity cohorts will be given. It was felt that those just becoming active would be more likely to be sources of new forces in the party than those just coming of political age. This was felt to be so because of the extent to which socialization tends to produce youth who do not differ significantly from the political characteristics of their parents. Correlations between the switching cohorts and the activity cohorts also indicated overlap.[3] Yet since the switchers were few in number compared with the activity cohorts and were expected to be an important source of new influence in the party, both the switchers and the activity cohorts were examined.

DEMOGRAPHIC CHARACTERISTICS

Research on party activists has consistently demonstrated that they tend to be recruited from the ranks of higher socioeconomic status (Verba and Nie 1972). The research by Kirkpatrick (1976) on national party conventions indicated that far from reducing this tendency, the reforms in the Democratic party seem to have produced delegates who differ even more significantly in terms of socioeconomic status.

The data on state convention delegates also contain no convincing evidence of increased involvement by lower socioeconomic groups among the newer cohorts. Tables 10.1 and 10.2 indicate that the recent switchers and those who have recently become active do tend to have a larger percentage of people in the lower income ranks than do those more

Table 10.1 Demographic bases of party support by length of party activity

	Democrats			Republicans		
	Less than 10 yrs. % (N)	10-20 years % (N)	More than 20 yrs. % (N)	Less than 10 yrs. % (N)	10-20 years % (N)	More than 20 yrs. % (N)
Race						
% Black	6.9 (354)	8.3 (138)	8.9 (142)	0.7 (38)	0.7 (14)	1.1 (15)
% Hispanic	2.3 (120)	1.9 (31)	1.2 (19)	0.4 (22)	0.2 (4)	0.1 (1)
Religion						
% Catholic	23.6 (1,166)	23.2 (377)	21.6 (341)	10.9 (561)	9.3 (172)	7.2 (100)
% Jewish	2.6 (129)	2.2 (35)	1.0 (16)	0.7 (36)	0.6 (11)	0.2 (3)
Education						
Less than high school	2.1 (153)	3.5 (58)	10.8 (170)	2.1 (107)	3.1 (57)	5.4 (76)
High school graduate	12.4 (632)	15.8 (259)	22.3 (351)	10.3 (536)	10.6 (197)	15.0 (210)
Some college	27.2 (1,390)	25.7 (420)	29.4 (463)	32.0 (1,666)	30.6 (567)	32.7 (457)
College graduate	22.9 (1,169)	16.1 (264)	13.8 (218)	26.9 (1,379)	26.2 (485)	22.1 (309)
Post college	34.6 (1,771)	38.8 (634)	23.7 (373)	28.7 (1,491)	29.5 (546)	24.6 (344)
Income						
$ 0 - 14,999	23.1 (1,064)	15.0 (243)	19.2 (283)	14.3 (712)	10.0 (176)	13.3 (171)
15 - 24,999	32.6 (1,625)	30.5 (493)	25.9 (382)	26.2 (1,308)	22.8 (400)	22.2 (286)
25 - 34,999	23.4 (1,165)	24.9 (403)	22.9 (338)	24.8 (1,239)	25.6 (449)	21.0 (271)
35 - 44,999	12.0 (596)	14.4 (233)	13.9 (206)	14.3 (716)	16.7 (293)	15.1 (194)
45 - 59,999	5.6 (278)	7.8 (127)	9.3 (137)	9.9 (493)	10.4 (182)	11.6 (150)
$60+	5.1 (256)	7.4 (120)	8.9 (131)	10.5 (522)	14.4 (253)	16.8 (216)

Table 10.2. Demographic bases of party support by switchers

	Democrats				Republicans			
	Recent switchers % (*N*)	Sixties switchers % (*N*)	Pre-sixties switchers % (*N*)	Non-switchers % (*N*)	Recent switchers % (*N*)	Sixties switchers % (*N*)	Pre-sixties switchers % (*N*)	Non-switchers % (*N*)
Race								
% Black	2.5 (8)	1.2 (3)	3.9 (21)	8.5 (584)	1.9 (11)	1.7 (8)	1.1 (10)	0.6 (37)
% Hispanic	1.3 (4)	0.8 (2)	1.1 (6)	2.2 (150)	0.2 (1)	1.1 (5)	0.2 (2)	0.3 (17)
Religion								
% Catholic	12.8 (38)	8.9 (20)	17.9 (94)	24.4 (1631)	16.9 (99)	14.4 (68)	10.8 (99)	8.7 (528)
% Jewish	1.7 (5)	1.2 (3)	1.1 (6)	2.3 (155)	0.9 (5)	1.3 (6)	1.0 (9)	0.5 (29)
Education								
Less than high school	1.5 (5)	0.4 (1)	4.8 (26)	4.7 (321)	1.3 (8)	1.7 (8)	2.0 (19)	3.0 (132)
High school	6.6 (21)	5.2 (12)	13.1 (71)	15.5 (1056)	8.3 (48)	10.0 (47)	11.0 (102)	11.4 (700)
Some college	25.0 (79)	19.0 (44)	26.9 (145)	28.0 (1906)	32.0 (184)	30.8 (144)	31.4 (292)	32.1 (1971)
College Graduate	19.0 (60)	15.1 (35)	18.7 (101)	20.2 (1378)	25.4 (146)	25.6 (120)	25.4 (236)	26.3 (1614)
Post college	47.8 (151)	60.3 (140)	36.5 (197)	31.6 (2150)	32.9 (189)	31.8 (149)	30.1 (280)	27.2 (1669)
Income								
$ 0 - 14,999	20.2 (63)	10.8 (25)	19.0 (100)	19.7 (1304)	17.2 (100)	8.8 (40)	8.2 (72)	13.6 (793)
15 - 24,999	29.8 (93)	29.7 (69)	27.5 (145)	31.3 (2073)	27.9 (162)	19.7 (90)	20.3 (178)	25.7 (1500)
25 - 34,999	22.8 (71)	29.3 (68)	24.3 (128)	23.4 (1548)	21.4 (124)	23.9 (109)	24.9 (218)	24.4 (1423)
35 - 44,999	14.1 (44)	16.8 (39)	13.9 (73)	12.8 (844)	13.8 (80)	18.4 (84)	17.5 (153)	14.6 (852)
45 - 59,999	5.8 (18)	7.8 (18)	8.7 (46)	6.6 (438)	8.8 (51)	12.1 (55)	13.0 (114)	10.0 (581)
$60+	7.4 (23)	5.6 (13)	6.6 (35)	6.2 (412)	10.9 (63)	17.1 (78)	16.1 (141)	11.6 (678)

traditional cohorts. Yet is is more plausible to argue this is due to the age of these groups rather than the greater involvement of lower socioeconomic status groups.

The overlap between age and length of activity has already been pointed out. The recent switcher cohorts in both parties had a larger percentage of people under thirty than did either of the other switching cohorts or the nonswitchers in the parties (29.9 percent among recent Democratic switchers and 26.5 percent among recent Republican switchers). The argument that their low income level may be only due to their stage of life is buttressed by the fact that newest cohorts also have the highest levels of education of any of the comparison groups, with a single exception. The exception is that group which switched to the Democratic party in the 1960s. Given the high correlation between education and income, it can be expected that the newest cohorts will attain higher income levels as they become more established in their careers.

Racial and religious groups have been important components of party coalitions. Axelrod (1972) identified nonwhites and Catholics as part of the New Deal Democratic coalition and whites and Protestants as Republicans. It has also been the case that Jews have traditionally been Democratic. Examination of these data indicate no major change in these patterns. An investigation of the activity cohorts indicates that by far the largest number of black delegates are Democrats, but the percentage of blacks appears to be declining slightly in both parties. This may be evidence that blacks are becoming politically disaffected and are withdrawing from traditional party politics, but it must be emphasized that the changes are small.

Other racial groups have been increasing in political activity, but there are relatively few of their representatives among these convention delegates. Hispanics are the only other minority group with a sizable representation at these conventions. By far the largest percentage of Hispanics are Democrats. If these increasing numbers among recent Democratic activists is an indication of a longitudinal trend, this may presage the creation of a new political force within the Democratic party. But again the numbers are small. The numbers of Hispanics among the switching cohorts in both parties are too tiny to warrant any generalizations.

Catholics and Jews are still predominantly Democrats. In both parties the percentage of Jews and Catholics among those who have recently become active is greater than among those active more than ten years. This increasing political presence may be related to the increasing importance of issues relevant to these groups—the viability of Israel for Jews and the banning of abortion for Catholics—although the direction of the relationship cannot be ascertained. Alternatively, since these groups include a high percentage of second and third generations of immigrant families, it may simply be the case that the increasing percentage of Catholics and Jews among recent activists may be due to increasing acculturation. Regardless of the reason for the increase, their increasing numbers may indicate their increasing importance in both parties, as well as an openness to these groups. Examination of the switching cohorts indicates there is a clear pattern of an increasing percentage of Catholics among recent switchers to the Republican party. This is very likely due to the fact that the Republican party has seemed to be more supportive of a constitutional amendment to ban abortion.

The evidence concerning the permeability of the parties by those with demographic characteristics which differ from those of traditional party activists is mixed. There is little reason to believe that these convention delegates are becoming any more representative of the population in terms of socioeconomic status. While these data in no way indicate the parties are not permeable by lower socioeconomic groups by design, they do indicate few representatives of the poor were present at these conventions. There was some evidence that fewer blacks were becoming active, but at the same time there were larger percentages of Hispanics, Jews, and Catholics among the new cohorts. The vast bulk of these groups were present in the Democratic party. Both Jews and Catholics were part of the traditional New Deal Democratic coalition and thus they do not indicate a major change in the coalitional base of that party. Two changes which may be important are the relatively large percentage of Catholics among recent switchers to the Republican party and the increasing percentage of Hispanics among recent Democratic activists. While the raw numbers in both cases are small, both groups are new additions to their present political homes, indicating some permeability.

No major changes are evident when the pre- and postreform activity cohorts were examined. However, those who switched to the Democratic party in the 1960s do differ in several ways from the other switching cohorts in that party. There are smaller percentages of blacks, Hispanics, Catholics, and Jews among the 1960s Democratic switchers. In addition, they have the highest level of education of any of the cohorts examined.

Table 10.3. Organizational membership by length of party activity

	Union	Ed. org.	Prof. org.	Business org.	Church group	Women's rts.	Civil rts.	Ecology	Pub. int.	Anti-abor.	Farm org.
Democrats											
Active less than 10 yrs.	14.7	25.8	19.6	11.3	24.3	18.8	18.3	14.7	20.0	5.1	8.5
(N)	(786)	(1,373)	(1,045)	(605)	(1,295)	(1,004)	(974)	(785)	(1,068)	(274)	(455)
Active 10-20 years	18.8	29.5	24.8	15.2	29.2	20.3	24.0	17.1	26.2	5.9	13.1
(N)	(330)	(516)	(434)	(267)	(512)	(356)	(421)	(300)	(459)	(103)	(229)
Active more than 20 yrs.	19.6	23.4	20.3	19.4	32.2	13.3	16.1	10.5	25.9	6.3	21.8
(N)	(335)	(400)	(346)	(332)	(549)	(227)	(275)	(179)	(442)	(108)	(372)
Republican											
Active less than 10 yrs.	2.9	13.2	21.1	22.0	36.4	4.1	2.1	6.2	13.8	11.6	8.6
(N)	(158)	(715)	(1,145)	(1,194)	(1,977)	(225)	(114)	(337)	(748)	(629)	(468)
Active 10 - 20 years	3.0	15.1	25.0	28.7	37.4	5.2	2.6	8.4	20.5	9.8	13.3
(N)	(57)	(292)	(483)	(555)	(721)	(101)	(50)	(162)	(395)	(189)	(256)
Active more than 20 yrs.	2.0	15.5	25.4	34.0	37.8	4.0	2.5	9.7	22.9	9.5	22.7
(N)	(30)	(229)	(377)	(504)	(560)	(59)	(37)	(144)	(340)	(141)	(336)

This evidence seems to indicate that one legacy of the 1960s is a group of people who switched to the Democratic party although differing from the demographic characteristics of the party. This finding parallels Kirkpatrick's (1976) discovery of the new professionals who became active in the national conventions in the 1970s. Further evidence for the uniqueness of this group can be found in the next section which examines the organizational membership of both the activity and the switching cohorts in each party.

ORGANIZATIONAL MEMBERSHIP

A second way of identifying changes in the party coalitions is to examine the organizational memberships of party activists. While activists may not always use their party strictly to further goals of their groups, it seems safe to assume that such memberships reflect the interests of the members and may provide a clue concerning what issues may be of concern to the party. Increasing involvement by members of organizations not previously represented in the party is an indicator of the openness of the party conventions.

Tables 10.3 and 10.4 provide information on the organizational memberships of the switching and length of activity cohorts of both parties. The pattern among the Democrats is virtually the same both among the activity cohorts and the switching cohorts. In both sets of cohorts the percentage of members of unions, farm, and church organizations is less among the newer cohorts. Also evident in both sets of cohorts is the uniqueness of those who switched to the Democratic party in the 1960s or who became active during that period. Those groups had high percentages of members in educational, professional, women's rights, civil rights, ecology, and public interest groups. The high percentage of educational and professional memberships is probably due to their high level of education noted earlier. The high percentages in the other groups, however, may well be a legacy of 1960s, for the issues which those groups represent were prominent during that period. The pre-1960s switchers also have high percentages of members of professional and public interest groups, but what seems to be most notable about them is the high percentage of church and farm memberships. This may simply be a reflection of the effects of the socialization process experienced by those who are old enough to have switched parties more than twenty years ago.

Table 10.4. Organization membership by switching cohorts

	Union	Ed. org.	Prof. org.	Business org.	Church group	Women's rts.	Civil rts.	Ecology	Pub. int.	Anti-abor.	Farm org.
Democrats											
Recent switchers	11.3	28.4	20.4	13.7	20.4	22.0	16.5	15.2	22.6	4.0	9.5
(N)	(37)	(93)	(67)	(45)	(67)	(72)	(54)	(50)	(74)	(13)	(31)
Sixties switchers	18.0	40.0	24.9	13.9	24.5	24.9	25.3	27.3	25.7	4.1	8.2
(N)	(44)	(98)	(61)	(34)	(60)	(61)	(62)	(67)	(63)	(10)	(20)
Pre-Sixties switchers	14.6	27.4	19.2	15.1	31.1	18.1	15.3	16.0	21.9	6.2	15.3
(N)	(82)	(154)	(108)	(85)	(176)	(102)	(86)	(90)	(123)	(35)	(86)
Non-switchers	16.8	25.5	20.7	13.6	26.9	17.7	19.4	13.6	22.6	5.5	12.2
(N)	(1211)	(1837)	(1491)	(979)	(1939)	(1273)	(1393)	(981)	(1624)	(396)	(875)
Republicans											
Recent switchers	6.4	15.6	22.5	22.6	42.2	4.9	5.4	6.5	13.0	19.5	7.8
(N)	(39)	(96)	(138)	(139)	(259)	(30)	(33)	(40)	(80)	(120)	(48)
Sixties switchers	3.1	14.8	27.6	29.2	34.7	3.9	3.3	8.0	18.7	12.9	10.1
(N)	(15)	(72)	(130)	(142)	(169)	(19)	(16)	(39)	(91)	(63)	(49)
Pre-Sixties switchers	2.7	13.9	26.6	27.1	34.5	3.8	2.0	7.7	20.0	9.3	10.3
(N)	(26)	(135)	(258)	(263)	(335)	(37)	(19)	(75)	(194)	(90)	(100)
Non-switchers	2.3	13.8	22.0	25.4	37.0	4.4	1.9	7.1	16.6	10.1	12.9
(N)	(149)	(882)	(1412)	(1626)	(2373)	(280)	(124)	(454)	(1063)	(648)	(825)

Among Republicans, when both the activity and the switching cohorts are examined, the only major changes seem to be decreases in the percentage of business, public interest, and farm organizations. No other changes are evident among the activity cohorts, but an examination of the switching cohorts shows some increases in the percentage of members of unions, church groups, and anti-abortion groups among recent switchers. While the percentages are small, the increase in the union memberships confirms the impression that union members are no longer solidly locked into the Democratic party. The increase in percentages of church and anti-abortion group memberships also confirms the fact that the Republican party has greater appeal to those who favor a constitutional amendment to ban abortion. This finding is probably related to the fact that larger percentages of Catholics are switching to the Republican party now than in the past.

Because these data are based solely on closed-ended questions, there is no way to tell if members of other groups have joined either of these parties. Yet, looking only at these organizations there is some evidence of the permeability of the parties. Whether one looks at switchers or those who became active in the 1960s, it is clear that the Democratic party was the recipient in the 1960s of new identifiers who differed in the percentage of members in organizations associated with issues prominent at that time. Conversely it would appear that currently it is the Republican party which is the recipient of those concerned about the moral issues which are prominent in political debate. Thus it would appear that both parties are permeable by delegates representing certain organizations in larger numbers than had previously been the case.

The evidence concerning the effect of the reforms on this permeability is not clear. Among the Republicans the increases in members of certain groups occurred among recent switchers, which may be some slight evidence that the reforms made the party more permeable. But it must be remembered that the Republican party was not affected by the reforms to the same degree as was the Democratic party. In addition, it might be expected that given its current leadership and position, the Republican party would be a more logical political home to church and anti-abortion groups than would the Democratic party. Thus the involvement of these group members may well have occurred regardless of the reforms.

Among the Democrats, the cohorts which stand out are those who became active in the 1960s and the 1960s switchers. There is no way of

Table 10.5. Mean index scores by switchers

	New issues		Traditional domestic		Strong America	
Category	Repub-licans	Demo-crats	Repub-licans	Demo-crats	Repub-licans	Demo-crats
Recent switchers	11.50	7.23	16.37	12.16	4.13	7.73
Sixties switchers	11.99	5.94	16.70	10.64	3.27	9.40
Pre-sixties switchers	11.72	7.28	16.68	10.18	2.94	7.61
Non-switchers	11.26	7.26	16.35	10.80	4.00	7.77

Note: The smaller the number the greater the support. All comparisons are significant at the .05 level.

knowing if those who became active in the 1960s also differed at that time. If the differences did exist at that time, it would indicate the party was permeable before the reforms. However, it is also intriguing to note that of the 1960s switchers, 64.1 percent have been active for less than ten years—after the time of the switch. This compares with 56.9 percent of the Republicans who switched in the 1960s and have been active for less than ten years. Again, it is impossible to prove that those who switched in the 1960s differed in terms of organizational memberships at the time of the switch. However the large numbers who became active after the reforms may indicate some greater openness of these party conventions to delegates with organizational memberships which differ from those of more traditional activists.

It must also be pointed out that the major differences occur between rather than within the parties. A higher percentage of Democrats than Republicans are active in unions, educational organizations, women's rights and civil rights organizations, ecology, and public interest groups.

ISSUE POSITIONS

The information presented so far contains only circumstantial evidence concerning how these cohorts differ in terms of issue positions. While socioeconomic status and organizational membership are related to political beliefs, the relationship is not perfect. The involvement of those with different demographic or organizational characteristics may not indicate much about the openness of the party if the new activists do not differ significantly on positions they take on issues which are politically rele-

Table 10.6. Mean index scores by length of activity

Length of activity	New issues		Traditional domestic		Strong America	
	Repub-licans*	Demo-crats	Repub-licans*	Demo-crats	Repub-licans*	Demo-crats
Less than 10 years	11.31	7.07	16.34	10.87	4.04	8.42
10-20 years	11.25	7.13	16.38	10.91	3.94	7.22
More than 20 years	11.25	8.01	16.33	11.04	3.78	6.04

Note: The smaller the number the greater the support.

*ANOVA not significant at the .05 level.

vant. This section will examine directly how the cohorts differ on positions they take on issues.

Questions concerning thirteen issues were included in these data. The responses were factor analyzed. Eleven of the thirteen questions loaded on one of three factors (see chapter 5 note 2 for results of factor analysis). The resulting factors were named Traditional Domestic (affirmative action, national health insurance, wage and price controls, and oil and gas deregulation), New Issues (ERA, abortion, and SALT II), and Strong America (nuclear power, defense spending, the draft, and Middle East). Additive scales were constructed for each factor, running from 4 to 20 for Traditional Domestic and Strong America and from 3 to 15 for New Issues; low scores indicate support for Traditional Domestic and Strong America positions and liberalism on New Issues (see appendix, question 19). Mean scores on these scales were then computed for each cohort and analysis of variance was used to determine if there were significant differences among the cohorts. The results appear in tables 10.5 and 10.6

Among the switching cohorts, all of the differences are significant, although in most cases the differences are not large. Among the Democrats, the 1960s switchers again stand out on two of the scales: New Issues and Strong America. That cohort was the most supportive of the New Issues index and the least supportive of Strong America. Again there is no way to know if those in this cohort had these positions at the time of their switch, yet their presence now among the delegates to these state party conventions indicates the liberal and pacifist concerns prominent in the 1960s are still being represented today. Among the Republicans, the 1960s switchers also stand out on the New Issues scale, on which they are the least supportive. This means that on that scale the 1960s switchers in the two parties are exact opposites of each other. On the Strong America scale, the pre-1960s switchers are the most supportive and on the Traditional Domestic issues all groups are extremely close.

Once again the major differences appear when comparing the parties. The largest difference (1.98) between the highest and lowest means of the four switching cohorts within a party occurs among Democrats, intriguingly on the Traditional Domestic issues. Among the Republicans, only on the Strong America scale is the difference between the highest and lowest mean greater than one point (1.19). In fact, the average difference between highest and lowest mean within the Democratic party cohorts is 1.70 and within the Republican party it is 0.67, indicating the Republicans are more consensual than the Democrats. Yet when the means between the parties are compared, for only two cohorts are the differences less than four points. When comparisons between the parties are made, the average difference between the means of comparable cohorts is 4.94.

These same between-party differences are also evident when the activity cohorts are examined. Yet there are even smaller differences within the parties among these cohorts. In fact, on the Traditional Domestic index there were no significant differences among the activity cohorts in either party. These issues represent the traditional divisions between the parties. Those just becoming active in the parties have apparently been socialized to accept this basic cleavage. In addition, there were no significant differences among these cohorts in the Republican party on the New Issues index. Of the cohort comparisons that produced significant differences, the pattern is linear. The newer Democratic activists were more supportive of the New Issues and in both parties the newer activists were more opposed to Strong America, although the Democrats were consistently more opposed than were the Republicans. The opposition of the newest activists to the Strong America index may well be due to the large numbers of people under thirty in that cohort.

In these data it would appear that of the two sources of new party activists who may differ in issue concerns from the mainstream of the party, those who switch to the party differ more than those who have recently become active in the party. The party switcher cohorts consistently produced significant differences on these indices. In the Republican party only on the Strong America index were there significant differences among the activity cohorts and in the Democratic party there were significant differences on both the New Issues and Strong America indices. In neither party were there significant differences on the Traditional Domestic index, which is composed of those issues which have traditionally divided the parties.

Among the Democrats it was clear that those who switched to the party in the 1960s are now espousing issue positions which are more liberal and more pacifist than those of any other cohort. This would seem to be an indicator of the permeability of that party. Again, the fact that 64.1 percent of these 1960s switchers did not become active until the seventies may indicate that the reforms did increase the openness of the party to new activists who differ from the mainstream. This conclusion must be tempered, however, by the fact that 60.3 percent of all Democrats had also been active for less than ten years. It thus may simply be the fact that few people stay active in party politics for more than ten years and the numbers may reflect this rather than the effect of reforms ten years ago to make the party more open. It may also be the case that those who switched parties simply needed a period of acculturation in their new party before becoming active.

For the Republicans, while the differences among the switching cohorts are significant, they are also small. The 1960s and pre-1960s switchers seem to be similar to each other and seem to be more conservative and hawkish than the recent switchers or the nonswitchers.

There was concern that the indices might have masked the differences among some cohorts. The factor analysis on which the indices were based was run using the entire data set. It may well be that the separate cohorts view the interrelationship among the issues differently. In fact when factor analyses are run for the cohorts, different factors are produced. Therefore separate analyses of variance were calculated for each of the issues within the cohorts.[4] The results appear in tables 10.7 and 10.8.

Among the Democratic switching cohorts, all differences were significant. Once again the uniqueness of the 1960s switchers is obvious. Of the thirteen issues, the 1960s switchers stand out on ten. They are the most supportive of ERA, affirmative action, and SALT II; and they are the most opposed to an anti-abortion amendment, increased defense spending, development of nuclear power, spending cuts, anti-inflation measures which may increase unemployment, draft registration, and the U.S. military presence in the Middle East—all positions that one might expect of a 1960s liberal.

Among the Republicans, three of the thirteen issues produced no

Table 10.7. Mean issue scores by switchers

	ERA	Anti-abortion	Defense spending	National health insurance	Nuclear power	Spending cuts	Affirmative action	Dereg. oil	Wage-price	Anti-inflation	Draft	SALT II	Military in Mideast
Republicans													
Recent switchers	3.95	3.31	4.38	4.44	3.85	4.00*	3.76	4.03*	4.04*	3.50	3.83	4.24	3.74
(*N*)	(603)	(600)	(603)	(604)	(597)	(599)	(598)	(590)	(594)	(586)	(593)	(591)	(591)
Sixties switchers	4.18	3.18	4.66	4.50	4.11	4.12	3.91	4.02	4.05	3.72	4.08	4.43	3.89
(*N*)	(480)	(474)	(477)	(479)	(479)	(476)	(471)	(473)	(471)	(466)	(472)	(474)	(475)
Pre-sixties switchers	4.00	3.06	4.48	4.45	4.14	3.97	3.72	4.07	3.97	3.66	3.96	4.28	3.82
(*N*)	(954)	(945)	(949)	(950)	(945)	(945)	(933)	(934)	(937)	(910)	(936)	(921)	(938)
Non-switchers	3.95	3.15	4.43	4.52	3.98	4.00	3.69	4.02	3.96	3.66	3.81	4.26	3.74
(*N*)	(6288)	(6266)	(6289)	(5952)	(6256)	(6252)	(6173)	(6171)	(6188)	(6076)	(6204)	(6133)	(6170)
Democrats													
Recent switchers	2.00	2.21	2.93	2.99	2.70	2.88	2.60	3.10	3.21	3.05	3.26	2.67	3.11
(*N*)	(325)	(322)	(323)	(321)	(319)	(321)	(320)	(319)	(323)	(318)	(321)	(318)	(322)
Sixties switchers	1.72	1.81	2.47	2.47	2.46	2.49	2.38	2.86	3.10	2.64	2.94	2.27	2.90
(*N*)	(242)	(240)	(241)	(243)	(241)	(241)	(239)	(239)	(240)	(237)	(234)	(240)	(241)
Pre-sixties switchers	2.26	2.40	3.03	2.81	2.87	2.76	2.67	2.87	3.09	2.93	3.35	2.70	3.09
(*N*)	(544)	(538)	(544)	(542)	(541)	(534)	(531)	(533)	(533)	(534)	(531)	(527)	(532)
Non-switchers	2.05	2.47	2.92	2.49	2.74	2.79	2.42	2.89	2.86	2.85	3.28	2.56	3.14
(*N*)	(6967)	(6907)	(6880)	(6120)	(6852)	(6784)	(6806)	(6696)	(6734)	(6707)	(6796)	(6627)	(6784)

*ANOVA not significant at the .05 level.

Table 10.8. Mean issue scores by length of activity

	ERA	Anti-abortion	Defense spending	National health insurance	Nuclear power	Spending cuts	Affirmative action	Dereg. oil	Wage-price	Anti-inflation	Draft	SALT II	Military in Mideast
Republicans													
Active less than 10 years	3.98*	3.17	4.41	4.50*	3.92	3.98*	3.72*	3.98	3.97*	3.59	3.84*	4.28	3.76*
(*N*)	(5232)	(5218)	(5255)	(4987)	(5211)	(5208)	(5161)	(5145)	(5155)	(5073)	(5167)	(5118)	(5160)
Active 10-20 years	3.93	3.05	4.44	4.54	4.04	4.04	3.72	4.06	3.97	3.68	3.83	4.27	3.71
(*N*)	(1899)	(1884)	(1893)	(1823)	(1882)	(1882)	(1858)	(1855)	(1875)	(1831)	(1873)	(1846)	(1859)
Active more than 20 years	3.94	3.19	4.49	4.51	4.13	4.01	3.66	4.06	3.93	3.79	3.86	4.20	3.76
(*N*)	(1428)	(1421)	(1436)	(1331)	(1421)	(1412)	(1394)	(1400)	(1398)	(1361)	(1401)	(1388)	(1392)
Democrats													
Active less than 10 years	1.94	2.30	2.76	2.55*	2.53	2.70	3.39	2.88	2.95	2.80	3.11	2.60	3.01
(*N*)	(5140)	(5117)	(5114)	(4399)	(5100)	(5072)	(5071)	(5000)	(5023)	(5009)	(5048)	(4971)	(5047)
Active 10-20 years	2.03	2.45	2.88	2.53	2.78	2.75	2.44	2.87	2.89	2.84	3.31	2.46	3.16
(*N*)	(1697)	(1683)	(1676)	(1520)	(1675)	(1656)	(1655)	(1631)	(1632)	(1628)	(1658)	(1610)	(1645)
Active more than 20 years	2.46	2.83	3.41	2.52	3.34	3.08	2.64	2.99	2.76	3.10	3.75	2.56	3.42
(*N*)	(1582)	(1549)	(1542)	(1449)	(1527)	(1498)	(1505)	(1491)	(1511)	(1495)	(1529)	(1462)	(1524)

*ANOVA not significant at the .05 level.

significant differences. Of the ten remaining issues, the 1960s and the pre-1960s switchers stand out as the most conservative on ERA, affirmative action, SALT II, increased defense spending, draft registration, and the U.S. military presence in the Middle East. Thus, when the separate issues are examined, the 1960s switchers to both parties appear as polar opposites. Again, the differences between the parties are greater than those within the parties.

When the Democratic activity cohorts are examined, only on the issue of national health insurance were there no significant differences. Of the remaining twelve issues, nine produced a linear pattern with the newer cohorts more liberal on ERA, affirmative action, an anti-abortion amendment, increased defense spending, development of nuclear power, spending cuts, anti-inflation measures, and the U.S. military presence in the Middle East. There is thus much similarity in the issue positions of the 1960s switchers and of those who recently became active.

Among the Republicans, on seven of the thirteen issues there were no significant differences among the activity cohorts. On three of the remaining six issues, there is a linear pattern parallel to that in the Democratic party, with the recent activists more liberal on increased defense spending, nuclear development, and anti-inflation measures. But all of the Republican cohorts are more conservative on these issues than any Democratic cohort.

This examination of the activity cohorts indicates the Democrats are experiencing an influx of new activists who are more liberal than the mainstream activists. The pattern is linear, with no major changes apparent following the reforms. The new activists in the Republican party, however, do not differ significantly from those active for longer periods on seven of the thirteen issues examined.

Our purpose in this chapter was to examine the permeability of state party conventions in eleven states which still choose national convention delegates by the caucus-convention method. The permeability of these conventions by new social forces is of major importance both because it may affect the composition of the national conventions and because it determines the degree to which the parties can legitimately claim to act as linkage mechanisms between the population as a whole and governing officials. It must be reiterated that failure to find changing representation among the new activists does not necessarily indicate the parties are deliberately denying entrance to new groups. Rather it may simply be that such groups are remaining out of politics or using other means besides the parties to participate.

Before the results of the cohort analysis are reviewed, it is important to point out that 61 percent of the convention delegates in the Republican party and 60.3 percent in the Democratic party have been active for less than ten years. In addition, 23.4 percent of the Republican delegates and 12.9 percent of the Democratic delegates had once considered themselves members of the opposite party. In fact 8.3 percent of the Republicans and 5.6 percent of the Democrats had switched in the last ten years. The fact that those new activists could be chosen as delegates to the state party conventions is itself an indicator that the conventions are not composed solely of a closed elite. Yet such numbers mean little in terms of representation if the new activists are similar or identical to those active in the party for longer periods of time.

Examination of the demographic characteristics of the new activists did not indicate any major change. Research has indicated that national convention delegates tend to have higher socioeconomic status than the population as a whole. This paper provides evidence that state party convention delegates also have higher income and education levels than the population. While the new activists have slightly lower incomes, than mainstream activists, they also have higher education levels. This would seem to indicate the lower incomes are due to life cycle rather than being an indicator of increasing representation of lower socioeconomic groups. No large influx of new religious or racial groups was evident in either party. In fact the percentage of blacks is less among recent cohorts than among the mainstream cohorts. There is, however, some evidence that Catholics are switching to the Republican party. In general there appears to be no evidence of major change in the demographic characteristics of new activists compared with the mainstream cohorts.

In many ways those who switched to the Democratic party in the 1960s stand out, but they were even less representative of the population as a whole. There were fewer blacks, Hispanics, Jews, and Catholics among that cohort and they had an extremely high level of education. This is similar to what Kirkpatrick (1976) found in her examination of national convention delegates in the 1970s. Among these delegates, that did not seem to foretell a continuing pattern since recent switchers and recent activists don't share the characteristics of the 1960s switchers. Examination of the organizational membership of the new cohorts also indicated few major changes. For the most part, the pattern seemed to be that of declining percentages of members in the organizations examined rather than increasing percentages. The exception to this pattern occurred among the Republicans where slightly larger percentages of members of unions, church groups, and anti-abortion groups appeared among recent switchers. Once again the switchers to the Democratic party in the 1960s stand out. Larger percentages of that cohort than any other cohort were members of groups representing concerns which were dominant at the time that they switched parties. Since the information on organizational membership was gathered by closed-ended questions, there was no way to know if members of other groups are becoming more active in these party conventions. Yet there is evidence here that both parties have been permeable to larger percentages of members of some groups. The evidence on the effect of the reforms is not clear since the data are not longitudinal. It may, however, be important that 64.1 percent of the Democratic switchers who do differ in organizational memberships did become active within the last ten years, perhaps indicating the reforms increased the permeability of the party.

While there is evidence that the parties are permeable to delegates with differing organizational affiliations, it must also be kept in mind that there is much more difference between the parties than within them. Therefore, while permeable, the parties have apparently not been the object of invasion by groups which would change in a major way the basic characteristics of the parties.

This same conclusion can be drawn from an analysis of the issue positions of the cohorts. Greater differences occur between rather than within parties. This is especially true in the case of the length of activity cohorts within the Republican party. On two of the three indices and seven of the thirteen issues there were no significant differences among these cohorts. There are significant differences among the switching cohorts in both parties on the indices and for most of the separate issues. In the Democratic party the 1960s switchers stand out as the most liberal and in the Republican party the 1960s and pre-1960s switchers are the most conservative. The fact that these switchers are delegates at the state conventions although having once been a member of the opposite party and differing in issue positions is itself evidence of the permeability of the parties.

These differences may well point to something else besides the permeability of the parties. Many have argued for the creation of responsible parties which would take clear positions on issues and which would therefore provide the voter with clear alternatives. During the 1960s a movement toward such parties apparently began. There was during that time an incipient realignment with liberals moving out of the Republican party and into the Democratic party and conservatives making the reverse move. These liberals are more liberal than the mainstream of the Democratic party and the conservatives are more conservative than the mainstream of the Republican party.

Of these liberals, 64 percent did not become active until after the reforms. Yet one must be cautious in concluding the reforms made the party much more permeable to them. Looking at the opposite side of the coin, 36 percent became active at approximately the same time that they switched parties—before the reforms. It may be that the reforms made it easier for this group to get involved, yet the party was certainly not closed to them before. As argued before, the switchers may simply have needed time to become acculturated to their new party before becoming active. Or, it may be that this group previously used other means than party politics to express their views and are only now moving into traditional party politics.

It is only possible to speculate about what effects these switchers have had or may have on the parties. Presumably their goal would be to pull the parties away from the traditional centrist politics. Predictably, the Republican switchers were strongly supportive of Ronald Reagan, who is seen as a spokesman for conservative positions. Yet what is not as predictable is the fact that a majority of the Democrats who switched in the 1960s were supportive of Jimmy Carter, despite the fact that they perceived themselves as more liberal than Carter. Their support may be due to the fact that a large majority believed Carter had a good chance to win in 1980. Presumably, the traditional goal of party politics—winning—was more important than ideology. This shows that they were then willing to play the party game, which may minimize the effect they would have on changing the party. In addition, they represent only a small percentage (3.4 percent) of the delegates at these conventions, which also minimizes their influence.

On the other hand, these 1960s switchers had high levels of party activity. Indices were created from questions dealing with other forms of

Table 10.9. Activity levels among switchers/non-switchers

Category	Republicans			Democrats		
	Party activity	Campaign activity	N	Party activity	Campaign activity	N
Recent switchers	1.32	2.43	(674)	1.62	3.00	(328)
Sixties switchers	2.36	3.18	(487)	2.21	3.93	(245)
Pre-sixties switchers	2.18	3.01	(970)	1.73	2.95	(562)
Non-switchers	2.10	2.87	(6413)	1.89	3.15	(7195)

Note: All comparisons significant at the .05 level.

party and campaign activities in which these delegates had taken part.[5] As Table 10.9 shows the 1960s switchers in both parties had the highest scores of any of the switching cohorts on the campaign index and second highest on the party index. Thus, while small in numbers they have the potential of influence because of their activity levels.

If these switchers were to have an effect on the parties, the change would be felt more by the Democrats. The Republican switchers stand out, but not to the same extent as do the Democrats. The Democratic delegates in general are less consensual than the Republican delegates, which means that change is thus more likely among the Democrats. This is especially the case because the delegates in the Democratic party who had been active for less than ten years were similar to the 1960s switchers in terms of issue positions. It may be that the high activity levels of the 1960s switchers in the Democratic party has created an image of the party which makes it attractive to new activists who share the views of the switchers.

Regardless of the impact of the 1960s switchers, their presence at these state party conventions is an indicator of the permeability of the conventions by those who differ from the traditional activist cohorts. Yet for the most part, the differences found are not large. The parties have not been invaded by activists who differ dramatically from the traditional activists, but rather by those who take basically the same, but slightly more extreme stands on the issues. Differences between the parties are consistently larger than differences within the parties on both issue positions and organizational affiliation. Only on socioeconomic status do the two parties look similar. Both Republican and Democratic conventions had delegations with higher income and education levels than the population as a whole, indicating these conventions are not as representative of the general electorate as Rubin (1980) and Kritzer (1980) found the primaries to be.

The fact that more than 60 percent of each party has been active less than ten years would seem to indicate that access is open to new participants. Since the 1960s switchers to the Democratic party are ideologically distinct from other groups and since about two-thirds have been active less than ten years one can speculate that reform has made the party more permeable. On the other hand the conventions appear to have been open prior to reform. Perhaps, the reforms simply made it easier for new activists. In general it appears that while large percentages of these delegates are new activists and while parties are permeable by those who do differ, the differences are more a difference in degree than a difference in kind. Winning is still important regardless of ideological orientation. As the French would say, "Le plus ça change, le plus c'est la même chose."

NOTES

1. For a contrary argument on the need to close parties and encourage opening the electoral system to new parties, see Ceaser (1980).

2. In this paper, the term activist is used to refer to these convention delegates. It is recognized that attendance at a state convention is not necessarily an indicator of participation in other forms of party activity. Information on the level of party and campaign activity of these delegates is presented later in the paper.

3. Among the Democrats, of the 5,438 who had been active less than ten years, only 491 (9 percent) had switched parties in the last ten years. Among the Republicans, the comparable numbers are 730 of 5,332 (14 percent).

4. While analysis of variance assumes a normal distribution, it has been shown that the accuracy of the F statistic is not seriously threatened by relaxing this assumption (Lindquist 1953, 86).

5. For the party activity index, the number of positions respondent had held in the party (question 6 in the appendix) were counted. For the campaign activity scale, the number of different campaign activities respondent had done were summed (question 10 in the appendix).

REFERENCES

Axelrod, Robert. 1972. "Where the Votes Come From: An Analysis of Electoral Coalitions, 1952-1968." *The American Political Science Review* 66 (March): 11-20.

Bode, Kenneth A. and Carol F. Casey. 1980. "Party Reform: Revisionism Revised." In *Political Parties in the Eighties,* edited by Robert A. Goldwin, Washington, D.C.: American Enterprise Institute.

Ceaser, James W. 1980. "Political Change and Party Reform." In *Political Parties in the Eighties*, edited by Robert A. Goldwin, Washington, D.C.: American Enterprise Institute.

Congressional Record. 1968. "Hughes Committee Report: The Democratic Choice," October 14: E. 9172.

Cousins, v. *Wigoda* (1975), 419 U.S. 477.

Keefe, William J. 1980. *Parties, Politics and Public Policy in America*, 3rd ed. New York: Holt, Rinehart, & Winston.

Kirkpatrick, Jeane, J. 1976. *The New Presidential Elite*. New York: Russell Sage.

Kritzer, Herbert M. 1980. "The Representativeness of the 1972 Presidential Primaries." In *The Party Symbol*, edited by William Crotty. San Francisco: W. H. Freeman.

Lindquist, Everet F. 1953. *Design and Analysis of Experiments in Psychology and Education*. Boston: Houghton-Mifflin.

Pitkin, Hannah. 1967. *The Concept of Representation*. Berkeley: University of California Press.

Pomper, Gerald M. with Susan S. Lederman. 1980. *Elections in America: Control and Influence in Democratic Politics*, 2nd ed. New York Longman.

Ranney, Austin, 1974. "Comment on 'Changing the Rules Changes the Game.' " *The American Political Science Review* 68 (March): 43-44.

Rossiter, Clinton. 1960. *Parties and Politics in America*. Ithaca: Cornell University Press.

Rubin, Richard. 1980. "Presidential Primaries: Continuities, Dimensions of Change, and Political Implications." In *The Party Symbol*, edited by William Crotty. San Francisco: W.H. Freeman.

Verba, Sidney and Norman H. Nie. 1972. *Participation in America: Democracy and Social Equality.* New York: Harper & Row.

Wayne, Stephen J. 1980. *The Road to the White House: The Politics of Presidential Elections*. New York: St. Martin's.

11

Extremist Delegates: Myth and Reality

CHARLES S. HAUSS, L. SANDY MAISEL

Both major parties were "opened up" considerably after the tumultuous 1968 Democratic convention. State laws and party rules were changed to make primaries the dominant way we select delegates to state and national conventions. Even where primaries are not used, the caucus procedures were changed to give grassroots party members more influence.

But the open party has also been the subject of much criticism, at least since the nomination and overwhelming defeat of Senator McGovern in 1972. Each party has enacted a wave of counter-reforms designed to cure the modern "mischief of faction" often attributed to the new, more open procedure (Ranney 1975). Most recently the Democrats have adopted the Hunt Commission reforms, which went into effect for the 1984 convention. Those reforms are typical of the changes taking place in both parties. Among other things, the reforms shorten the delegate selection "season," presumably to limit some of the alleged irrationalities produced by the primary system (Kirkpatrick et al. 1980; Lengle 1981). The commission has also tried to blunt the impact of the post-1968 reforms by increasing the role party leaders played at the 1984 convention and afterward.

These counter-reforms are all in some way inspired by criticisms of the open party levelled by the so-called neoconservatives (Kirkpatrick 1976; Ranney 1975). In their eyes, the open party has brought the "wrong" kinds of people into the parties—ideologues who would make disastrous choices such as nominating McGovern.

The neoconservatives are by no means the first group of observers to make this kind of criticism. In the 1950s and 1960s such activists were described as amateurs who did not share the winning-is-all-that-counts focus of the so-called professionals.

The neoconservatives are following a similar line of reasoning when they argue that rules changes have given ideological extremists an opportunity to take over one or both of the major parties. They continue by claiming that these individuals are more likely to have an amateur role orientation and to be more concerned with the adoption of their own political views as a basis for party platforms rather than seeking one which serves the good of the party, most frequently defined as nominating a candidate and adopting a platform which will most likely lead to victory in November (Wildavsky 1965; Soule and Clarke 1970; Sullivan et al. 1974; 1977; Kirkpatrick 1976; Nakamura and Sullivan 1981).

In short, the neoconservatives are worried that ideologues are encouraged to enter the delegate selection process because of the openness of that process and that they will place principle above pragmatism, adopt platforms which hurt the parties' efforts to form majority coalitions, and will nominate "pure" candidates who will lose the November election. They feel that takeover of the parties by activists who can be characterized by ideological extremism, tactical amateurism, and devotion to purist, issue-oriented candidates will have serious negative consequences for the parties and for politics in general, consequences that go beyond the nomination of a losing candidate like McGovern to the evolution of a system in which public policy directions swing vastly from administration to administration in a way which would be detrimental to American policy at a time when consistency and stability, not chaos, is required (for a British version of this argument, see Rose 1980).

The party leaders responsible for the Hunt Commission and other reforms clearly accept at least the broad outlines of the neoconservative analysis, since they have tried to increase the influence of party regulars in the nomination process. Yet, oddly, that analysis has never been subjected to the kind of empirical analysis it warrants. Serious research on the new, open party and its strengths and weaknesses is just beginning nearly a decade after the McGovern debacle and the beginnings of the neoconservative movement.

Austin Ranney organized a panel at the 1981 annual meetings of the American Political Science Association to begin dealing with the neoconservative critique of the nominating process in a systematic fashion. Robert Nakamura and Denis Sullivan (1981) presented a cogently argued critique of the most frequent criticisms of that process. In this chapter, we continue that investigation and reinforce this skeptical reaction to the criticisms of the new party and its activists.

Delegates to state conventions which selected delegates to the national conventions without presidential preference primaries provide us with another view of the impact of the post-1968 reforms. Despite the fact that these delegates were not chosen in primaries, they were selected in a manner which was open, which was marked by proportional representation of presidential preferences (at least for the Democrats), and which was certainly susceptible to take-over by nonregulars. (Nakamura and Sullivan 1981, 5ff.). Those observing caucuses which selected state convention delegates in these states were often struck by the fact that the first-level caucuses looked more like primaries in which the polls were only open for a short period of time than the closed door caucuses of an earlier era (see Maisel, chapter 2). Hence, while we cannot use the data from the state party delegate study to test the entire neoconservative argument, we can use them to continue exploring one of its most important empirical elements—the role of activists—and see if there are many of those the neoconservatives fear. And we can determine what their influence on party life is and get some idea as to how likely they are to take over either of the major parties in the near future.

IDEOLOGUES IN THE PARTIES

The first task in evaluating the neoconservative theory is to identify those delegates who qualify as the type of ideologues the neoconservatives fear.[1] Neither our questionnaire nor the professional literature provides the convenient indicators of the main aspects of the neoconservatives' critiques—ideological identification, attitudes on issues, and attitude on the role of party. We have constructed indices which identify those delegates with whom we are concerned.

First, we identified ideologues on issues. For each delegate we totaled the number of issues on which s/he responded with an extreme position—on the left for the Democrats and on the right for Republicans (see appendix, question 19).[2] Second, we developed a similar index which taps an individual's attitude about proper party strategy (question 14). We gave a score of 1 for each ideological answer to the questions regarding whether or not a candidate should compromise his/her values in order to win, whether the party platform should avoid controversial issues, and so on. (It would have been useful to examine the effects of these variables on candidate choice as well. However the anti-organizational extremist candidates that were present in 1964, 1972, and 1976, were absent in 1980,

Table 11.1. Number of extreme answers on issues and party tactics

	Issues (Percent)		Party tactics (Percent)	
	Democrats	Republicans	Democrats	Republicans
None	19.5	4.5	14.9	16.3
1	18.6	7.5	19.8	18.6
2	17.3	8.2	20.8	18.0
3	12.4	10.2	19.4	17.7
4	9.5	10.5	13.8	15.9
5	6.6	11.0	11.3	13.5
6	5.1	10.6		
7	3.6	9.8		
8	2.8	9.2		
9	2.0	7.8		
10	1.3	6.0		
11	1.0	3.5		
12	0.3	1.3		
N	6429	7246	7656	7884

with the possible exception of the short-lived Crane campaign.)

Table 11.1 presents the distributions on these indicators. Even a most cursory analysis shows that there is a major flaw in the neo-conservatives' analysis. Ideologues do not dominate either party. Only 4.6 percent of the Democrats and 18.6 percent of Republicans gave extreme answers on nine or more of the twelve issues. While one could claim that these are not insignificant numbers, none of the questions posed permitted us to identify true radicals or reactionaries. If one scored a twelve on our scale, one could still fall within the mainstream of our political system, a liberal or a conservative to be sure, but not necessarily a radical or a reactionary. Yet only 1.3 percent of Republicans and 0.3 percent of Democrats did so.

Similarly 25.1 percent of the Democrats and 29.4 percent of Republicans qualified as ideologues on the question of party tactics, by taking the nonprofessional extreme on at least four of the five questions posed. Again, though these numbers are far from meaningless, one could easily take the extreme position on all of these questions, achieve the perfect score of five on the tactical scale, and still not be someone only interested in ideology and issues and not in winning. Again, only slightly more than one in ten respondents fell into the most extreme category.

Table 11.2. Interrelationships among ideological indicators

	Issues		Party tactics	
	Democrats	Republicans	Democrats	Republicans
Party tactics	.14	.22	—	—
	(5951)	(6707)	—	—
Political philosophy[a]	−.45	.40	−.05	.20
	(6242)	(7114)	(7432)	(7771)

Note: Entries are Kendall's tau-*b*s.

[a]Response to the question "How would you describe your own political philosophy?" Answers run from very liberal to very conservative.

CHARACTERISTICS OF THE EXTREMISTS

To this point we have defined ideologues as those who qualify on either one of the dimensions indicated. The neoconservatives argue, however, that these factors, ideological extremism, and an amateur definition of the role of party, are part and parcel of a common approach to party politics. If this is so, then these dimensions should be highly correlated and related as well to an individual's self-perception of his/her placement on a liberal/conservative spectrum.

Not surprisingly, the individuals who call themselves "very liberal" Democrats or "very conservative" Republicans are likely to score high on our indices. The conclusion from table 11.2 is that the delegates' ideological self-perceptions relate mainly to their views on the issues of the day. But significantly, self-described liberals in the Democratic party and conservatives in the Republican party are not of one mind on questions relating to the role of party.

Perhaps asking the ideologues we have identified to fit neatly into one view of politics is demanding too much of the neoconservatives. At the heart of their criticism is not just that these individuals are ideologues, but that they are not loyal party members. Massachusetts Congressman Barney Frank has described participants of this type as "tumbleweeds," because they blow in and out of the major parties, touching down as active participants only when the candidates and issues turn them on.

We compiled an index to measure respondents' past involvement in party life in order to test the "tumbleweed" hypothesis. We looked at whether or not the respondent had been a delegate before, whether s/he

Table 11.3. Ideologues and party loyalty

	Activism in the past		Ever switch party identification		1976 vote[a]	
	Demo-crats	Repub-licans	Demo-crats	Repub-licans	Demo-crats	Repub-licans
Issue	−.04	−.07	.01	−.03	−.05	.04
	(6353)	(7149)	(6269)	(7060)	(6242)	(7077)
Party role	.06	.06	.01	−.04	.05	−.05
	(7566)	(7775)	(7354)	(7668)	(7366)	(7670)

Note: Entries are Kendall's tau-b correlations between issues and party role ideologue scales and loyalty measures.

[a]Vote is coded as 1 Carter, 2 did not vote, 3 Ford.

had been involved in earlier campaigns or held party office, how long the delegate had been active in party life, whether s/he had voted in the 1976 presidential election. If the ideologues had "tumbleweed" tendencies, they should have shown up at some point—a disloyal vote, limited past involvement in party life, prior affiliation with the other party.

Table 11.3 reveals that ideological thinking in the ways we have measured it has nothing to do with a history of loyalty or commitment to the party. Tactical and ideological extremists have been as active as anyone else and among Republicans were even slightly less likely than mainstream delegates to have ever identified with the other party. In addition among the Republicans, tactical ideologues were slightly more loyal to President Ford in 1976 than were mainstream delegates. For these individuals, commitment to extreme views and desiring a more ideological party have not been impediments to long standing party involvement, an involvement very much in the mainstream of party life.

From our analysis to this point we conclude that it will result in a more accurate description if we view the ideologue in a light very different from that posited by the neoconservatives. They feared that the two major parties were susceptible to takeover by large groups of delegates who thought alike on the two types of issues we have examined here. They saw the conventions populated by two sharply divergent groups, namely the party regulars and the ideologues. We have found no such major division. At the state conventions in 1980, the large majority of delegates in both parties eschewed the extreme views which the neoconservatives feared.

Table 11.4. Ideologues and social characteristics

	Issues		Party role	
	Democrats	Republicans	Democrats	Republicans
Age	−.10	.06	.05	.05
	(6294)	(7094)	(6565)	(7327)
Sex	−.09	.09	−.08	−.03
	(6302)	(7131)	(7461)	(7731)
Race	.13	−.02	.05	.01
	(6211)	(7073)	(7375)	(7679)
Fundamentalist	.13	−.14	−.04	−.16
	(4500)	(4000)	(5475)	(4448)
How religious	.17	−.13	−.07	−.19
	(6194)	(7042)	(7332)	(7635)
Education	.10	−.01	−.09	−.07
	(6148)	(6967)	(7306)	(7570)
Income	−.07	.01	−.09	−.09
	(6086)	(6724)	(7180)	(7278)

Note: Entries are Kendall's tau-b correlations between issues and party role ideologue scales and social characteristics.

Even those delegates who tended toward extremism in one respect were not notably different from the mainstream delegates in others.

The analysis to this point leaves us somewhat puzzled about the neoconservatives' fears. Perhaps, we reasoned, the real fear was that the party was susceptible to takeover by people "not like them." Certainly stereotypes of ideologues in both parties are clear in the minds of many active politicians. In the Republican party, we expect advocates of the New Right to be newly wealthy, bright, young, predominantly male born-again Christians or fundamentalists. Democratic ideologues should come from urban (or perhaps rural, but not suburban) areas, they should be highly educated though not necessarily wealthy, and they should have rejected conventional political and moral standards. These two groups are not only different from each other; they should also be clearly distinguishable from the average delegate to the party convention.

Table 11.4 reveals that these expected differences simply did not materialize. In no case are the correlations for either party as high as .20. Republican issues ideologues and tactical extremists do tend to be slightly more religious and fundamentalist than the mainstream Republicans, but these differences are minimal. On the other factors which we have identified, they look very much like the rest of the Republican delegates. In short, the Republican ideologues are very much like those who were less ideological.

Among the Democrats, the correlations are similarly weak. Once again, born-agains and the very religious are more conservative and more purist than the mainstream delegates. The only other factor correlating at even .10 is education (and here only with issue extremists). The most important finding here, however, is not the direction of the correlations, but their weakness. This is not a distinct, divergent group. At best, it might be described as a faint shadow of what the stereotypical view of ideologues would lead us to expect.

Why then are the neoconservatives' images of the ideologues so far off? We can only speculate. Perhaps they were swayed by the first impressions of the most visible ideologues—those who have passed out petitions or been visible and vocal at the conventions. Many of the highly ideological speeches at the state conventions were in fact given by individuals who seem to fit the stereotypical mold, but our data show that these "spokespersons" may well have been echoes of a distant past. They cannot be identified through analysis of sociological traits. If equivalents of those who took over the Democratic party in 1972 were present in 1980, they were few and far between.

ACTIVISM OF THE EXTREMISTS

Finally, it seems worthwhile to look at the most important tenet of the neoconservative critique to see if it can be sustained for even the small groups of ideologues we have identified. The neoconservatives hold that the presidential nominating system is open and susceptible to takeover by individuals who have no enduring interest in party affairs and politics as usual. That is, they argue that the parties need commitment to politics from their activists in order to fulfill their role in our system, and that those who participate out of allegiance to issues or a particular candidate do not have this commitment.

The convention delegate questionnaire contains many items dealing with delegates' involvement which we grouped into three types. The first is the individual's involvement in the public campaign activities of the party; we constructed a simple index measuring the number of such

Table 11.5. Ideologues and party and interest group activism

	Campaign activities		Position in party hierarchy		Interest group memberships	
	Democrats	Republicans	Democrats	Republicans	Democrats	Republicans
Issues	.10	.01	−.05	.02	.16	.02
	(6429)	(7246)	(6429)	(7246)	(6429)	(7246)
Party role	−.09	−.11	−.09	−.08	.03	.03
	(7656)	(7884)	(7656)	(7884)	(7656)	(7884)

Note: Entries are Kendall's tau-b correlations between issues and party role ideologue scales and activism measures.

activities that an individual claims to participate in regularly. Second, we examined the individual's position in the formal party hierarchy, whether or not the delegate holds an office in the party at the state or local level. Finally, we constructed a simple index measuring the number of other organizations (e.g., labor unions, environmental groups) to which the individual belongs. The neoconservatives would lead us to expect that the extremists would be much less involved in public campaign activities of the two parties, that they would not hold party offices, but that they would be likely to be involved in other political organizations.

Table 11.5 reveals once again what has become a familiar pattern. On almost every indicator, the ideologues are not very different from the mainstream delegates. There are some differences between the two parties, but all of the correlations are quite weak.

Democratic ideologues are more active in public campaigning than are the mainstream delegates, not less so as the neoconservative argument would predict. On the other hand, they are somewhat less involved in the party hierarchy than their numbers would warrant; again, however, the divergence is much less than one might imagine. The only place where the expected pattern is revealed is that the ideologues do tend to be distinctly more active outside of the Democratic party than is the case for the rest of the Democratic delegates.

In the Republican party, patterns are even less clear. Those who score highest on the ideological measure seem to be more, not less, active than other delegates. The conclusion from these data for the Republicans is that ideologues were those who felt strongly about issues and/or their candidate but were still very much involved in the Republican party and its activities.

This section of our analysis supports our earlier conclusions. The neoconservatives have been simply wrong in their depiction of the impact that the reform rules have had on those involved in party decision-making; the "mischief of faction" is more apparent than real (Ranney 1975). Whether we analyzed what ideologues thought, what they looked like, or what they acted like, we were unable to find any evidence of the existence, much less the threat of an ideologically coherent, unusually active, dangerously ideological element in either party.

We were frankly surprised by just how inaccurate the neoconservative analysis of the parties is. Nothing in our analysis lends any support to their fears of an ideological takeover of either major party. In 1980 few ideologues were to be found; those whom we were able to identify did not hold most of the views nor take most of the actions regarding party life the neoconservatives had led us to expect.

It is possible, of course, that some different, more representative sample would reveal a larger, more influential cluster of ideologues. However, we do not believe this to be the case. Our sample is drawn from a number of states which used a variety of procedures in selecting delegates. Delegates were chosen at differing points in the nominating process under differing political circumstances. It seems unlikely that activists in other states would be markedly different.

To the contrary, we feel this sample should have revealed as many ideologues as could have been involved in the 1980 nominating process.[3] It is often said that the caucuses are ripe for the plucking by ideological groups, yet their presence at and impact on these conventions was negligible. The system "worked," if by that one means that the parties were dominated by their mainstream elements, rather than by ideologues.

Our findings suggest that, far from the neoconservatives' expectations, both parties seem dominated by well-informed activists who are committed to traditional electoral strategies and mainstream electable candidates. The parties are not likely to be taken over by extremist activists whatever rules are in force.

Although the absence of extreme candidates in 1980 must temper our conclusions, counter-reforms such as those proposed by the Hunt Commission now seem unnecessary even from the neoconservatives' perspective. If the neoconservatives were right for the Democrats in 1972 or the Republicans in 1964, the parties have clearly "learned" since then. Again, if one accepts the neoconservative notion that one wants moderate parties whose activists are committed to nominating candidates who can win, our data are in line with Will Rogers' aphorism, "If it ain't broke, don't fix it."

NOTES

1. We will use the terms "ideologue" and "extremist" interchangeably here. There is no commonly accepted term to describe these activists, and in earlier versions we used extremists, amateurs, radicals, and even flakes. We are convinced that extremist and ideologue best describe the values and activism the neoconservatives fear.

2. We eliminated one of the thirteen issues listed in question 19. The question on national health insurance was not asked in Maine. Its inclusion would have skewed our results as many of the delegates who favored Governor Brown came from Maine.

3. It is possible that there were many other ideologues who had dropped out of the party leaving us with a now much smaller group of these activists, limited only to those with the most staying power. Unfortunately, we have no way of knowing if this was the case.

REFERENCES

Kirkpatrick, Jeane. 1976. *The New Presidential Elite*. New York: Russell Sage.

______. Michael J. Malbin, Thomas E. Mann, Howard R. Penniman and Austin Ranney. 1980. *The Presidential Nominating System*. Washington, D.C.: American Enterprise Institute.

Lengle, James. 1981. *Representation and Presidential Primaries*. Westport, Conn.: Greenwood Press.

Nakamura, Robert and Denis Sullivan. 1981. "A Critical Analysis of the Neoconservative Critique of the Presidential Nomination Reform." Paper presented at the 1981 annual meeting of the American Political Science Association, New York.

Ranney, Austin. 1975. *Curing the Mischief of Faction: Party Reform in America*. Berkeley: University of California Press.

Rose, Richard. 1980. *Do Parties Make a Difference?* Chatham, N.J.; Chatham House.

Soule, John and James Clark. 1970. "Amateurs and Professionals: A Study of Delegates to the 1968 Convention." *American Political Science Review* 64:888.

Sullivan, Denis G., Benjamin I. Page, Jeffrey L. Pressman, and John Lyons. 1974. *The Politics of Representation*. New York: St. Martin's.

———. Jeffrey L. Pressman, F. Christopher Arterton, and Martha Weinberg. 1977. "Candidates, Caucuses, and Issues: The Democratic Convention of 1976." In *The Impact of the Electoral Process*, edited by L. Maisel and J. Cooper. Beverly Hills: Sage Publications.

Wildavsky, Aaron. 1965. "The Goldwater Phenomenon: Purists, Politicians, and the Two-Party System." *Review of Politics* 27:386.

Appendix

THE 1980 DELEGATE SURVEY

1. How long have you lived in (name of state)?
   1. Less than 5 years ( )
   2. Between 5 and 10 years ( )
   3. Between 10 and 20 years ( )
   4. More than 20 years ( )
2. How long have you been active in party politics in (name of state)?
   1. Less than 5 years ( )
   2. Between 5 and 10 years ( )
   3. Between 10 and 20 years ( )
   4. More than 20 years ( )
3. How would you describe the area where you now live?
   1. City with over 250,000 population ( )
   2. Suburb of city with over 250,000 population ( )
   3. City with between 100,000 and 250,000 population ( )
   4. Suburb of city with between 100,000 and 250,000 population ( )
   5. City with between 50,000 and 100,000 population ( )
   6. City with between 10,000 and 50,000 population ( )
   7. Town with less than 10,000 population ( )
   8. Rural area ( )
   9. Other ( )
4. What county is that in?
5. What congressional district do you live in?
6. Please indicate which, if any, of the following positions you now hold or have held in the past. (Check as many as apply.)

	Hold Now	Held in Past
Member of a local (city, county, or town) party committee....................	( )	( )
Chairman of a local party committee......	( )	( )
Other local party office..................	( )	( )
Member of congressional district party committee...........................	( )	( )
Member of state central committee........	( )	( )
Elected to state or national office........	( )	( )
Elected local office.....................	( )	( )

This survey was previously published in *Nomination Politics: Party Activists and Presidential Choice,* by Alan I. Abramowitz and Walter J. Stone (New York: Praeger, 1984). It is reproduced here with the permission of the publisher.

Appointed government or political office .. ( ) ( )
Paid campaign staff for candidate......... ( ) ( )

7. Before this convention, had you ever been a delegate to a state or national party convention?
   1. Yes ( ) 2. No ( )
8. How often have you been actively involved in recent state and national political campaigns?
   1. Active in all ( ) 3. Active in a few ( )
   2. Active in most ( ) 4. Active in none ( )
9. What kinds of campaigns have you been active in? (Check as many as apply.)
   Local ( ) State Legislative ( ) Congressional ( )
   Stateswide offices ( ) Presidential ( ) Other ( )
10. Which of the following activities, if any, have you performed in political campaigns? (Check as many as apply.)
    Clerical work ( ) Writing ads, press releases ( )
    Door-to-door canvassing ( ) Speechwriting ( )
    Telephone canvassing ( ) Planning strategy ( )
11. How would you describe your own party affiliation:

    In state politics?
    1. Strong Democrat ( )
    2. Democrat, but not too strong ( )
    3. Independent, closer to Democrats ( )
    4. Completely independent ( )
    5. Independent, closer to Republicans ( )
    6. Republican, but not too strong ( )
    7. Strong Republican ( )

    In national politics?
    1. Strong Democrat ( )
    2. Democrat, but not too strong ( )
    3. Independent, closer to Democrats ( )
    4. Completely independent ( )
    5. Independent, closer to Republicans ( )
    6. Republican, but not too strong ( )
    7. Strong Republican ( )
12. DEMOCRATIC DELEGATES: Was there ever a time when you considered yourself a Republican?
    1. Yes ( ) 2. No
    REPUBLICAN DELEGATES: Was there ever a time when you considered yourself a Democrat?
    1. Yes ( ) 2. No ( )
13. IF YOU HAVE EVER CHANGED YOUR PARTY AFFILIATION: In what year did you last change your party affiliation?
    Year ______

14. Please indicate your opinion about each of the following statements. There are no right or wrong answers, so just give your personal opinion.

	1 Strongly Agree	2 Mildly Agree	3 Not Sure	4 Mildly Dis-agree	5 Strongly Disagree
A political party should be more concerned with issues than with winning elections	( )	( )	( )	( )	( )
The party platform should avoid issues that are very controversial or un-popular	( )	( )	( )	( )	( )
I'd rather lose an election than compromise my basic philosophy	( )	( )	( )	( )	( )
A candidate should ex-press his convictions even if it means losing the election	( )	( )	( )	( )	( )
Broad electoral appeal is more important than a consistent ideology	( )	( )	( )	( )	( )

15. We're interested in your reasons for becoming actively involved in this year's presidential campaign. Please indicate how important each of the following factors was for you.

	1 Very Impor-tant	2 Some-what Impor-tant	3 Not Very Impor-tant	4 Not at All Impor-tant
To support my party	( )	( )	( )	( )
To help my own political career	( )	( )	( )	( )
To enjoy the excitement of the campaign	( )	( )	( )	( )
To meet other people with similar interests.........	( )	( )	( )	( )

To support a particular candidate I believe in	( )	( )	( )	( )
To work for issues I feel very strongly about......	( )	( )	( )	( )
To enjoy the visibility of being a delegate	( )	( )	( )	( )
To fulfill my civic responsibilities..................	( )	( )	( )	( )

16. How would you describe your own political philosophy?
    1. Very liberal ( )
    2. Somewhat liberal ( )
    3. Middle-of-the-road ( )
    4. Somewhat conservative ( )
    5. Very conservative ( )

17. Please indicate your opinion about each of the following state and national political figures.

	1 Very Favorable	2 Somewhat Favorable	3 Neutral	4 Somewhat Unfavorable	5 Very Unfavorable
Jimmy Carter.....	( )	( )	( )	( )	( )
Edward Kennedy..	( )	( )	( )	( )	( )
Jerry Brown......	( )	( )	( )	( )	( )
Ronald Reagan....	( )	( )	( )	( )	( )
George Bush......	( )	( )	( )	( )	( )
John Anderson....	( )	( )	( )	( )	( )
John Dalton	( )	( )	( )	( )	( )
Harry Byrd, Jr...	( )	( )	( )	( )	( )
John Warner......	( )	( )	( )	( )	( )
Charles Robb.....	( )	( )	( )	( )	( )
Marshall Coleman..	( )	( )	( )	( )	( )

18. Was there any particular issue that caused you to become involved in this year's election campaign?
    1. Yes ( ) 2. No ( )
    IF YES: What issue was that? ______________________

    ____

19. Please indicate your position on each of the following issues.

	1 Strongly Favor	2 Favor	3 Undecided	4 Oppose	5 Strongly Oppose
The Equal Rights Amendment to the U.S. Constitution	( )	( )	( )	( )	( )

A constitutional amendment to prohibit abortions except when the mother's life is endangered	( )	( )	( )	( )	( )
A substantial increase in defense spending even if it requires cutting domestic programs	( )	( )	( )	( )	( )
A government sponsored national health insurance program	( )	( )	( )	( )	( )
More rapid development of nuclear power	( )	( )	( )	( )	( )
Across-the-board cuts in nondefense spending to balance the federal budget..................	( )	( )	( )	( )	( )
Affirmative action programs to increase minority representation in jobs and higher education	( )	( )	( )	( )	( )
Deregulation of oil and gas prices	( )	( )	( )	( )	( )
Mandatory wage-price controls to deal with inflation	( )	( )	( )	( )	( )
Stronger action to reduce inflation even if it increases unemployment substantially............	( )	( )	( )	( )	( )
Reinstituting draft registration.............	( )	( )	( )	( )	( )
Ratification of the SALT II Treaty..................	( )	( )	( )	( )	( )
Increasing U.S. military presence in the Middle East	( )	( )	( )	( )	( )

20. How would you rate the political philosophy of each of the following presidential candidates?

	1 Very Liberal	2 Some-what Liberal	3 Middle-of-the-Road	4 Some-what Conserv-ative	5 Very Conserv-ative
Jimmy Carter.....	( )	( )	( )	( )	( )
Edward Kennedy..	( )	( )	( )	( )	( )
Jerry Brown......	( )	( )	( )	( )	( )
Ronald Reagan....	( )	( )	( )	( )	( )
George Bush......	( )	( )	( )	( )	( )
John Anderson....	( )	( )	( )	( )	( )

21. Please rank your preferences for your party's presidential nomination.
    1st choice: ____________________
    2nd choice: ____________________
    3rd choice: ____________________
22. Are you pledged to support a particular candidate at the convention?
    1. Yes ( )   2. No ( )
    IF YES: Which candidate is that? ____________________
23. How good a chance do you think each of the following candidates would have of winning the November election if nominated by his party?

	1 Definitely Would Win	2 Probably Would Win	3 Might Win	4 Probably Would Lose	5 Definitely Would Lose
Jimmy Carter.....	( )	( )	( )	( )	( )
Edward Kennedy..	( )	( )	( )	( )	( )
Jerry Brown......	( )	( )	( )	( )	( )
Ronald Reagan....	( )	( )	( )	( )	( )
George Bush......	( )	( )	( )	( )	( )
John Anderson....	( )	( )	( )	( )	( )

24. Which, if any, of your party's candidates would you be unable to support in the November election? (Check as many as apply.)
    DEMOCRATS: Carter ( )   Kennedy ( )   Brown ( )
    I could support any of these ( )
    REPUBLICANS: Reagan ( )   Bush ( )   Anderson ( )
    I could support any of these ( )
25. How did you vote in the 1976 presidential election?
    1. Carter ( )   2. Ford ( )   3. Neither, didn't vote ( )

26. How would you rate the effectiveness of the Democratic and Republican state party organizations in (name of state)?

	1 Very Effective	2 Fairly Effective	3 Not Very Effective	4 Not at All Effective	8 Not Sure
Democratic organization..	( )	( )	( )	( )	( )
Republican organization..	( )	( )	( )	( )	( )

27. At present, how important a role does your state party organization play in each of the following areas?

	1 Very Impor- tant	2 Some- what Impor- tant	3 Not Very Impor- tant	4 Not at All Impor- tant	8 Not Sure
Providing campaign assist- ance to candidates	( )	( )	( )	( )	( )
Taking positions on issues to influence elected officials	( )	( )	( )	( )	( )
Providing services and information to elected officials and local party organizations between campaigns	( )	( )	( )	( )	( )
Recruiting candidates.....	( )	( )	( )	( )	( )
Informing the electorate about party goals and positions	( )	( )	( )	( )	( )

28. How important a role do you think your state party organization _should_ play in each of the following areas?

	1 Very Impor- tant	2 Some- what Impor- tant	3 Not Very Impor- tant	4 Not at All Impor- tant	8 Not Sure
Providing campaign assist- ance to candidates	( )	( )	( )	( )	( )
Taking positions on issues to influence elected officials................	( )	( )	( )	( )	( )

Providing services and information to elected officials and local party organizations between campaigns	( )	( )	( )	( )	( )
Recruiting candidates.....	( )	( )	( )	( )	( )
Informing the electorate about party goals and positions................	( )	( )	( )	( )	( )

29. In which of the following groups, if any, have you been politically active? (Check as many as apply.)
    Labor unions ( )
    Educational or teachers organizations ( )
    Other professional organizations ( )
    Business organizations ( )
    Church-related groups ( )
    Women's rights groups ( )
    Civil rights groups ( )
    Conservation or ecology groups ( )
    Public interest groups ( )
    Antiabortion groups ( )
    Farm or agricultural organizations ( )
    Other issue-related groups ( )
30. How politically active were your parents when you were growing up?

	Father	Mother
1. Very active	( )	( )
2. Fairly active	( )	( )
3. Not very active.....	( )	( )
4. Not at all active.....	( )	( )
5. Not sure	( )	( )

31. In what state did you spend most of your childhood?

    ____
32. How would you describe your parents' party affiliation at the time when you were growing up?

	Father	Mother
1. Strong Democrat	( )	( )
2. Democrat, but not too strong........	( )	( )
3. Independent, closer to Democrats....	( )	( )
4. Completely independent	( )	( )
5. Independent, closer to Republicans..	( )	( )
6. Republican, but not too strong......	( )	( )

7. Strong Republican ( ) ( )
8. Not sure ( ) ( )

33. What is your approximate age?
1. 18-24 ( ) 5. 40-44 ( ) 9. 60-64 ( )
2. 25-29 ( ) 6. 45-49 ( ) 10. 65-69 ( )
3. 30-34 ( ) 7. 50-54 ( ) 11. 70 or over ( )
4. 35-39 ( ) 8. 55-59 ( )

34. What is your sex? 1. Female ( ) 2. Male ( )

35. What is your race?
1. White ( ) 3. Hispanic ( ) 5. American Indian ( )
2. Black ( ) 4. Oriental ( )

36. What is your religious preference? (For example, Baptist, Methodist, Roman Catholic.)
Religious preference ______________________

36a. Do you consider yourself to be either a fundamentalist or born-again Christian?
1. Yes ( ) 2. No ( )

37. In general, how religious do you consider yourself?
1. Very religious ( ) 3. Not very religious ( )
2. Fairly religious ( ) 4. Not at all religious ( )

38. How much formal schooling have you completed?
1. None ( )
2. Grade school only ( )
3. Some high school ( )
4. Graduated high school ( )
5. Some college ( )
6. Graduated college ( )
7. Post college ( )

39. What would you estimate your family's income will be this year before taxes?
1. 0-$14,999 ( ) 4. $35,000-44,999 ( )
2. $15,000-24,999 ( ) 5. $45,000-59,999 ( )
3. $25,000-34,000 ( ) 6. $60,000 or more ( )

Contributors

Alan I. Abramowitz is associate professor of political science, State University of New York-Stony Brook.

Tod A. Baker is professor of political science, The Citadel.

Robert C. Benedict is associate professor of political science, the University of Utah.

Jeffrey L. Brudney is associate professor of political science, the University of Georgia.

John G. Francis is associate professor of political science, the University of Utah.

Charles S. Hauss is associate professor of government, Colby College.

Mary Grisez Kweit is professor of political science, the University of North Dakota.

Robert W. Kweit is professor of political science, the University of North Dakota.

L. Sandy Maisel is professor of government, Colby College.

Jean G. McDonald is assistant professor of political science, the University of Oklahoma.

John McGlennon is associate professor of government, College of William and Mary.

Laurence W. Moreland is associate professor of political science, The Citadel.

Ronald B. Rapoport is associate professor of government, College of William and Mary.

Steven E. Schier is assistant professor of political Science, Carleton College.

Robert P. Steed is professor of political science, The Citadel.

Walter J. Stone is associate professor of political science, the University of Colorado.

Index